Montgomery
and The River Region
In Focus

Beers & Associates would like to thank the following
for their support and cooperation in the creation of this volume

The City of Montgomery

The Town of Pike Road

The Montgomery Area Chamber of Commerce

The Prattville Area Chamber of Commerce

The Wetumpka Area Chamber of Commerce

Montgomery
and The River Region
In Focus

By Jennifer Stewart Kornegay
Corporate Profiles by Minnie Lamberth

**FOREWORD BY MONTGOMERY MAYOR TODD STRANGE
AND MONTGOMERY COUNTY COMMISSION CHAIRMAN ELTON DEAN**
WITH PRATTVILLE MAYOR BILL GILLESPIE, WETUMPKA MAYOR JERRY WILLIS, PIKE ROAD MAYOR GORDON STONE,
MILLBROOK MAYOR AL KELLEY AND TALLASSEE MAYOR JOHN HAMMOCK

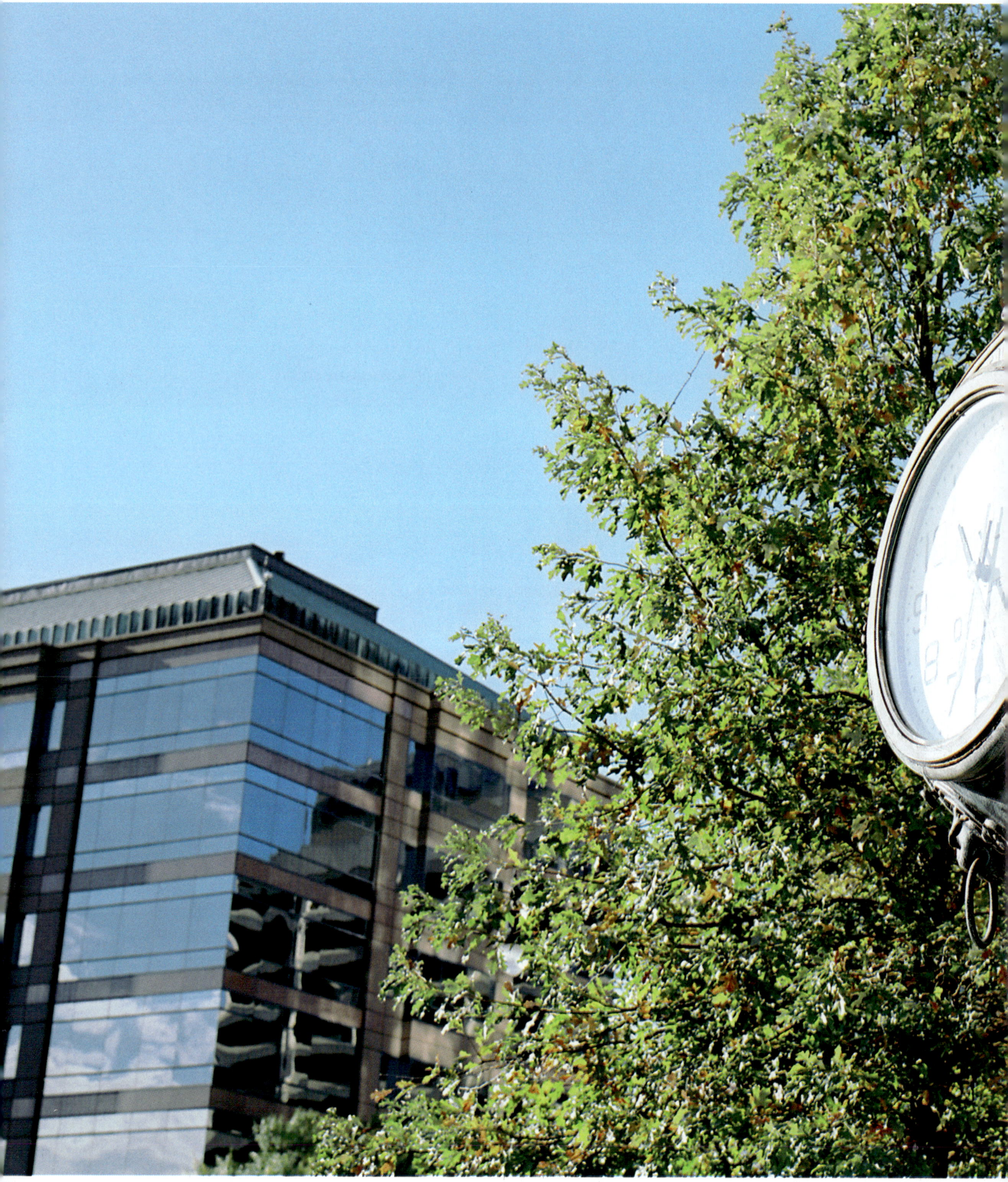

Montgomery & the River Region | In Focus

Foreword by
Montgomery Mayor Todd Strange and
Montgomery County Commission Chairman Elton Dean
with Prattville Mayor Bill Gillespie, Wetumpka Mayor Jerry Willis, Pike Road Mayor Gordon Stone, Tallassee Mayor John Hammock and Millbrook Mayor Al Kelley

Introduction by
Leslie Sanders, Golson Foshee, Clay McInnis, Ashley Jernigan Brandle and **Dr. Y.T. Tsai**

Written by
Jennifer Stewart Kornegay with company profiles written by **Minnie Lamberth**

Featuring the photography of
Becca Beers, Madelaine Burkhardt, Barry Chritzerburgh, Bryan Carter, Elmore DeMott, Nancy Fields, Robert Fouts, Brooke Glassford, Jonathon Kohn, Michelle Consuegra Lambert, Josh Moates, Aubrie Moates, Sam Moody, Grace O'Connor, Scooter Painter, Stephen Poff, Eric Salas and Josh Whitman with photos contributed by the Montgomery CVB, the Montgomery Area Chamber of Commerce and @exploremgm

BEERS
& ASSOCIATES

Ronald P. Beers, Publisher
Rachel Fisher, Managing Editor
Erika Tracy, Designer
Amye King, Designer
Wendi Lewis, Proofreader
Becca Beers, Staff Photographer
Ed Willcoxon, Sales Assistant

Printing and Production by Friesens Corporation
Cover image by Stephen Poff

Beers & Associates, LLC
113 Washington Avenue, Montgomery, Alabama 36104
beersandassociates.net
334-396-2896

© 2018 Beers & Associates, LLC
All Rights Reserved
Published 2018
First Edition
ISBN: 978-0-9796601-0-8
Library of Congress Control Number: 2018931795

Every effort has been made to ensure the accuracy of the information herein. However, the authors and Beers & Associates are not responsible for any errors or omissions that may have occurred.
Printed in Canada

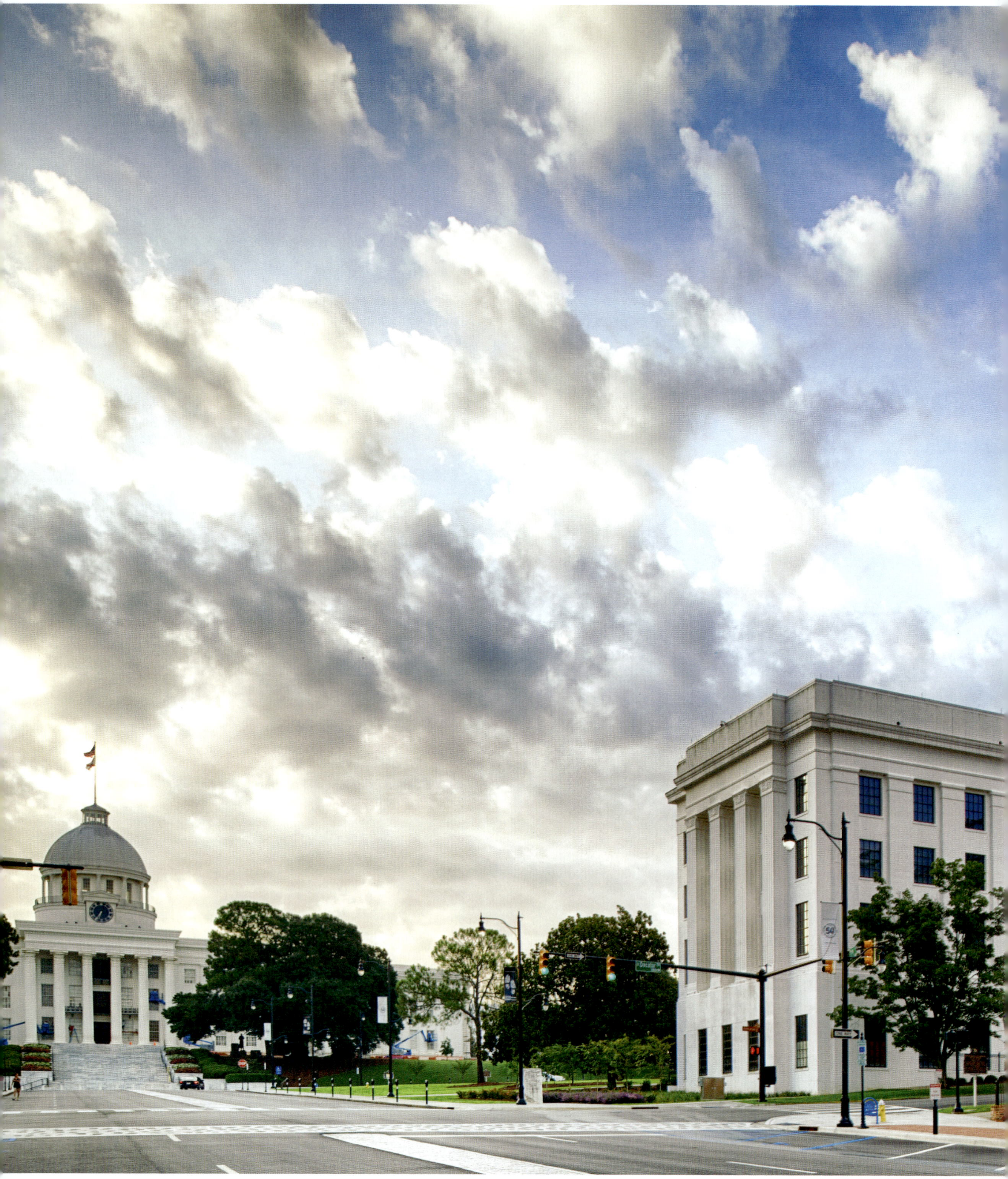

CONTENTS

Foreword 12

Introduction 18

Montgomery & the River Region |
At the Intersection of History 38

Center of It All | Downtowns
of the River Region 56

Making the Grade | Education 78

Living Well in the River Region |
Health & Wellness 112

Sustaining Mind, Body & Spirit |
Community Organizations
& Non-Profits 132

Building the River Region |
Communities & Neighborhoods 148

On the Forefront of Business & Industry |
Business & Economic Development ... 172

Foundation for Progress |
Politics & Government 236

The Force is With Us |
Maxwell Gunter AFB 250

Lightning Speed |
High-Tech & Global Connectivity 260

Made in the River Region |
Manufacturers, Creatives, Makers
& Entrepreneurs 278

Quality of Place | Events, Tourism, the
Arts, Sports & Recreation 310

Photo by Josh Whitman

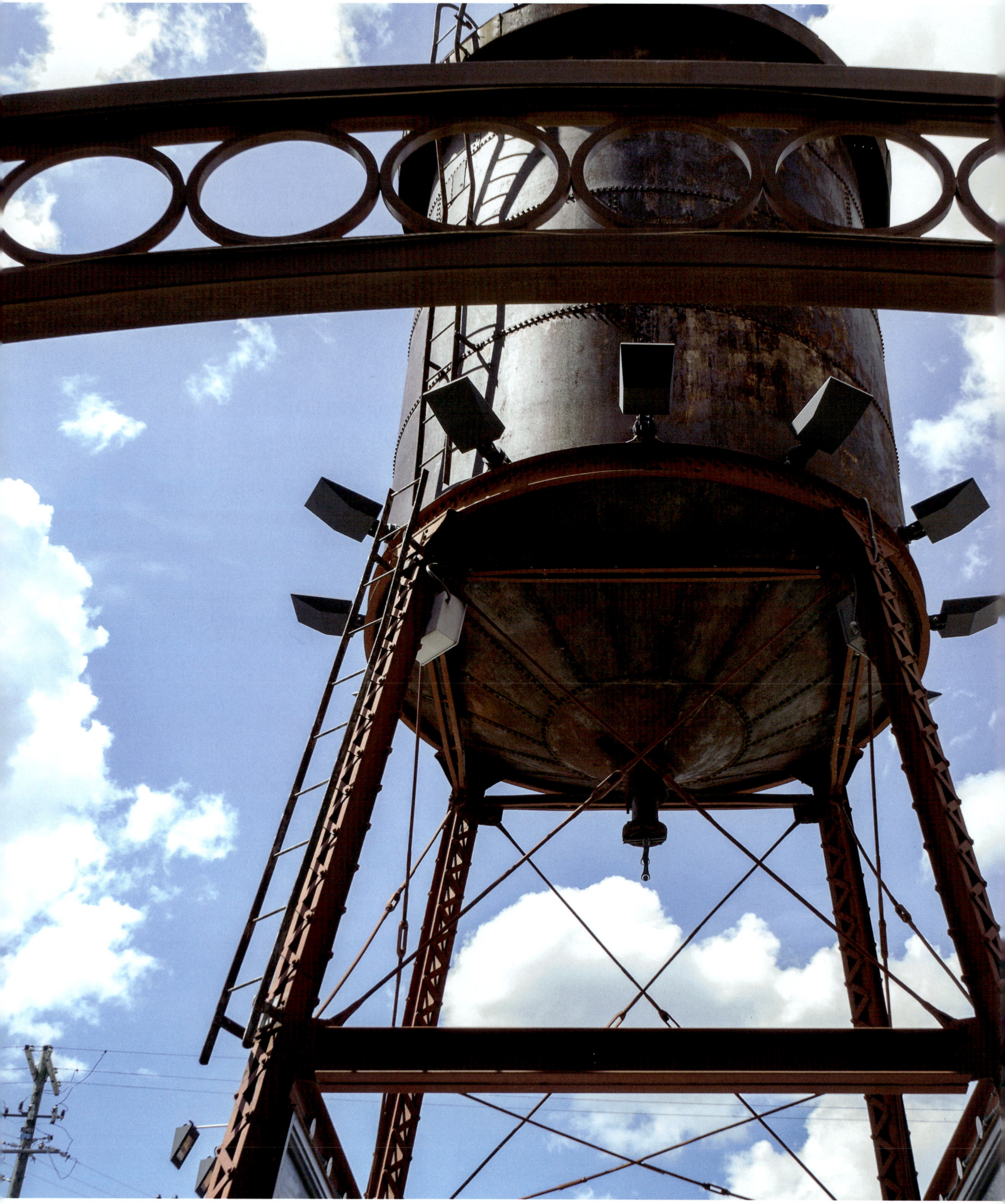

Companies and Organizations Profiled

Company	Page
Adams Family Enterprises, LLC	60
AIDT	96
Alabama Christian Academy	111
Alabama Machinery & Supply Company	296
Alabama Power Company	271
ALFA	188
Amridge University	104
Answered Prayer Home Care Services	131
Aronov Realty Management	158
Auburn University at Montgomery	80
Bacheler Technologies	277
Baptist Health	114
Beers & Associates	306
Borden Morris Garner Consulting Engineers	231
Brown Studio Architecture	204
Burt Steel, Inc.	288
Capital City Gastroenterology	127
Capitol Container, Inc.	305
Cedric Bradford	220
Central Alabama Community College	92
Chip Nix, Attorney at Law	241
DAVMOOR	208
Edwards Plumbing and Heating	196
eSolution Architects	217
Fastening Solutions, Inc.	300
Faulkner University	101
Frazer United Methodist Church	169
Garner Electric	228
Goodwyn, Mills and Cawood	209
Holt Street Memorial Baptist Church	43
Information Transport Solutions	275
Jackson Hospital	121
Jackson Thornton	225
Jenkins Tire & Automotive	235
JMR+H Architecture, P.C.	180
The Joe Hubbard Law Firm	247
Jones Drugs	130
Joy to Life Foundation	136
The Kelly Fitzpatrick Memorial Gallery	341
Kountry Air RV Park	338
Larry E. Speaks & Associates, Inc.	212
Lear Corporation	304
The Lilly Baptist Church	162
McPhillips Shinbaum, LLP	243
Merrill Lynch	224
The Montgomery Academy	105
The Montgomery Area Chamber of Commerce	176
Montgomery Catholic Preparatory School	108
The Montgomery Museum of Fine Arts	314
Montgomery Regional Airport	264
The Montgomery Symphony Orchestra	318
Montgomery Water Works & Sanitary Sewer Board	268
Montgomery Zoo & Mann Wildlife Museum	324
Neptune Technology Group	284
Prattville Area Chamber of Commerce	201
Prattville Christian Academy	110
Prattville YMCA	145
Production Automation, Inc.	301
Publications Press, Inc.	192
Ralph Smith Motors	233
Renal Associates of Montgomery, P.C.	124
Realty Connection	163
Regitar U.S.A.	292
Riverfront Facilities	65
River Region Dermatology and Laser	125
River Region United Way	146
Robinson and Associates Architecture, Inc.	221
Ross-Clayton Funeral Home, Inc.	232
Sabel Steel Service, Inc.	280
SABIC	308
Saint James School	100
ServisFirst Bank Montgomery	184
Stanley Steemer	230
The Town of Pike Road	152
Trenholm State Community College	84
Trinity School	109
Troy University	88
United Heating and Air	229
VT Miltope	297
Warren Averett CPAs and Advisors	205
Warren Averett Technology Group	273
Wealth Management Partners, LLC	213
Wesley Gardens Retirement Community	129
WestRock	309
Wetumpka Area Chamber of Commerce	203
Wingate by Wyndham	340
Woolard Brothers Commercial Contracting, Inc.	216

Photo by Eric Salas

Visionaries

The Water Works & Sanitary Sewer Board — Montgomery, Alabama

Baptist Health

Joy to Life
joytolife.org

ADAMS FAMILY ENTERPRISES

BROWN STUDIO ARCHITECTURE

JACKSON HOSPITAL

HOLT STREET BAPTIST CHURCH

ESA eSolution Architects

INFORMATION Transport SOLUTIONS, Inc.

The success of the effort to bring the Air Force's fleet of Lockheed Martin's F-35 Lightning II jets to Montgomery marks one of the area's most important economic development accomplishments in decades. These jets — the most sophisticated and advanced aircraft in the Air Force — will be home-based in the capital city with the historic 187th Fighter Wing.

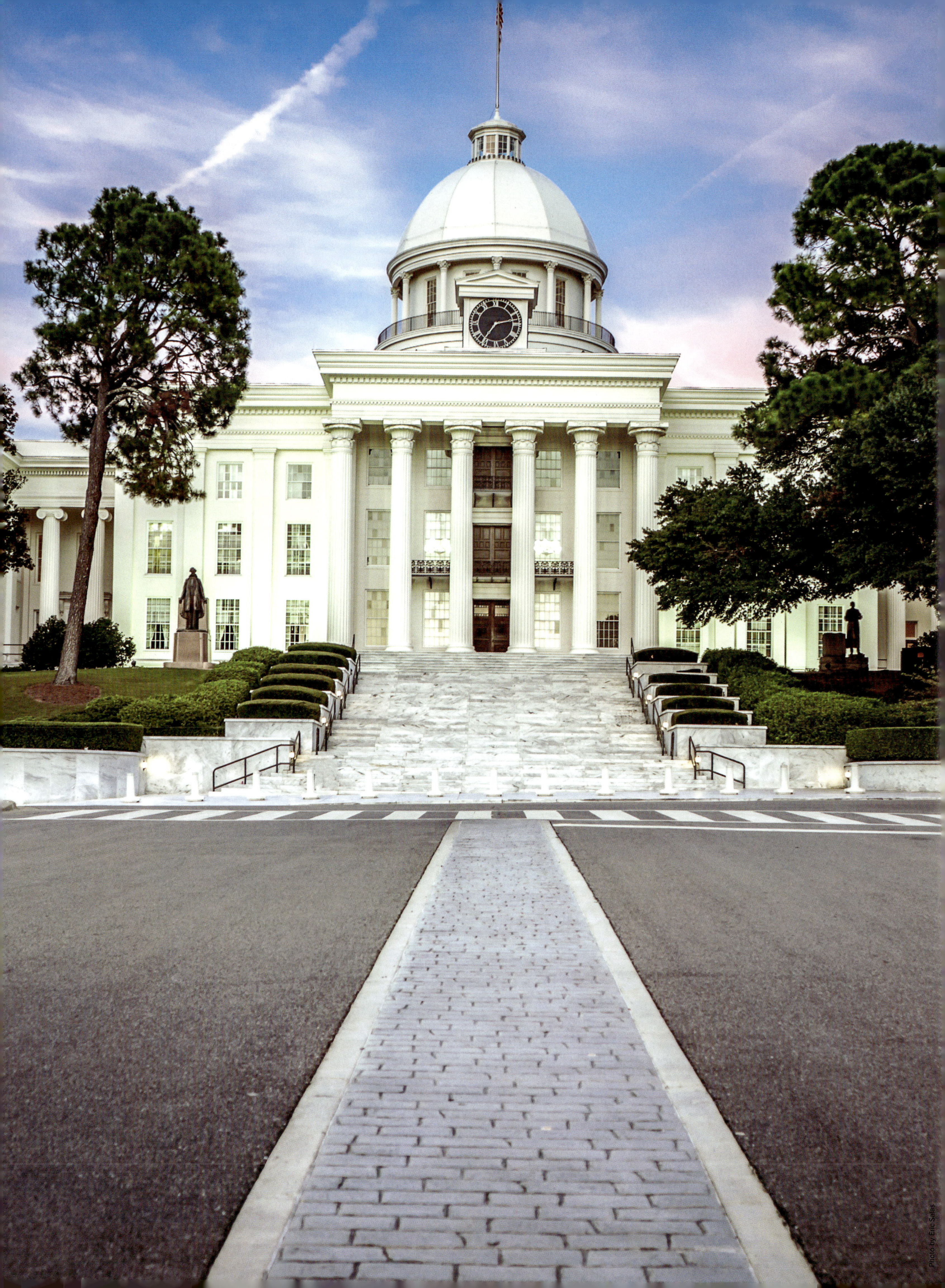

Foreword

Montgomery is at the center of everything: We're at the center of the mountains, center of the lakes, center of the beaches and the center of state government. The renewed vibrancy of our downtown has broad appeal, as do the distinct charms of our multiple communities and neighborhoods. A lot of attention is paid to our history, too. While this city's and this region's heritage are without a doubt unique and compelling, what's on the horizon is even more exciting. We have a spirit that pushes us to reach out, to reach higher and to always ask "What's next?" We remember and celebrate our past, but we are constantly striving for the things that will propel us into the future. That drive makes Montgomery and the River Region special, and interacting with the people who possess it is my favorite part of my job. I love collaborating with our citizens. I love facing our challenges together and unifying in support of the work that gets things done. As we look ahead, our city and our region will continue to embrace and share the stories and lessons from our history, while at the same time developing new frontiers in technology. Our perseverance, persistence and our forward-thinking attitude will help us become that "beloved community" envisioned by Dr. Martin Luther King, Jr.

- Montgomery Mayor Todd Strange

I've served on the Montgomery County Commission since 2000. In that time, I've realized how many opportunities there are here. There's a saying that in the past has been true: The seeds have been planted, but they've never been harvested. It refers to the potential here in our area, potential that at times has been left to wither. But we're capitalizing on it now. And we're doing it by working together. One of the things that makes our region so unique and so special is the collaboration and teamwork that exists between the county, the city of Montgomery and the entire River Region on projects that affect our entire area. That's my hope for our future, for the people I love representing, that we all continue to work together for the good of all citizens, be it in establishing a quality education system or bringing in the next big company. It's a hope that I feel is founded in reality. I know we can do it, because we've done it before.

- Montgomery County Commission Chairman Elton Dean

The River Region

The cities and communities that surround Montgomery in Autauga, Elmore, Lowndes and Montgomery counties combine with the capital city to create the River Region, a special spot in central Alabama that's far greater than the sum of its parts. Thanks to the diverse communities that stand as individuals yet stay linked in common heritage and common aspirations, the outlook for all of the area's residents remains full of hope and promise.

Wetumpka is known as the "City of Natural Beauty." Nestled at the foothills of the Appalachians and on the banks of the Coosa River, it boasts a picturesque landscape and even has a feature that's heaven-sent, a massive crater created by a meteor blast 85 million years ago. It's one of only two marine impact craters in the United States, and the unique geological wonder draws hundreds from around the country every year. These and other components of Wetumpka's rich natural resources allow for a positive flow of new residents and visitors, making the Elmore County seat the economic center of the county too. In turn, the local and regional economies are sparked by increased property values, municipal revenues and talented workers. Downtown Wetumpka has been revitalized, offering a mix of retail, dining and office spaces. As much as folks enjoy visiting Wetumpka, our residents love living here even more, due to the small-town charm, leisurely lifestyle and an abundance of trails and waterways ideal for outdoor enthusiasts. Events like Wetumpka's River and Blues Music & Arts Festival, Christmas on the Coosa, Arbor Day, Wetumpka Crater Tour, Mardi Gras parade, 4th of July Celebration and more mean there is always something to do and something to see. And the people of Wetumpka are a big family. We work and play together, we eat and laugh together, and we support and help one another. This allows Wetumpka to keep growing, to offer great education and to enhance our medical services with the latest technologies available. But we want to maintain our small-town feel too. We know that's our real appeal.

-Wetumpka Mayor Jerry Willis

"The Fountain City" was our original motto, and "The Preferred Community" came along somewhere in the 1990s. I've modified that a little bit to say we are "The Preferred Fountain City." Our roots run very deep, and our history has helped define all of Autauga County. When Daniel Pratt came to Alabama, he settled here because of the proximity to needed natural resources, and we've been growing ever since. Prattville is known as the birthplace of industry in Alabama because of Pratt's cotton gin, which kept the then-rural economy going. Autauga Creek that flows in the center of town is one of the main reasons he came here; the creek was the power source that helped run the gin. Today, the creek with a Creek Walk and a canoe trail is a tourism draw. The Robert Trent Jones Golf Course in the city has also brought thousands of visitors and put Prattville on the map worldwide. The view is gorgeous, and the course has hosted a prestigious LPGA tournament for several years. Prattville's located right off the interstate, offering multiple shopping options, and development continues to boom all over, including downtown. Pratt's old gin is still standing, and now this cornerstone of the city is being refurbished. We've brought the James Hardy Corporation to the city, which represents a $200 million-plus investment, and there are more similar announcements to come. But we're being careful to not outgrow our pace. We want to protect the quality of life we've built. We don't have a lot of big buildings, but we do have so many different amenities and services. And one of the things that really makes us is our people; we have so many forward-thinking residents who love their city and are dedicated to keeping it a safe and caring place while also helping us move ahead.

-Prattville Mayor Bill Gillespie

The Town of Pike Road is a community of people with a passion who are deeply in love with their way of life. The people of the area incorporated the Town of Pike Road more than two decades ago. Since that day, the people have been its focus, its driving force, and its greatest resource. From its earliest days, the town utilized intensive listening and planning sessions to guide the future of our young municipality. Residents identified Services, Planning, Quality of Life, and Education as our Four Pillars, priorities to be considered in every decision. Along with the mission statement, "maintaining character while planning for progress," the dedication of our citizens to these pillars has led the Town of Pike Road to population growth, the creation of an excellent and innovative public school system, and huge opportunities for economic growth. Expansive views of farmland and pastures conceal vibrant neighborhoods in tight-knit, historical communities. The ENHANCE initiative, designed to ensure quality of life, offers community programming across a spectrum of interests, from artistic to agricultural. The development of a Natural Trail system provides opportunities to connect with neighbors while enjoying our beautiful outdoors. Through the engagement of citizens in numerous community activities that bring people together, it is easy to see why our motto is Welcome Home. It is important to note the partnerships that make our growth possible. Collaboration with service providers, county and state government, and community groups allows the Town of Pike Road and its residents to move forward in ways that would not be possible on our own. With a focus on our vision for the future – the vision of our citizens – and practical daily decisions, our Town looks forward to continued growth while preserving the character and natural beauty of our community.

-Pike Road Mayor Gordon Stone

Tallassee has maintained her small-town charm in a family-oriented atmosphere. City officials and employees work hard to create and maintain a community that is attractive to visitors and those who choose Tallassee as their home. Home to well-known international industries as well as friendly, small-town residents, the city continues to grow and prosper, welcoming those who find the unique blend of old and new as charming as it is enlightening. Tallassee schools are part of its own school system. They serve approximately 1,700 students and employ 203 people. Tallassee is also home to Tallassee Community Hospital which employs over 400 people and has a level-three triage center. What makes Tallassee special, as with much of Elmore County, is the majesty of the rivers, streams and lakes bringing an incredible beauty to this place.

-Tallassee Mayor John Hammock

Located one interstate exit north of Montgomery, Millbrook is known for its casual and comfortable lifestyle. Its slogan, "Comfort, Convenience, Community," explains the success of our youthful and energetic city. Once here, visitors quickly adjust their pace to enjoy Millbrook's relaxed way of doing things, and begin to understand why lifelong locals and newcomers alike make Millbrook their home. From a stroll in the Village Green, to a leisurely nature walk at the Alabama Nature Center, to cheering on a little league baseball or softball game – all of these activities illustrate our comfortable way of life. Our city capitalizes on its central location in the River Region by attracting residents and providing convenient dining and shopping, education and employment, and recreation and entertainment. Our energized economic development program stands ready to assist all business sectors making Millbrook well positioned for future growth. It's easy to appreciate why so many people call Millbrook home. The people of Millbrook are the community. It is a privilege to serve them. Come and see us soon and experience first-hand "Comfort, Convenience, Community."

-Millbrook Mayor Al Kelley

Introduction

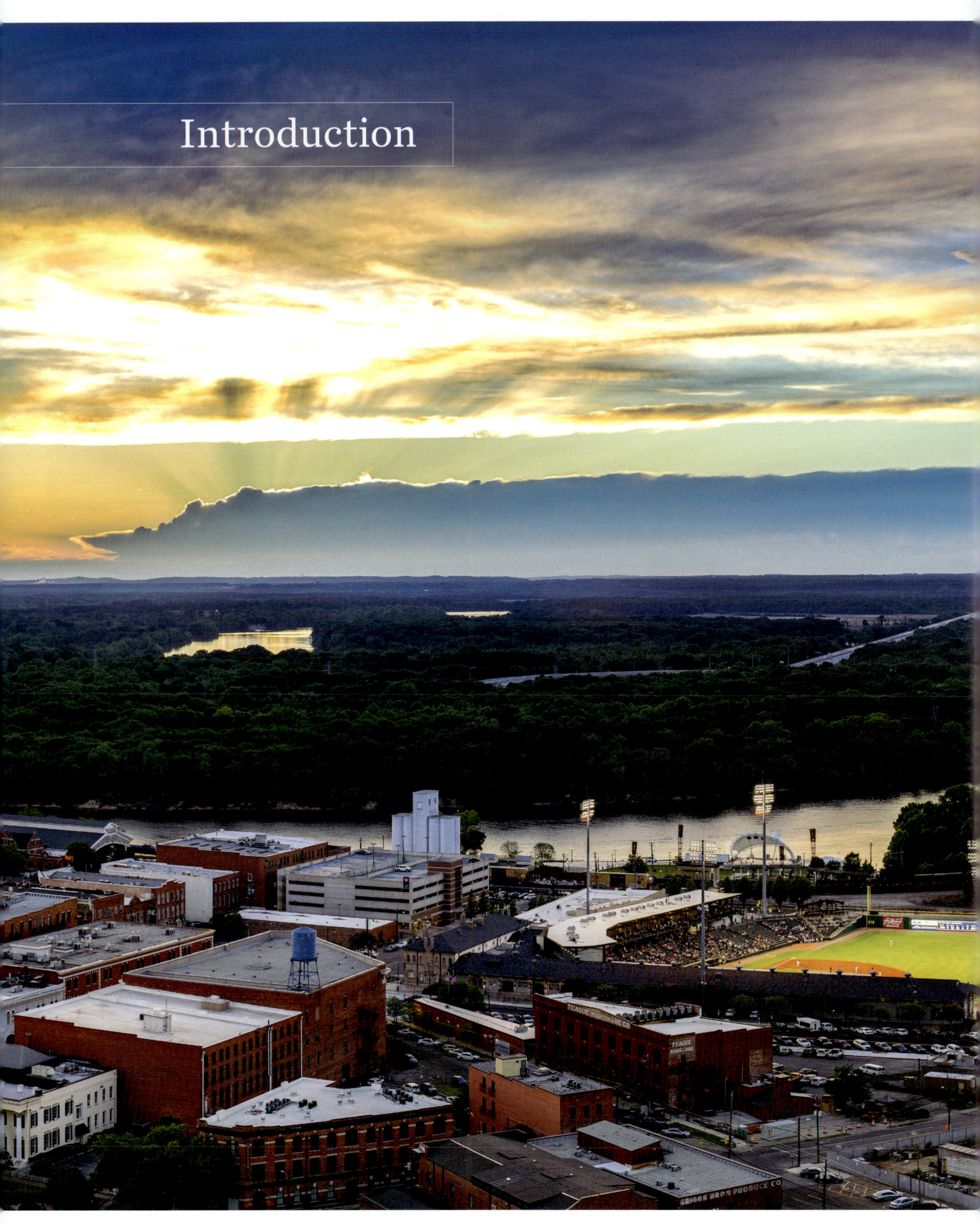

In the pages that follow, we shine a spotlight on Montgomery and the surrounding River Region — communities deeply rooted in their history and heritage, yet enthusiastically envisioning the future and moving ahead. Words and images paint a colorful portrait and tell an inspiring story of a modern region. It's a place mindful of its past and present challenges, yet undaunted by them as it pushes toward continued prosperity. Perhaps most notably, it's a place overflowing with the soul and character of its diverse people; the people who are its pulse and give it life. People like the five residents (two natives and three transplants) who've contributed their thoughts and hopes for the place they call home as this volume's introduction. As you read their words, you'll note their distinct voices and unique perspectives. But there's a clear and compelling thread that ties them together too: Their shared pride in the place where they have chosen to write their own stories and their eagerness to encourage others to come and do the same. Welcome to Montgomery. Welcome to the River Region. We're so glad you're here.

19

Leslie Sanders
Vice President,
Alabama Power

Several decades ago, my husband David and I moved to the capital city to chase our professional dreams. We soon realized that this community was much more than just a place where we worked; it became a place where we chose to raise our family and establish lasting friendships. In other words, Montgomery became our home.

Over the years, as we've watched our children grow, we have also watched our city grow and progress and have been blessed to be a part of this growth. Progress, however, is never a destination – It's a journey.

Montgomery County has been on that journey for just over 200 years, and the City of Montgomery will celebrate that 200-year milestone in 2019. A short walk up Dexter Avenue provides glimpses of the past – buildings still stand from the 1800s, and the legacy of the Civil Rights Movement is memorialized. One can hear the crack of a bat and cheers for our Montgomery Biscuits in one of the most impressive historic stadiums in the country or enjoy vibrant restaurants all around our town. While our City embraces its history, the people and leadership do not remain static.

Today, Montgomery is rapidly changing to take advantage of technological and business opportunities. When it opened its plant here, Hyundai brought opportunities to the River Region that may have only existed in the imaginations of a few. It, and the supplier network it requires, help fuel a diversifying economy. Commercial and industrial development has also accelerated throughout the region. If one were to look in any direction from downtown Montgomery, there is evidence of growth, revitalization and excitement.

The Montgomery Internet Exchange makes Montgomery a destination for companies requiring incredibly fast Internet access. With the exchange, Internet traffic no longer needs to be routed through another city, or two, before reaching a final destination – Montgomery is a direct connection to the world. We are a community determined to demonstrate to the world that we are comprised of visionary people who turn challenges and opportunities into reality.

No highlight of the River Region would be complete, however, without recognizing our military partners. Those associated with Maxwell-Gunter Air Force Base and the 187th Fighter Wing are incredibly important to the fabric of our community. They are integral to much more than helping provide a positive and strong economic impact. The support we all show each other was one reason Montgomery was successful in bringing the F-35 jet program here.

I am excited for today's Montgomery and the River Region. I am equally excited for the next chapter as well. There is an infusion of energy, innovation and competitiveness that underscores our wonderful sense of place.

Montgomery is indeed a "big little town." "Big" in the opportunities it affords its people and "little" in the feel of a hometown it offers all. Welcome to a new and exciting River Region. Welcome to an area reinvesting in itself and its people.

"Welcome to a new and exciting River Region. Welcome to an area reinvesting in itself and its people."

"Prattville is my home. Both the Doster and the Chambliss families settled in Autauga County in the early 1800s, and throughout history they have been leaders in politics, community organizations, social events and churches. The area has a wonderful history that is being preserved, but uses that history to develop a place for future generations.

My memories growing up in this idyllic region include spending hours outside playing games like 'Red Rover' and 'Kick the Can.' I'll never forget roller skating on closed streets on Saturday mornings. We adjusted our skates with the turn of a key — it was very important to keep that key around my neck! The community swimming pool was a gathering place along with the Rexall Drug soda fountain. Life was simple and fun.

Prattville was a delightful and safe place to raise my three children. Today, I enjoy sharing my Prattville with visitors. The Daniel Pratt Historical District and the Prattaugan Museum are always on the tour. The Autauga Creek Walk commences at the Daniel Pratt Fountain, which overlooks the dam and follows the creek to the park. It is a wonderful place to share with my grandchildren or just spend a quiet moment enjoying the view. A walk through the Bamboo Forest is delightful, and a short ride to tour Buena Vista, a colonial mansion built in the 1840s, is always a must see.

Community participation is an important part of Prattville. Community concerts, theatre, parades for all holidays, and street parties help develop a feeling of community for all citizens. A variety of shops and restaurants welcome locals and visitors. Today, I am still proud to say Prattville is my HOME!"

- **Melanie Walthall Chambliss,
Life-long Resident of Prattville**

"A variety of shops and restaurants welcome locals and visitors. Today, I am still proud to say Prattville is my home!"

Prattville

"Commenced" by Daniel Pratt in 1839

Proud to be a City of Character where *PROGRESS* and *PRESERVATION* go hand in hand.

"I believe Montgomery is on its way to becoming a place that embraces what makes us unique in so many ways."

Clay McInnis
President, Montgomery's Downtown Business Association

Today, many of us find ourselves looking down at our phone more than looking up, looking around and really seeing what our city has to offer. But if we pause a moment to consider both the power in our hands and the powerful potential all around us, amazing things can happen.

Since its founding, Montgomery's economic backbone has shifted from the river, to the rail, to the interstate and then to technology, exemplified in the smart phone. What does this trend mean for Montgomery? I believe it signals good things. There is a tremendous opportunity in Montgomery to grow to new heights.

Our rich history partnered with our growing and thriving downtown and the emergence of the Montgomery Internet Exchange makes for a bright forecast in a world that is more connected than ever. As a millennial, it inspires me to see Montgomery grow as a digitally connected city and a physically connected place where you can see friends on the streets of downtown or share coffee with out-of-towners and share stories about the rich history of Dexter Avenue.

Imagine a city where the citizens face the facts of its past so we can grow and learn. Imagine a city where citizens sit down with one another and respect each other's views and opinions no matter how different they are. Imagine a city where the next generation embraces smart growth strategies that will better physically connect the city. Imagine a city that thrives on technology and entrepreneurism, where the local economy is bustling with talent and energy.

I believe this city is Montgomery. I believe Montgomery is on its way to becoming a place that embraces what makes us unique in so many ways. We have sparked change and created societal innovations that have impacted the world through the Civil War, civil aviation and the Civil Rights movement. By walking alongside and behind the leaders who walked the streets of Montgomery before us, reaching for something far greater, we too will push our city to reach its full potential.

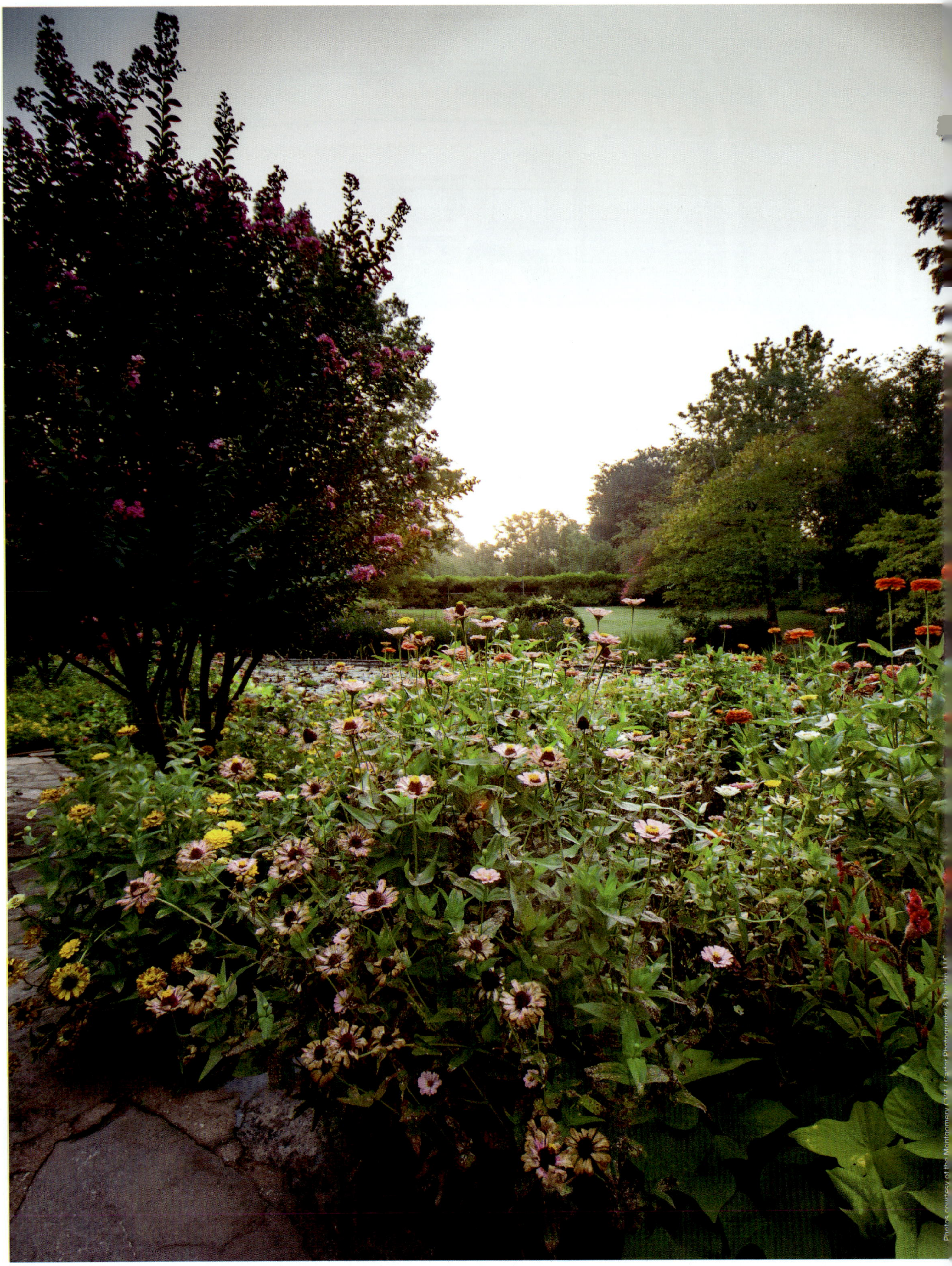

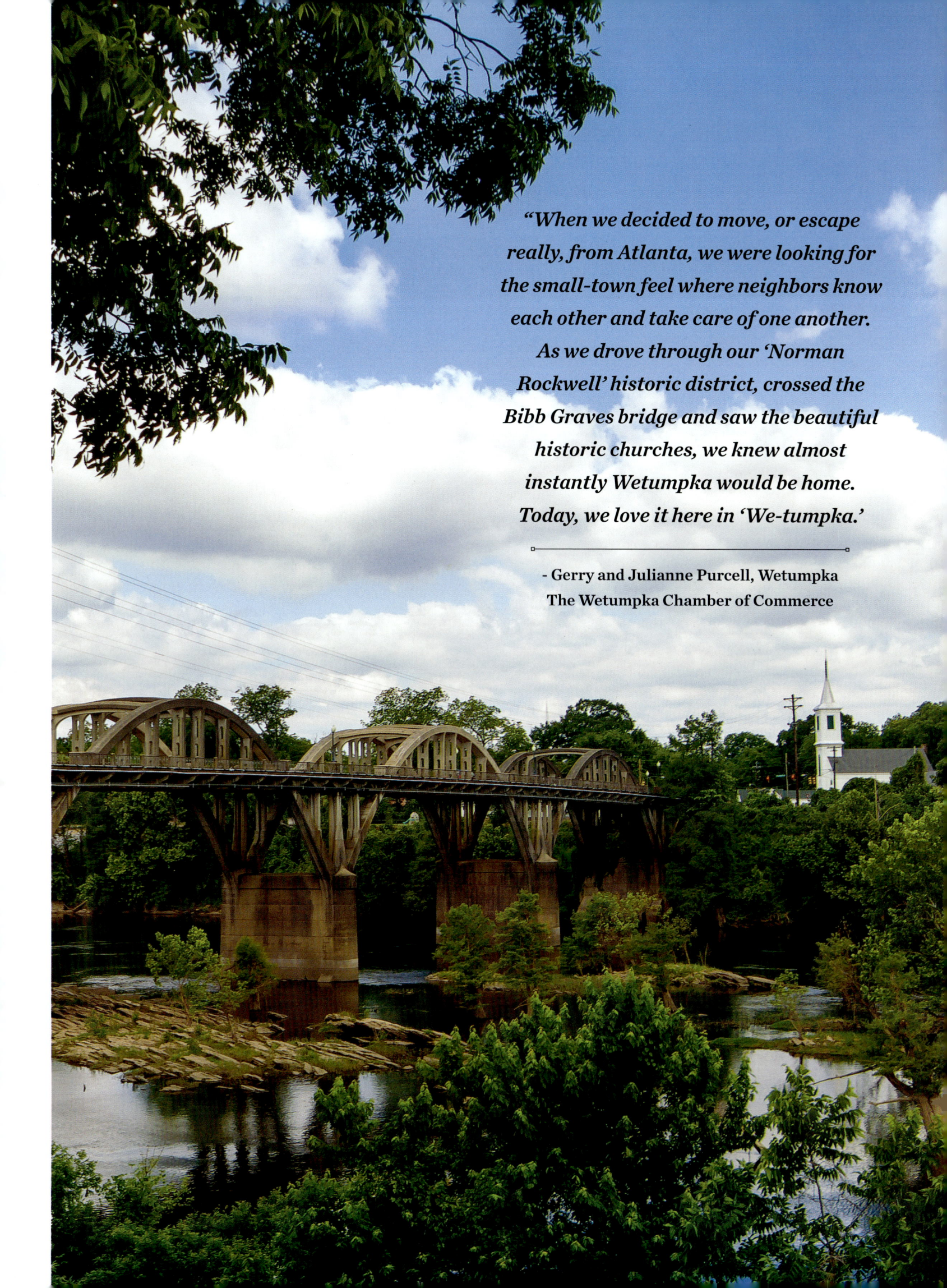

"When we decided to move, or escape really, from Atlanta, we were looking for the small-town feel where neighbors know each other and take care of one another. As we drove through our 'Norman Rockwell' historic district, crossed the Bibb Graves bridge and saw the beautiful historic churches, we knew almost instantly Wetumpka would be home. Today, we love it here in 'We-tumpka.'

- Gerry and Julianne Purcell, Wetumpka
The Wetumpka Chamber of Commerce

Ashley Jernigan Brandle
Founder & owner of JDB Hospitality, LLC

I moved to Montgomery from the San Francisco Bay Area in 2004 to attend Alabama State University on an academic scholarship. I came here sight unseen, but I could not say no to a free education. After graduation, I stayed, and that has turned out to be one of the best decisions I've ever made.

So much has changed in our area, and I've witnessed so much progress unfold. When I first came to Montgomery, the Alley Entertainment District was not developed yet. In fact, downtown Montgomery was not developed much at all. It has been amazing to see downtown full of life again, with a recent surge of hotels, restaurants and entertainment venues all within a one-mile radius.

What makes this piece of downtown's revitalization incredibly special is to know that my input, along with that of many other young professionals, was heard, and that our local government and private developers worked together to invest in downtown to add more options for all residents, but to also draw and retain young professionals.

Seeing our voices so valued has encouraged me to get even more involved in the community. Through my work in public relations and marketing for the

"Seeing our voices so valued has encouraged me to get even more involved."

hospitality industry, I'm constantly connected to many facets of the community, but I strive to further strengthen those bonds, too. I am the Past President of Emerge Montgomery, a young professional's organization dedicated to improving the life of YPs in the city. Being an Emerge Member has meant so much to me. Not only did it allow me to grow professionally, it created the space for me to share my opinions on effective change needed in the city. I continue to participate in Emerge so I can pay that forward and help other YPs learn how to love Montgomery the way I do.

I was also appointed by the governor to serve on the State of Alabama's Department of Tourism Board. This board allows me to ensure Montgomery is always represented when decisions are made on advertising tourism in Alabama and aligns perfectly with my passion for helping businesses in the hospitality industry.

It also gives me just one more outlet to tout and promote the many things that are special about this city and region. I enjoy the lower cost of living and the convenience of being just a few hours from the beach, the mountains and an international airport. I love how Montgomery has big-city amenities with a small-town feel, something that's been exemplified in the support I've received from both the City of Montgomery and the Chamber of Commerce as a small-business owner.

My peers are appreciating the same things, and it's driving them to engage and invest in their home. The young professional scene in Montgomery is growing. So many of us are starting businesses, spearheading nonprofits and running for office. And it's so diverse. We come from different backgrounds and cultures, yet we're coming together to accomplish major changes. This unity is something that I think makes Montgomery unique. There's so much to celebrate here, so much.

Photo by Eric Salas

"Moving to Pike Road, Alabama was like taking a positive step back in time for us. Memories of simpler times visiting my grandparents often pop into my head as I pass cows grazing next to white fields of cotton on my way to John Hall's Country Store to grab a biscuit that can only be matched at my Mama's table. Children run free all day and late into the evening playing games on the green at The Waters while parents grill out by the pool or roast marshmallows around the fire pit. They say you can't choose family but we did! We love our Pike Road family."

- Cindy Barganier, Pike Road
Owner, Cindy Barganier Interiors

Dr. Y.T. Tsai
Founder & Owner
of Regitar U.S.A.

I came to Montgomery in 1985 after receiving my Ph.D. degree from the University of Texas at Austin. I was offered an assistant professor position at Auburn University at Montgomery (AUM) teaching Information Systems. My wife, Dr. Chau Lee Tsai, who also received her Ph.D. from the University of Texas, joined me a year later at AUM. We enjoyed the opportunities and people at AUM, as well as Montgomery, and decided to stay here to raise our two boys, Gary and Henry. We eventually started and grew our company, Regitar U.S.A., here too.

In the 30-plus years that I've been here, I've seen Montgomery come a long way. There has been tremendous growth and development, not just physically across the city, in downtown, along the riverfront and in east Montgomery, but also culturally, as a wealth of diversity has improved the overall quality of life in Montgomery by allowing many businesses to generate new ideas to further innovate.

Other elements that continue to spur progress in our area include a business-friendly atmosphere fostered most notably by The Montgomery Area Chamber of Commerce, on whose board I now sit. The Chamber was important to the establishment of my company, Regitar U.S.A., and I wanted to give back and provide other businesses better tools and opportunities to succeed. We also have a good education system that is able to produce local talent; my belief in that fuels my service on the advisory boards for The University of Alabama and Auburn University. I also founded the Central Alabama Association for Chinese as another channel to network and share experiences among members of our region's Asian American community.

"As we continue to develop areas in and around Montgomery, we will continue to attract families of all backgrounds and experiences, as well as businesses across all industries."

I have now lived in Montgomery longer than I have lived anywhere else, and my love for this place only gets stronger every year. I love the progress I see all around me. I love that while we are a city, we still have that small-town feel. That's due to our friendly people. For someone who did not grow up here, I felt welcome from the moment my wife and I arrived. I love our rich history. And in terms of geographic location and from a business point of view, it is advantageous in its proximity to ports and major hubs.

Finally, I love that I see a bright future ahead for my city. As we continue to develop areas in and around Montgomery, we will continue to attract families of all backgrounds and experiences, as well as businesses across all industries. This is the way we'll propel Montgomery and the River Region to the next level. I'm looking forward to being a part of that future.

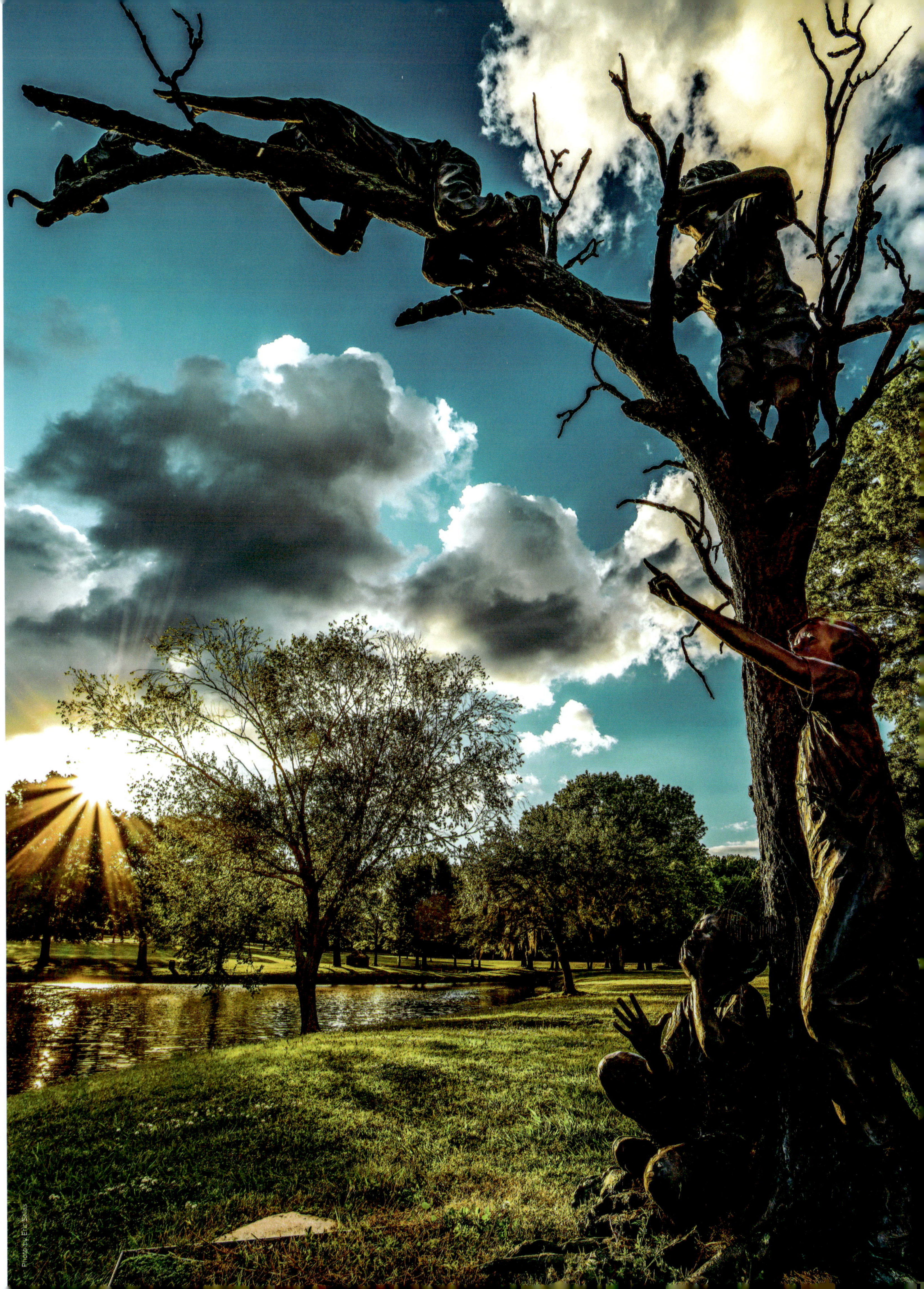

"Tallassee is a unique and intimate southern town in the middle of nowhere, close to everywhere, rich in beauty, culture and history."

- Tim Bianchi, Tallassee
VP of Engineering, Neptune Technology Group

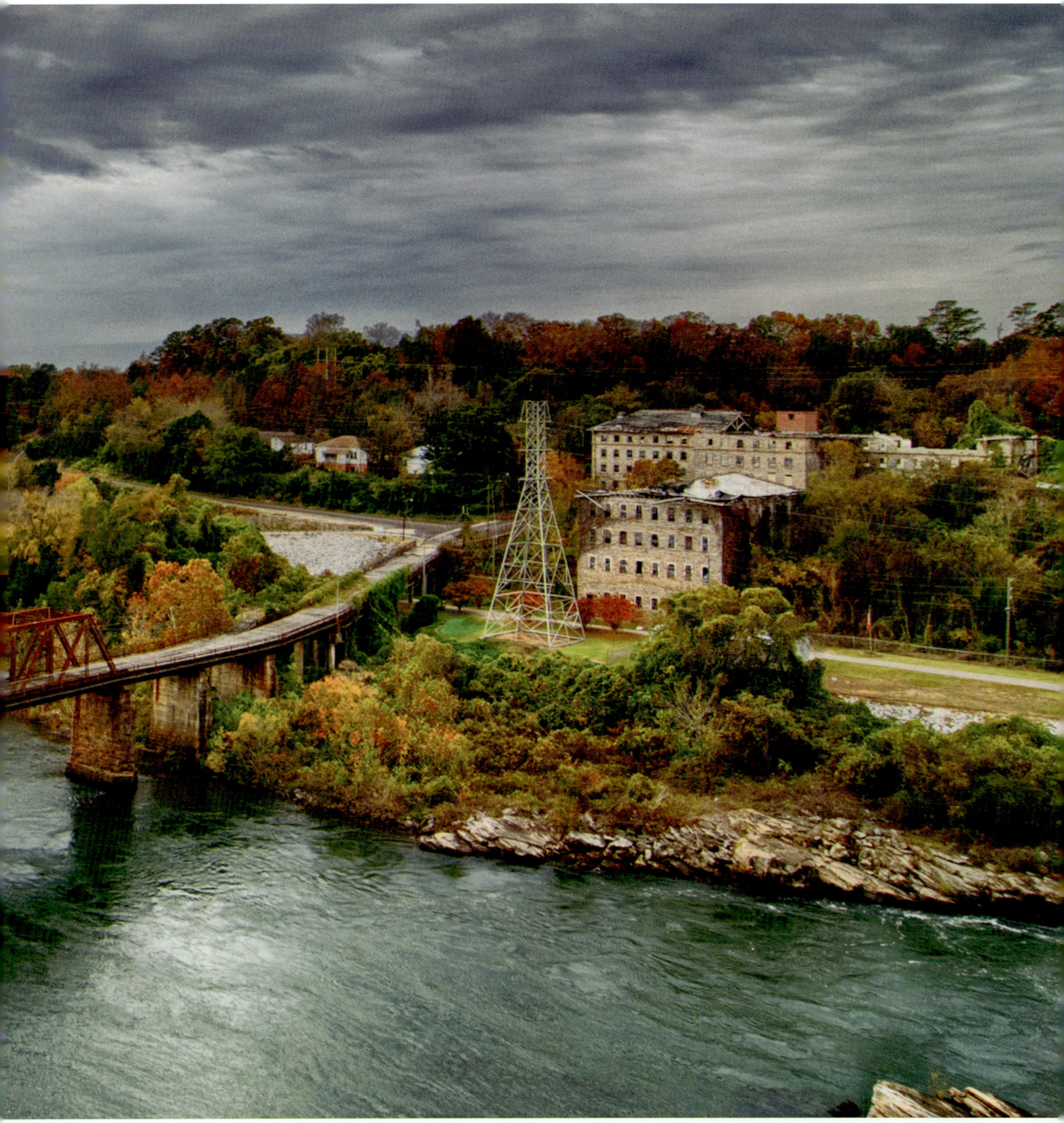

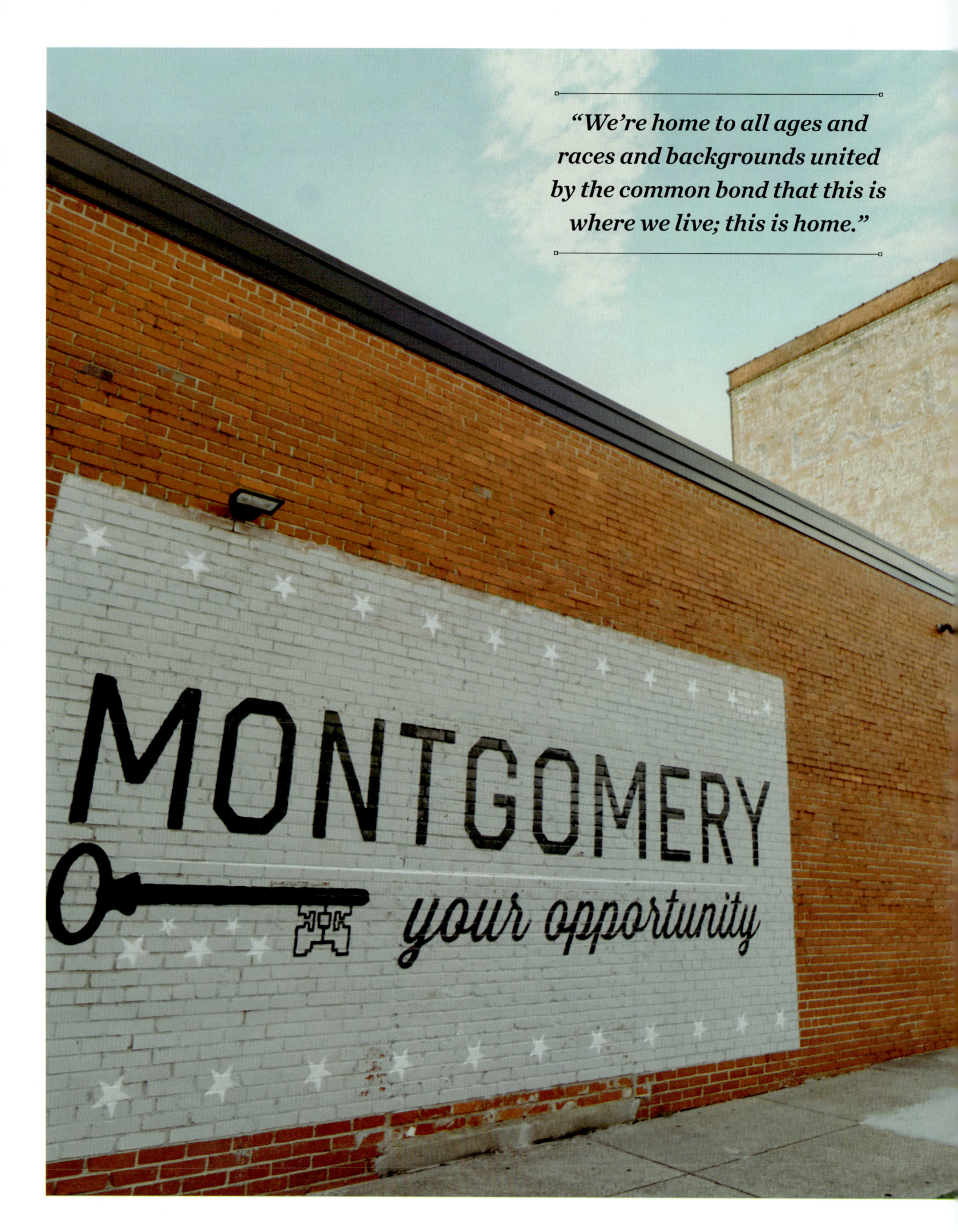

"We're home to all ages and races and backgrounds united by the common bond that this is where we live; this is home."

Golson Foshee,
Foshee Management

I was born in 1979 and, other than my time at Auburn University for college, I have lived here my entire life. There are so many things I love about this place, so many things that make it truly unique and make it stand out from other cities.

Where else can you stand in one place and see where the telegraph was sent to start the Civil War, where Rosa Parks boarded that now-famous city bus in 1965, where Jefferson Davis held his inaugural ball and where Dr. Martin Luther King preached on Sunday? Montgomery also has a strong moral fabric. This rich history, coupled with the opportunity for growth, help to make Montgomery a special place to live, work and raise a family.

As a real estate developer, I'm happy to be a part of the city and area's growth. I've enjoyed developing residential projects in east Montgomery, mixed use projects in downtown, and various other businesses. I'm especially excited about the revitalization of downtown and proud to see life being breathed back into the heart of our city.

These things are so visible. But there's a key piece of Montgomery's appeal that, I think, is sometimes overlooked: the rich cultural diversity here. We're home to all ages and races and backgrounds united by the common bond that this is where we live; this is home. Hundreds of people from around the world attend the International Officer School at Maxwell AFB's Air University each year, adding their experiences to our community mix.

And now, an increasing number of Montgomery's homegrown men and women are coming back home after college, ready to roll up their sleeves and make a positive impact here. That's our future, and it's bright.

37

Montgomery & the River Region
At the Intersection of History

Montgomery has always been an intersection, a place where people, cultures and ideas come together; sometimes in orderly mergers and sometimes in a collision. Its location on the banks of the Alabama River meant access to fresh water and, later, transportation, making it prime real estate. Once the site of a crucial crossroads in Creek Indian trade routes, it drew white settlers in search of prosperity in the early 1800s.

In 1819, the same year Alabama became a state, two towns that had sprung up at the river's bend joined to form Montgomery, and in 1846 the city became the capital. It was a major mark on the city's timeline, but certainly not the last. Montgomery has played a key role in events that have shaped not just our region or our state, but the nation and the world.

As the first capital city of the Confederacy, the spot where Jefferson Davis was sworn in as its president, Montgomery was a nucleus of Civil War leadership. At the end of the 19th century and start of the twentieth, the city embraced technological advancements. In 1886, it boasted the nation's first electric streetcar system, called The Lightning Route. In 1910, things really took off when Orville and Wilbur Wright chose the city to establish the first civilian flying school in the United States, and it was here that the first recorded "heavier-than-air" flight at night in aviation history occured.

Decades later, almost a century after the end of the Civil War, one of the most compelling chapters in the city's story played out, beginning a reconciliation long overdue. In 1955, Rosa Parks inspired the Montgomery Bus Boycott, which in turn gave rise to the Civil Rights Movement, led by Dr. Martin Luther King, Jr., who spread his message of peaceful resistance from the pulpit in his Montgomery church. In 1965, he led the final Selma-to-Montgomery march, the culmination of the Civil Rights struggle that brought about the passage of the Voting Rights Act. In the years following, the societal changes born in Montgomery swept the country and the globe.

Between its founding and now, Montgomery has undergone myriad changes and overcome as many challenges, but the city has always been focused on the future. Today, its people are still striving forward and making progress, but only because we've never stopped looking at and learning from our past.

Montgomery's Dexter Avenue is one of the most historic streets in America. Its sidewalks and storefronts have witnessed several world-changing moments: from the bronze star placed on the Capitol building steps to mark Jefferson Davis' inauguration as President of the Confederacy, to the spot where Rosa Parks boarded that infamous bus, and then full circle back to the front of the Capitol, where a century after the star was laid, Martin Luther King, Jr., delivered his rousing speech as the culmination of the final Selma-to-Montgomery march.

Photo by Jonathon Kohn

The Jefferson Davis statue on the grounds of the Capitol building.

Montgomery, April 11, 1861
General Beauregard, Charleston:

Do not desire needlessly to bombard Fort Sumter. If Major Anderson will state the time at which, as indicated by him, he will evacuate, and agree that in the meantime he will not use his guns against us unless ours should be employed against Fort Sumter, you are thus authorized to avoid the effusion of blood. If this or its equivalent be refused, reduce the fort as your judgment decides to be most practicable.

- L. P. Walker, Sec. of War. C.S.A.

The spiral staircases in the Capitol building, designed by architect Horace King, are remarkable examples of cantilevered stairways. The former slave's achievements here and in his other notable accomplishments are made all the more remarkable since he attained them while working among the prejudice against blacks and other minorities prevalent in Alabama and the South during his lifetime. He also served two terms in the Alabama Legislature.

Photo by Eric Salas

"How long? Not long, because the arc of the moral universe is long, but it bends toward justice."

– Martin Luther King, Jr.

Sitting in the shadow of the Capitol building, The Dexter Avenue King Memorial Baptist Church was founded in 1877 in a spot that was once a slave trader's pen. In the mid-1950s, it became the breeding ground for the Civil Rights Movement under the leadership of its young pastor, Dr. Martin Luther King, Jr. It now houses a museum, inviting visitors to gaze at the pulpit where Dr. King spread his message of peaceful protest and marvel at the moving mural depicting Dr. King's journey from Montgomery to Memphis where he would meet his tragic end. The church's parsonage around the corner, the house that was Dr. King's home from 1954 to 1960, is also open to visitors.

Photo by Madeline Burkhardt

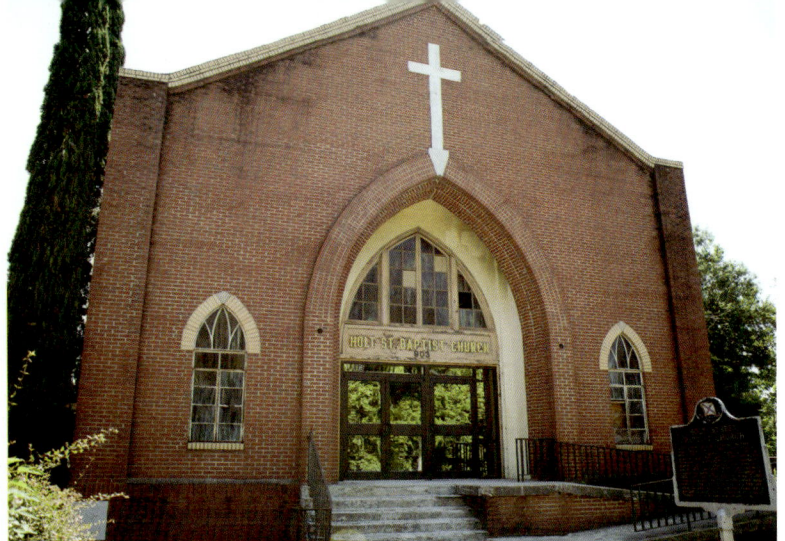

HOLT STREET MEMORIAL BAPTIST CHURCH

A Community of Faith with a Commitment to Its History

On Monday, December 5, 1955, Holt Street Baptist Church entered the history books as the site of the first mass meeting that launched the Montgomery Bus Boycott and gave birth to the nation's Civil Rights Movement. There, a 26-year-old Martin Luther King, Jr. delivered his first public address to a crowd of 5,000 that filled the pews and spilled into the parking lot and onto the streets. Rosa Parks was in attendance, having been arrested the previous Friday for her refusal to yield her seat on a Montgomery transit bus to a white man.

Events moved quickly after Parks' arrest, and organizations such as the Women's Political Council, the NAACP, and ultimately the Montgomery Improvement Association saw an opportunity to challenge unjust segregation laws. A one-day boycott of the bus system was hastily arranged for Monday to be followed by a mass meeting that night. Pastor Dr. A.W. Wilson offered Holt Street as the location for the gathering, and together the attendees made the fateful decision to stay off the buses until the segregation law was overturned.

Holt Street Baptist Church remained active as a church community at that site for more than 40 years. Then in 1998, Dr. Willie D. McClung, who began serving as pastor in 1992, led the church through a relocation that would provide for the growth of the congregation. At the same time, the church made a commitment to preserve its pivotal connection to U.S. history. With the addition of the word "Memorial," the original church name was retained.

Today, Holt Street Memorial Baptist Church is located on South Court Street on a campus known as The Village. A 1,000-seat sanctuary is the centerpiece for Sunday Worship at 8:15 a.m. and Wednesday Bible Study at 6 p.m. The educational building is home to a weekday preschool and a Christian Academy for grades K-6 and includes the 100-seat I.S. Fountain Chapel, the 120-seat Performing Arts Theatre, and 22 classrooms. The W. D. McClung Family Life Center is another facility designed to accommodate large events.

As the expansion of the facilities reached its culmination on South Court Street, the congregation was able to devote more attention to its original Holt Street location. Significant efforts have been undertaken to restore the original sanctuary and to add an interactive exhibit space for visitors. The Holt Street location recently reopened as a museum and is included on the state's Civil Rights Trail.

Photography by Brooke Glassford/Colorbox

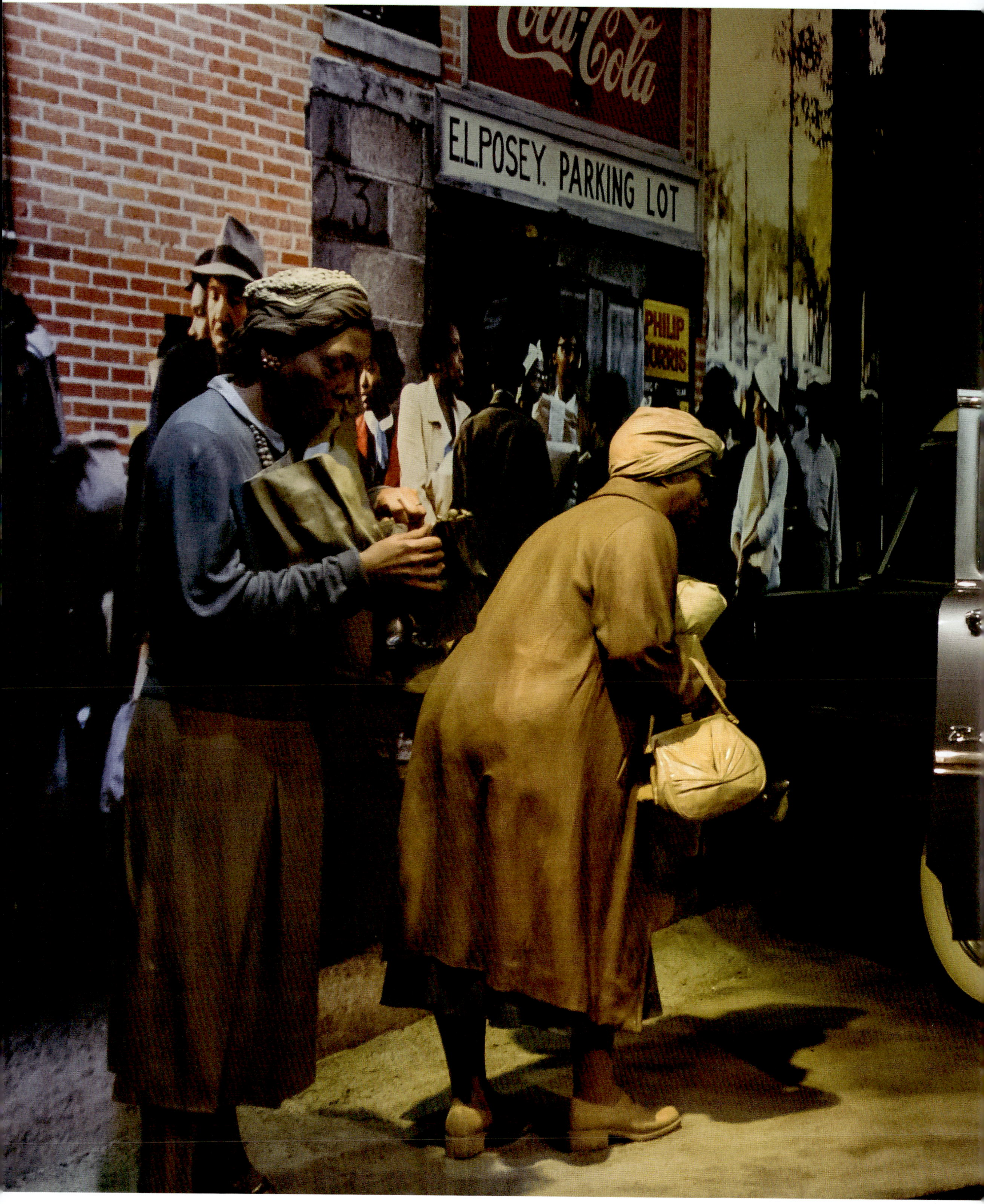
Coca-Cola
E.L.POSEY. PARKING LOT
PHILIP

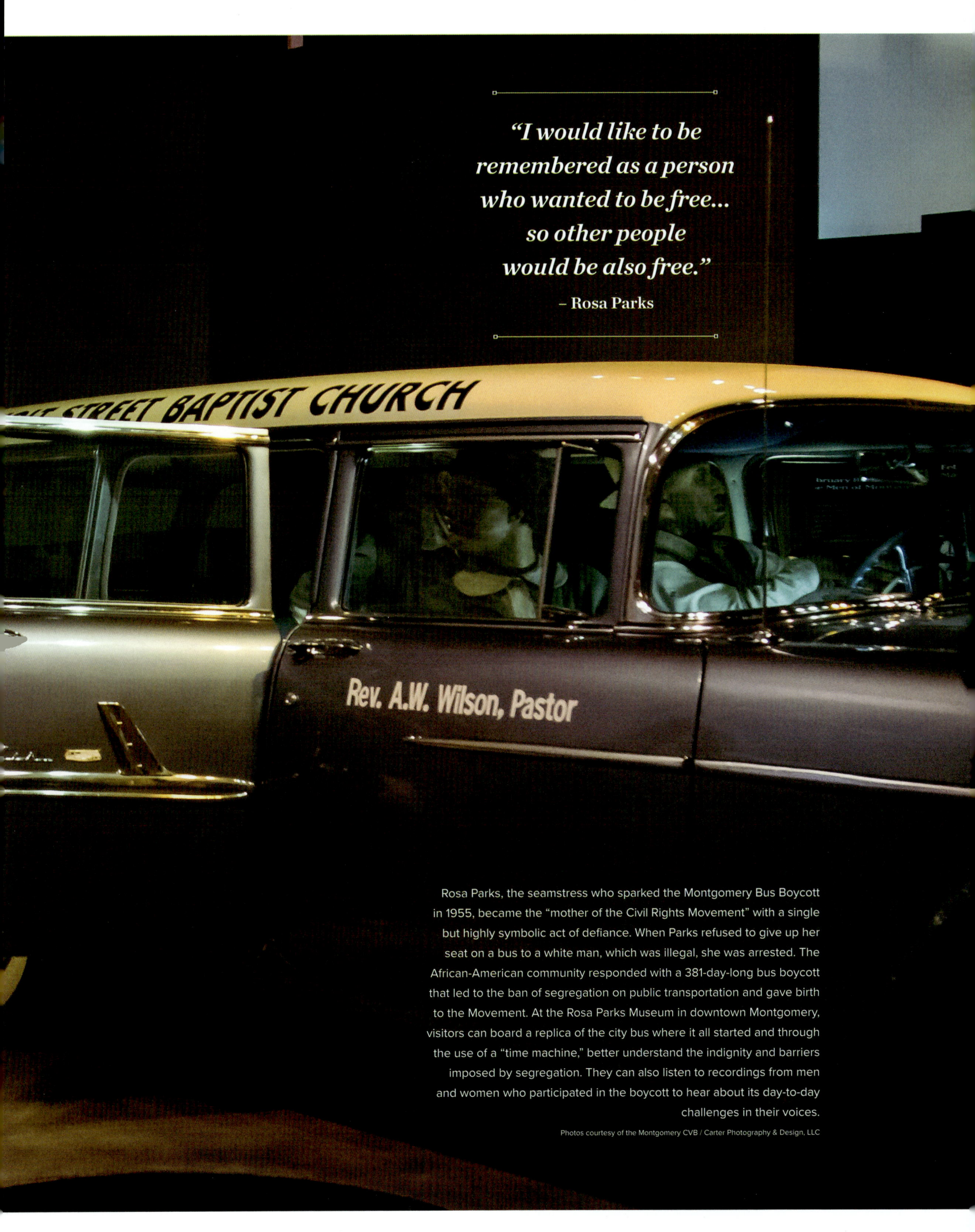

"I would like to be remembered as a person who wanted to be free... so other people would be also free."
– Rosa Parks

Rosa Parks, the seamstress who sparked the Montgomery Bus Boycott in 1955, became the "mother of the Civil Rights Movement" with a single but highly symbolic act of defiance. When Parks refused to give up her seat on a bus to a white man, which was illegal, she was arrested. The African-American community responded with a 381-day-long bus boycott that led to the ban of segregation on public transportation and gave birth to the Movement. At the Rosa Parks Museum in downtown Montgomery, visitors can board a replica of the city bus where it all started and through the use of a "time machine," better understand the indignity and barriers imposed by segregation. They can also listen to recordings from men and women who participated in the boycott to hear about its day-to-day challenges in their voices.

Photos courtesy of the Montgomery CVB / Carter Photography & Design, LLC

Barbara Gaston, Melanie Chambliss,
Dan Edgeworth and Ann Boutwell

A Story to Tell

"The early history of Prattville and Autauga County introduced economic diversity, not only to the River Region, but to the entire State and the South. Daniel Pratt is viewed as the one who introduced the Industrial Revolution to Alabama. Prior to Pratt's arrival in 1833, Alabama's economy was purely agriculturally based. Recognizing Alabama's wealth of rich natural resources, Pratt created Alabama's, and generally the South's, first industrial town when he modeled his new village after towns in his native New Hampshire. Today, his 'New England Village of the South,' is recognized as 'The Birthplace of Industry' in Alabama. The Autauga County Heritage Association has played a huge role in saving and promoting the legacy of Pratt. The downtown revitalization and the Prattaugan Museum display the rich history of our town. Currently, a team of volunteer archivists involved in the Daniel Pratt/Continental Gin Company Preservation Project are in the process of preserving 180 years of cotton ginning history. Prattville has a story to tell! Our future stands on the shoulders of a man with a vision and a town unlike any other in the South. Prattville and Autauga County will continue to attract businesses, families, and visitors alike. Pratt's innovative spirit lives on in the progress of our community."

**-Ann Boutwell,
Prattville and Autauga County historian**

All In the Family: A conversation with two generations of the Neeley Family

Anybody who knows much of anything about Montgomery knows that Mary Ann Neeley is the authority on the city's—and the area's—history.

If you don't know that already, you will know it within minutes of meeting her. Spunky and smart with her short bobbed hair and round, wire-rim glasses slightly hiding inquisitive eyes, Mary Ann is always ready and happy to regale anyone with tales of our city's significant — and sometimes troubled — past. Two of her grandsons, cousins Graham and Collier Neeley, have followed in her footsteps, both making history their life's work, Collier at the Alabama Historical Commission and Graham at the Alabama Department of Archives and History. The three Neeleys shed a little light on what about Montgomery's history inspires them, why preserving it is important, and what we can learn from Montgomery's specific story.

What makes Montgomery history unique?
Mary Ann: The diversity of it. It deals with three distinct cultures converging, the Creek Indians, whites and blacks. While we often think about the Selma-to-Montgomery march when we think of our history, another group, much earlier, was forced to march down Dexter Avenue, the Creek Indians, on their way to being removed. And then, in later years, Montgomery was the spot of the two most cataclysmic events in U.S. history, the Civil War and the Civil Rights movement. Montgomery and the River Region are a true cultural crossroads.

What about Montgomery's history and past inspires you?
Graham: I think Collier and I can both say our grandmother was a large part of our inspiration, but for me, watching the revitalization of Dexter Avenue is exciting. Seeing it pay homage to multiple sites that tell of such a rich history and showing the two stories, Civil War and Civil Rights, being told on the same street through the ages. It shows that plenty of people, not just historians, really care about our history.

Why does our history matter?
Collier: It is who we are and where we are going, and so there are many lessons to pull from that history. And it's not just big things like the final Selma-to-Montgomery march, but the day-to-day of people's lives that show how society and culture operate and how that led to things that happened.

Graham: History can be difficult to look at sometimes, but we have to examine it and learn from it.

What can we learn from it?
Mary Ann: A quote I love says, "The past can't be cured." What happened here did happen. We don't have to be proud of all of it, and we can move on from it, but we can't go back and change it, so we need to know about it and learn from it. One lesson we can learn is how did the Jim Crow era happen? What led to that? We have to understand it fully so when and if things that reek of it come our way again, we get it. That's how we stop it, but we have to see it clearly first.

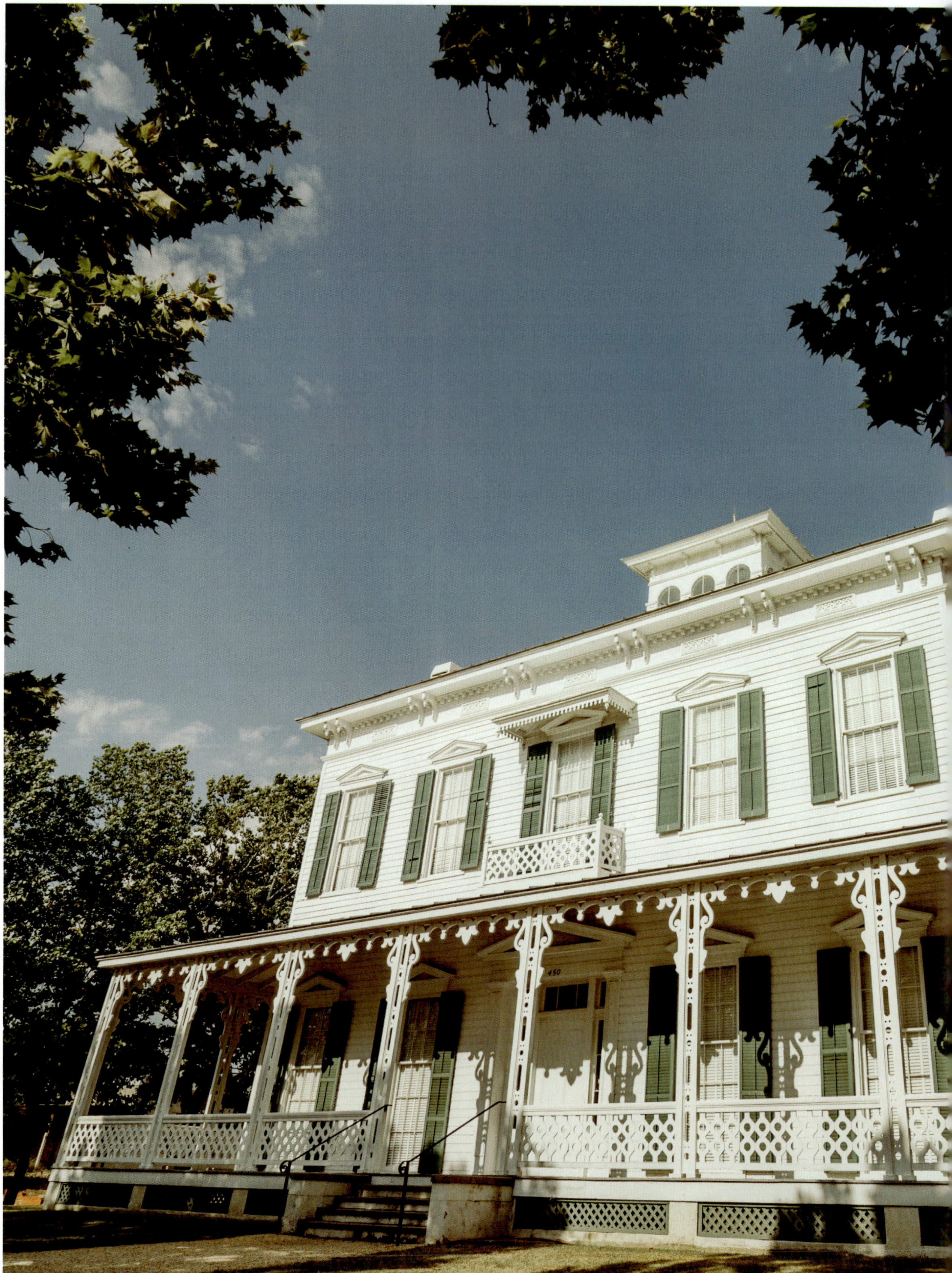

Old Alabama Town features completely authentic 19th and early 20th century homes and buildings that have been saved from demolition, carefully restored and reopened to the public as a history museum.

Photos by Becca Beers

49

The Alabama Department of Archives and History was the nation's first state department of its kind.

"Since 1901, the Alabama Department of Archives and History has been the home of Alabama history, a place where residents of our state and visitors from around the globe can surround themselves with fascinating collections connected to some of the most compelling history in the United States. From Native American societies to the Civil War and Civil Rights, our exhibits and programs help visitors understand Alabama's role in events that defined the American character.

Although our mission is to serve the entire state, the Archives and its Museum of Alabama have an obvious, special significance for the communities of the River Region. Along with the State Capitol, the Archives building anchors the east end of Montgomery's revitalized downtown and is an easy walk from the restaurants, shops and residences of Dexter Avenue and surrounding streets. Newcomers to Alabama will find the Archives to be a perfect introduction to their new home, and even lifelong residents are sure to learn something new during their visits.

More than just a window to the past, the Archives is a place where citizens can prepare to build a better future by investigating the decisions and values that shaped our present. We hope you will visit soon to find your story!"

-Steve Murray, Director of the Alabama Archives

Photo courtesy of the Fitzgerald Museum / Thomas Lucas

Infused with the creativity of the flamboyant couple who called it home and sharing their lives through letters, manuscripts and more, The Fitzgerald Museum gives residents and visitors a tangible way to connect with a bit of both F. Scott and Zelda Fitzgerald's energy, making it a literary landmark and a compelling addition to the capital city's cultural landscape.

Photo courtesy of the Fitzgerald Museum / Jonathon Kohn

A Legacy at Home

"The story of F. Scott and Zelda Fitzgerald fits perfectly in the middle of the history that makes Montgomery what it is: the Civil War history and the Civil Rights history. Their meeting here basically birthed the Jazz Age. Zelda, a native of Montgomery, remains an icon of independence for women all over the world. And Scott will forever be a literary giant. Their home, which is now the Museum, is the last of four surviving homes and the only dedicated museum to the lives and legacies of the Fitzgeralds in the world."

- Sara Powell, Executive Director of The Fitzgerald Museum

Man on the Street

Legendary country crooner Hank Williams was born in Butler County, Alabama, but began his musical career in Montgomery when he moved to the city in 1937 with his Silvertone guitar in hand hoping to make it big. Williams frequented many Montgomery restaurants, and he was known to often write songs while sitting at the lunch counter in Chris' Hot Dogs on Dexter Avenue. He got his break when he performed a few songs in a small studio at WSFA radio. It was the first time his distinctive voice traveled the airwaves, but it wouldn't be the last. Before his untimely death in 1953 at age 29, he created country music classics that have been hailed by critics and fans alike as some of the most important songs of all time, including 11 No. 1 hits. He and his wife Audrey are buried in the Oakwood Annex Cemetery on the edge of downtown. Both grave sites are marked by giant granite music notes, and Hank's is further embellished with a stone cowboy hat. His final resting place draws crowds, as does the Hank Williams Museum downtown, where the Cadillac in which he took his last ride is housed along with other memorabilia.

Located south of Wetumpka where the Coosa and Tallapoosa rivers meet to form the headwaters of the Alabama River, Fort Toulouse-Jackson National Historic Park invites visitors to discover more than 6,000 years of history.
Photo by Barry Chrietzberg

The clock at the former site of the First National Bank Building on Company Street in downtown Wetumpka is a local landmark that has been telling time for more than 100 years.

Photo by Brooke Glassford / Colorbox Photography

Photo by Becca Beers

Keeping History Alive

"Today it is vitally important to ensure the past is maintained in the present and carried into the future so we simply do not forget the roads we have traveled. After all, a society's history is the road map to where they have been and who they are and this is what we hope to communicate to visitors of Fort Toulouse-Fort Jackson Park. For the people of Alabama, more than 6,000 years of history is preserved at this site and it is that history that ties us to the land and rivers and connects us to past, present and future."

-Ove Jensen, Site Director, Fort Toulouse-Fort Jackson Park

Montgomery is home to several transportation firsts. The city boasted the country's first electric streetcar line, called the Lightning Route. In 1910, the nation's first civilian flying school was established in the capital city by the "fathers of flight," Orville and Wilbur Wright. The duo's school was located at what came to be known as Wright Field. The school only lasted a short time, but it set the stage for the establishment of Maxwell-Gunter Air Force Base in Montgomery.

Center of It All
Downtowns of the River Region

Fronting the banks of the Alabama River, downtown Montgomery's Riverwalk makes for an inviting stroll any time and is often host to special events like alfresco concerts and performances at the Riverwalk Amphitheater.

Photo courtesy of the Montgomery CVB / Benjamin Bevilacqua

A city's downtown area is its center; in its streets it contains the history, the heritage and the stories that imbue a spot with the qualities and personality that make it distinct. After decades of boarded-up windows and fading foot traffic, downtowns all across the River Region are once again thriving. Wetumpka's little downtown square is bustling. Prattville's is feeling a flow of enthusiasm to match the bubbling Autauga Creek running along its edge.

Downtown has always been Montgomery's heart. Yet, for a long stretch in the second half of the 20th century, our capital city's vital organ was barely beating. Suburban sprawl pushed people out to the city's edges, which in turn forced businesses to shutter, meaning even fewer people made their way to the area. But in the late 1990s, a few visionaries saw the truth: Without a vibrant city core, Montgomery itself would lack vitality. City and business leaders embarked on a bold plan to re-energize downtown, and today, while much progress has been made, the work is still ongoing.

Montgomery's skyline continues to change, yet the area's unique historic sites and breathtaking architecture are being painstakingly preserved. Downtown is now buzzing with life and emerging as a melting pot of arts, culture, business and government, all while giving a nod to our heritage.

Its easily walkable areas are burgeoning with retail, restaurants and nightlife pumping renewed excitement into residents, attracting tourists in droves and inspiring further development. Entertainment options abound, including the often winning and widely praised Biscuits Baseball team that continues to hit home runs with hometown fans and visitors alike. Old commercial spaces have been transformed into swank residential spaces that are bringing people to live downtown again, and so much more is on the drawing board.

Photos by Becca Beers

In Wetumpka, the Main Street organization is making great strides. Projects like the Tulotoma Snail Trail, a cultivated place project using art to tell the community's history, are adding to its downtown area's appeal.

The old Pratt cotton gin hints at the city's industrial past and anchors Prattville's charming downtown. Its streets are lined with quaint boutiques and tasty local eateries, in addition to a peaceful creek-side park.

Today, both leaders and residents of the entire tri-county area know that continued enhancements leading to improved experiences in flourishing downtowns are key to the River Region's future. Right now, that future is looking brighter than ever.

CITY OF MONTGOMERY

Two small villages, New Philadelphia, founded by Massachusetts lawyer Andrew Dexter in 1817, and East Alabama, established by Georgians led by John Scott in 1818, united in 1819 to form Montgomery, named for Revolutionary hero Gen. Richard Montgomery. Connecting at Court Square, the two towns' principal streets were Philadelphia's Market Street (Dexter Avenue) and East Alabama's Main Street (Commerce Street). First courthouse stood to west of artesian well which City enlarged in 1850s. Fountain erected in 1885.

(Continued on other side)
ALABAMA HISTORICAL ASSOCIATION

Photo by Eric Salas

ADAMS FAMILY ENTERPRISES, LLC

Samuel Adams, former CEO of Adams Life Insurance Company and a lawyer by training, was an early investor in the redevelopment of downtown Montgomery. "My wife, Mary, and I have made Montgomery our home for the last 30 years. We watched downtown Montgomery languish for decades as companies moved east," Sam recalled. They decided the best thing they could do to see a vibrant downtown Montgomery was to revitalize it so it would become a destination point for businesses, tourists and especially residents.

In the early 2000s, the Adams family began repurposing dilapidated century-old buildings into luxurious residential lofts and businesses. Sam shared, "We were the first major residential redevelopment in downtown Montgomery in many years."

These transformed structures have all the amenities of modern life, along with the charm and character of an historic building. Many of them stand in the midst of Montgomery's active entertainment district.

The Segall Ice Company, at the corner of North Court and East Jefferson Street, once manufactured blocks of ice. The second floor was used as a distribution center for Chiquita Bananas with a large skylight to help mature the bananas. "The bananas would come off the barges from the Alabama River and would be brought here to ripen in the indirect sunlight," reflected Mr. Adams.

Today, the new skylight stretches across two of the four luxury apartments that occupy the building's second floor. The aptly named Icehouse Lofts offer hardwood floors, granite countertops, 20-foot ceilings, spacious living areas, security systems and enclosed parking.

The first floor is the office space for the *Alabama Gazette*, a nearly 20-year old newspaper owned and operated by Loretta Grant and Sam. The newspaper has a circulation of approximately 20,000 and a strong online presence at www.alabamagazette.com.

While the building makes use of modern amenities, the historical touch is not lost. Several original and historic front-page articles decorate the walls, such as Neil Armstrong's walk on the moon and the sinking of the Titanic. An original framed area map of downtown Montgomery, circa 1887, hangs there too.

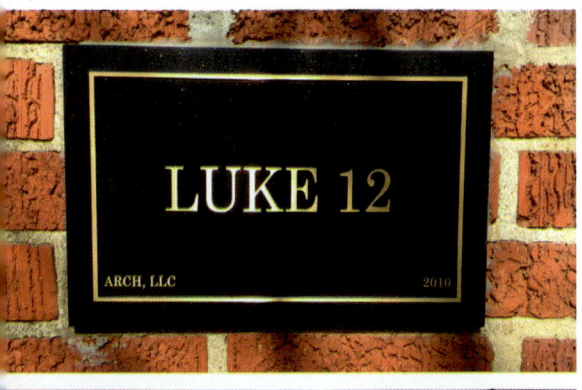

The original beams, while incredibly sturdy, still carry signs from the preparation of the ice. Prices for the blocks of ice can also be seen on the patina of the building. Twenty-foot windows replaced a portion of the bricks on the first floor that had deteriorated because of the chemical compound used to make the ice. One-hundred-year-old bricks on the pathway hold a special significance because they originate from Sam's grandfather's store in Samson, Alabama.

Across the street, at 241 North Court Street, The Gun Store Lofts are at the former location of Todd's Gun Shop, which had once been Alabama's longest active business. What began as a fur trade business and musket shop in 1822 was passed on as a family business from generation to generation, eventually settling in this location until closing its doors in 1986.

Today, the building houses a business on the first floor with residential units upstairs. The Gun Store Lofts offer seven one-bedroom floor plans featuring hardwood floors, exposed brick walls, granite, a private elevator, security systems and high fencing for the parking lot. That lot was made famous by the pivotal scene in the movie, *The Long Walk Home* starring Sissy Spacek and Whoopi Goldberg. A target range found in the basement was conveniently converted to storage cages for tenants' belongings.

When Mr. Adams moved to Montgomery in the '80s, he purchased a brick apartment complex strategically located on Adams Avenue. The property became a mixed-use structure that included an office space for Adams Life Insurance Company. After selling the company, he renovated the property for an exclusive residential setting.

Adams Ave. Flats are a mix of unique one-bedroom floor plans, each offering hardwood floors and vintage tile work. "The apartments have been modernized, but also retained some of the original hardware and checkered black-and-white tile that was popular in the '30s and '40s," commented Adams. Located one block from the state's Capitol, this represents the only residential property on Goat Hill.

The Printing Press Lofts, located at 215 North Court Street, were completed in 2014. The building was constructed in the early 1900s and originally purposed to be the headquarters for a newspaper. When the deal fell through, the property was transformed into a space for a lawyer's office, a barbershop, dress shops and even a broom-making store. The Printing Press Lofts are a unique mix of one-bedroom floor plans, each offering hardwood floors, exposed beams and custom tile work.

Each building has a bronze plaque on an outside wall referencing Scripture, which has a particular message for those who love and seek God. Sam is an active member of Trinity Presbyterian Church. He has also been a member of the Montgomery Rotary Club for 30 years and serves as District Governor for District 6880 in the 2018-19 Rotary year. Sam and Mary have been married for more than 30 years. They have been blessed with four children, Mary Elizabeth in New York, Ali in Atlanta, and Sarah Ross and Sam in Auburn as students. Sam concluded, "We are all but broken vessels, loving our God and our neighbors, while praying for His wisdom, love, and grace. To God be the Glory and may His blessings be with you always."

Montgomery's Kress building is full of light and life again, reopening in early 2018 as Kress on Dexter. It took $20 million and four years to transform the 90-year-old abandoned shell of the city's S.H. Kress Co. department store into a beautiful multi-use space combining retail, office and residential under one roof. The Kress redevelopment was a linchpin in the re-energizing of Dexter Avenue, one of our country's most historically significant streets.

Photo by Becca Beers

Photos by Jonathon Kohn

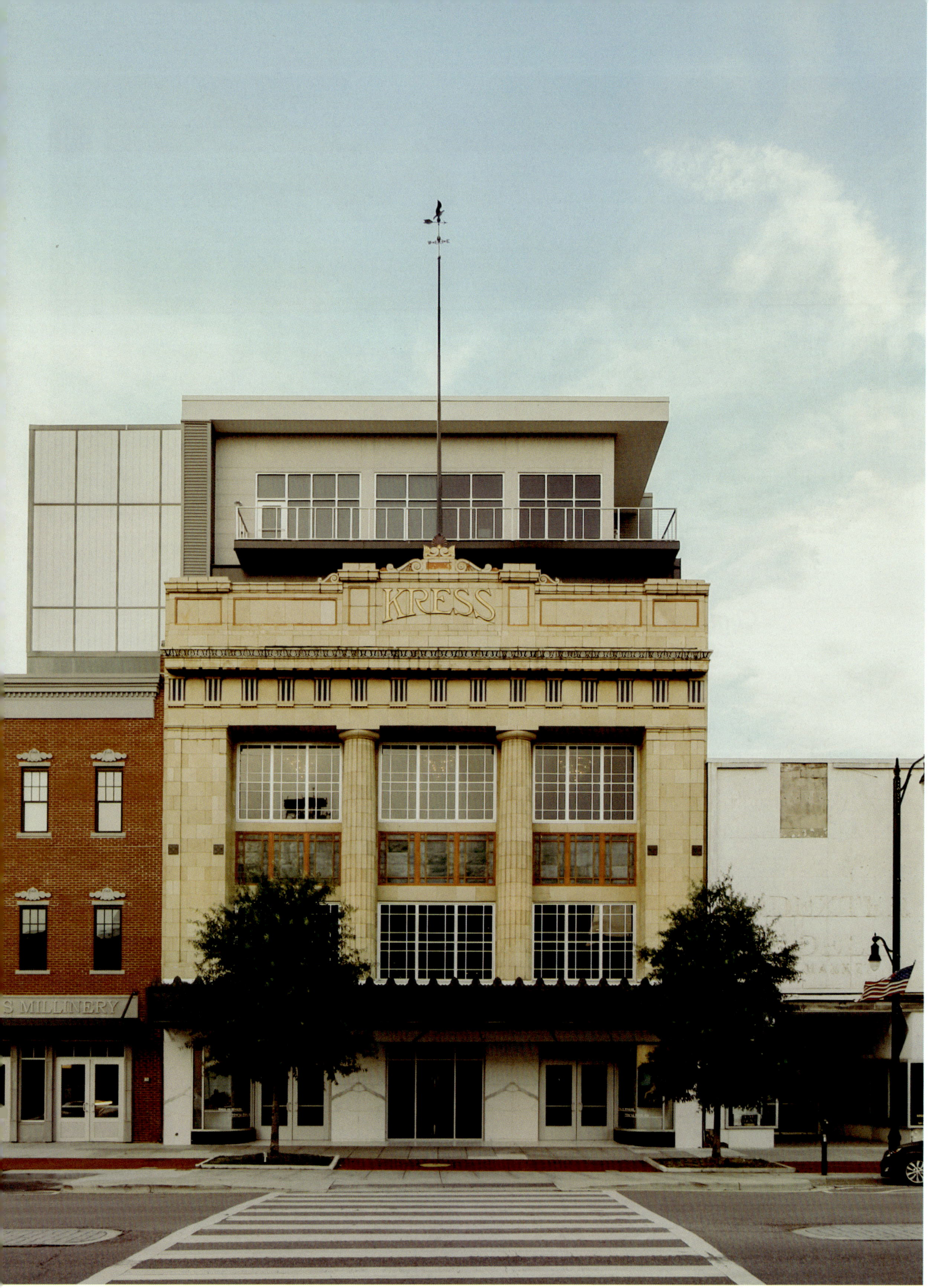
KRESS
S MILLINERY

Coming Home

"I was born and raised here, and when I moved back after college, I wasn't certain Montgomery was a place I wanted to stay. But now I know it is. There is so much opportunity here. From when the renaissance started downtown in the early 2000s, I've seen the rise of so many great things: the Biscuits, restaurants, residential spaces and more. But equally important are the soft assets downtown, the organizations and businesses working together to create an attitude that promotes quality of life and drives a narrative of inclusiveness. That's what the Downtown Business Association is really focused on."

– **Clay McInnis,
Executive Director,
Downtown Business Association**

RIVERFRONT FACILITIES

Downtown Montgomery has become a fun-filled destination for locals and tourists year-round. The City of Montgomery has several standout venues that bring a myriad of events to life, including the beautiful facilities of Riverfront Park, which include the Amphitheater, Pergola and Splash Pad, the historic Union Station Train Shed, enchanting cruises on the Harriott II Riverboat and festive occasions inside Riverwalk Stadium.

The City of Montgomery's Special Events Department helps give residents and tourists plenty of reasons to come enjoy the downtown area. Tom Pierce, who heads the department, says that their work is two-fold. "A large part of what we do is put on both ticketed and free events, while the other part of what we do is venue rental," he said.

Some of these events are sporting events, such as the Montgomery Half Marathon and 5K held in the spring. The Dragon Boat Festival along the Alabama River is a big draw in August for crowds watching dragon boat teams race on the Alabama River. At Riverwalk Stadium, home to the Montgomery Biscuits AA baseball team, fans gather as top-notch players deliver a season of exciting games.

Music is on the menu for the River Jam Music Festival and the Riverbend Brew Fest, both held in May. Summertime features a Rock the Park Battle of the Bands and an Independence Day celebration (with fireworks, of course!). Plus, the City of Montgomery hosts a family movie night at the Amphitheater during the summer on Monday nights.

In September, the Zombie Walk and Prom is another popular event for those dressed in zombie attire gathering to enjoy a block party and parade. In October, the Riverwalk Wine Festival is a savory event featuring more than 100 different wine samples and live music at the Riverwalk followed by a cruise on the Harriott II.

The holiday season launches with the Capital City Christmas Parade along historic Dexter Avenue and ends with a block party on Commerce Street for a New Year's Eve Downtown Celebration.

That's only the beginning of what's happening in downtown Montgomery – because there are many other events planned by organizers who lease these facilities for their own occasions.

Whether you're planning a festival, wedding, performance, competition or conference, you have many beautiful options for your venue. You can lease all or parts of Riverfront Park for your event, including the Riverwalk, Pergola and Amphitheater stage; the Historic Union Station Train Shed; the Harriott II Riverboat; or all or part of Riverwalk Stadium.

A "Cajun" in the Fountain City

—Mickey Thompson, owner, Uncle Mick's Cajun Cafe

Mickey Thompson has been an entrepreneur in the Montgomery River Region for the past 40 years. His interest in Cajun cuisine developed during his career as a real estate investor when he hired a Cajun carpenter for a two-week stint. Their relationship continued for another 15 years, and Mickey became fascinated with Cajun spices and cooking. "I came out of retirement in 2009 and started Uncle Micks. I've always enjoyed historical architectural structures and bought this building and one next door and remodeled it and opened my Cajun restaurant in the heart of downtown Prattville. We've been here ever since. I love being downtown. There's a lot going on and Prattville is a great place to do business."

The restaurant has been ranked the No. 1 restaurant in Prattville by Trip Advisor for four years in a row. Its authentic Cajun cuisine is cooked from scratch every morning. Not all of its food is spicy — They have a little something for everyone. "If you want to spice it up we have our own blend of hot sauce we make right here on location," said Mick. "We look forward to giving you a piece of Southern Louisiana right here in the Fountain City — serving up the best Cajun cuisine you can find between Birmingham and Mobile."

Photo by Brooke Glassford / Colorbox

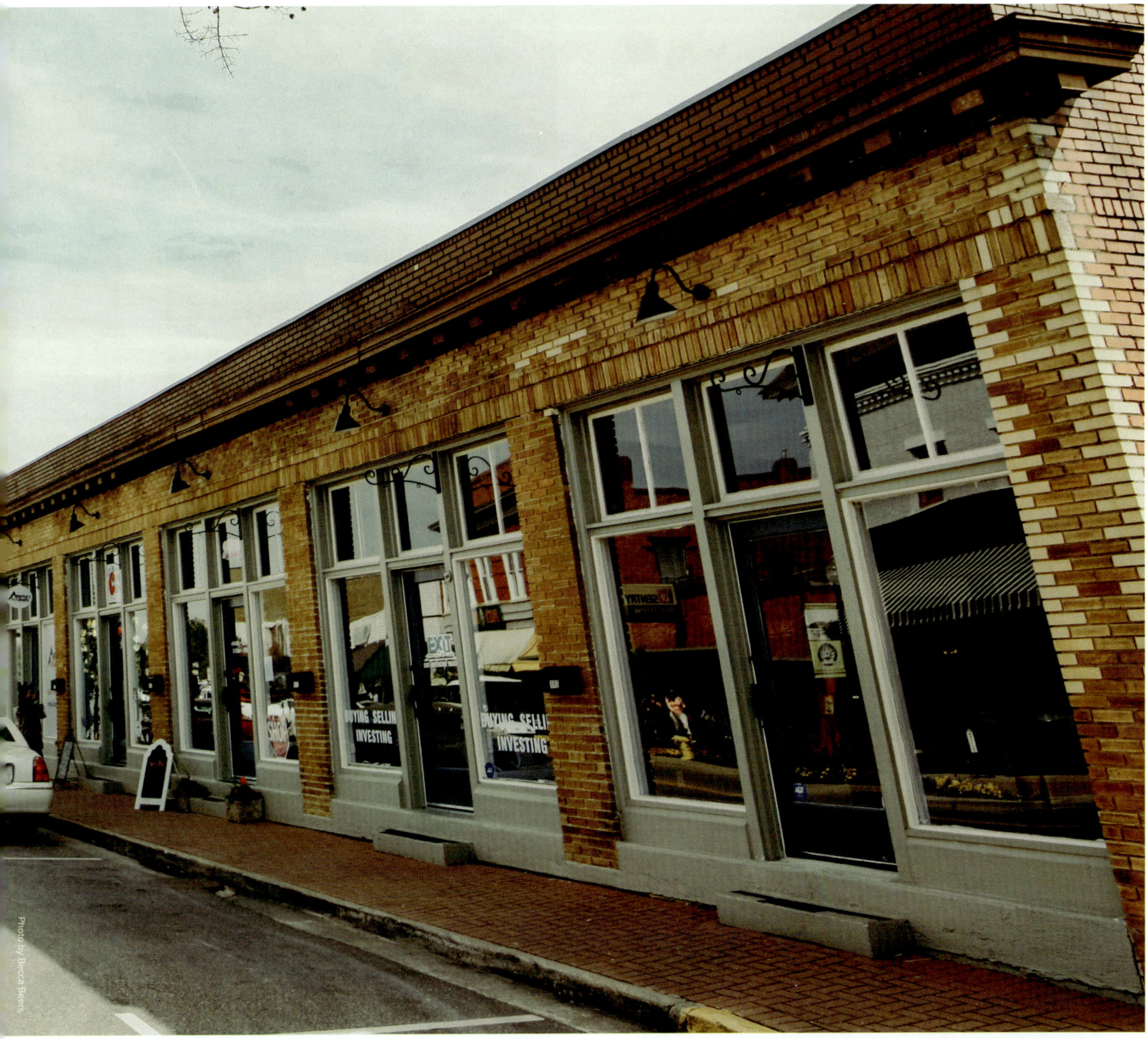

Photo by Becca Beers

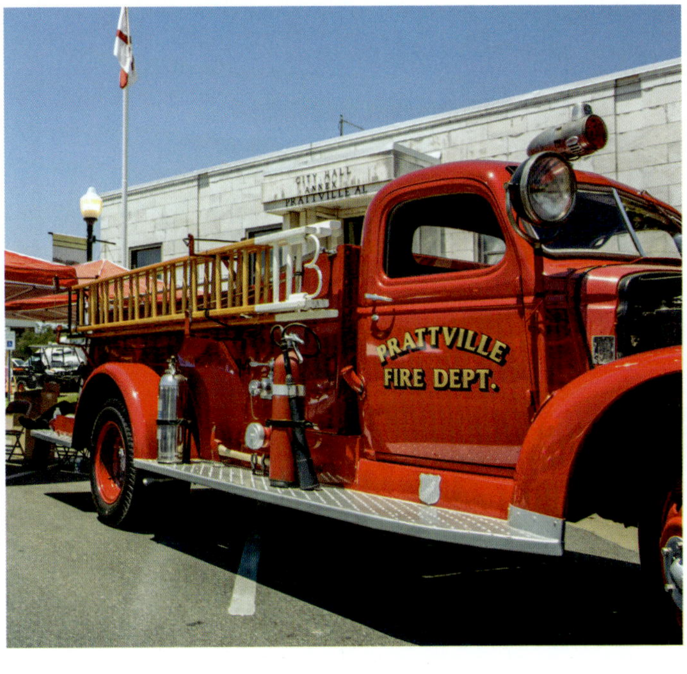

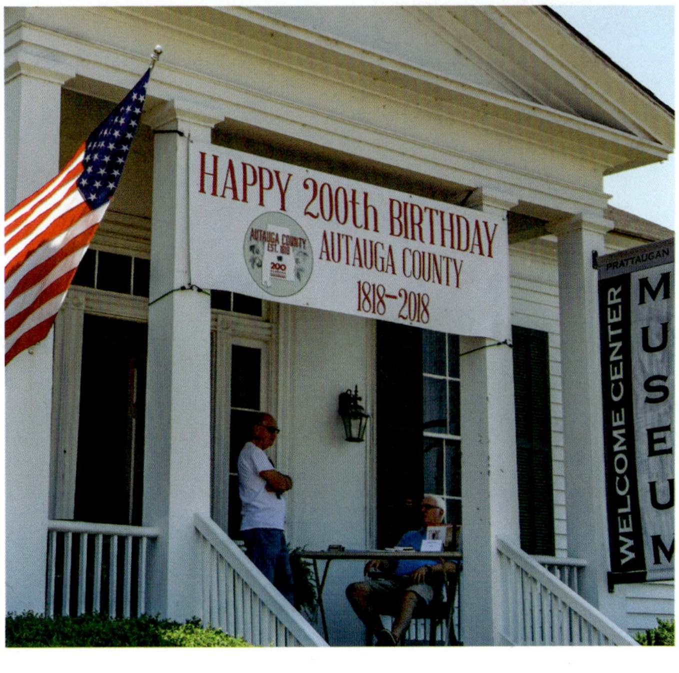

Photo by Becca Beers

Main Focus

"Main Street Wetumpka's mission is to revitalize downtown by incorporating economic vitality, design, promotion and organization. We have several projects just beginning, but we're really looking forward to the start of our downtown streetscape. I honestly believe the American identity is interwoven in its downtowns. There is a quaintness and charm found in downtowns that can't be replicated. Likewise, a history exists that gets lost when a vibrant downtown fades. A healthy downtown also leads to a more sustainable, locally focused economy. That's why the work we are doing is important."

–Jenny Stubbs, Executive Director, Main Street Wetumpka

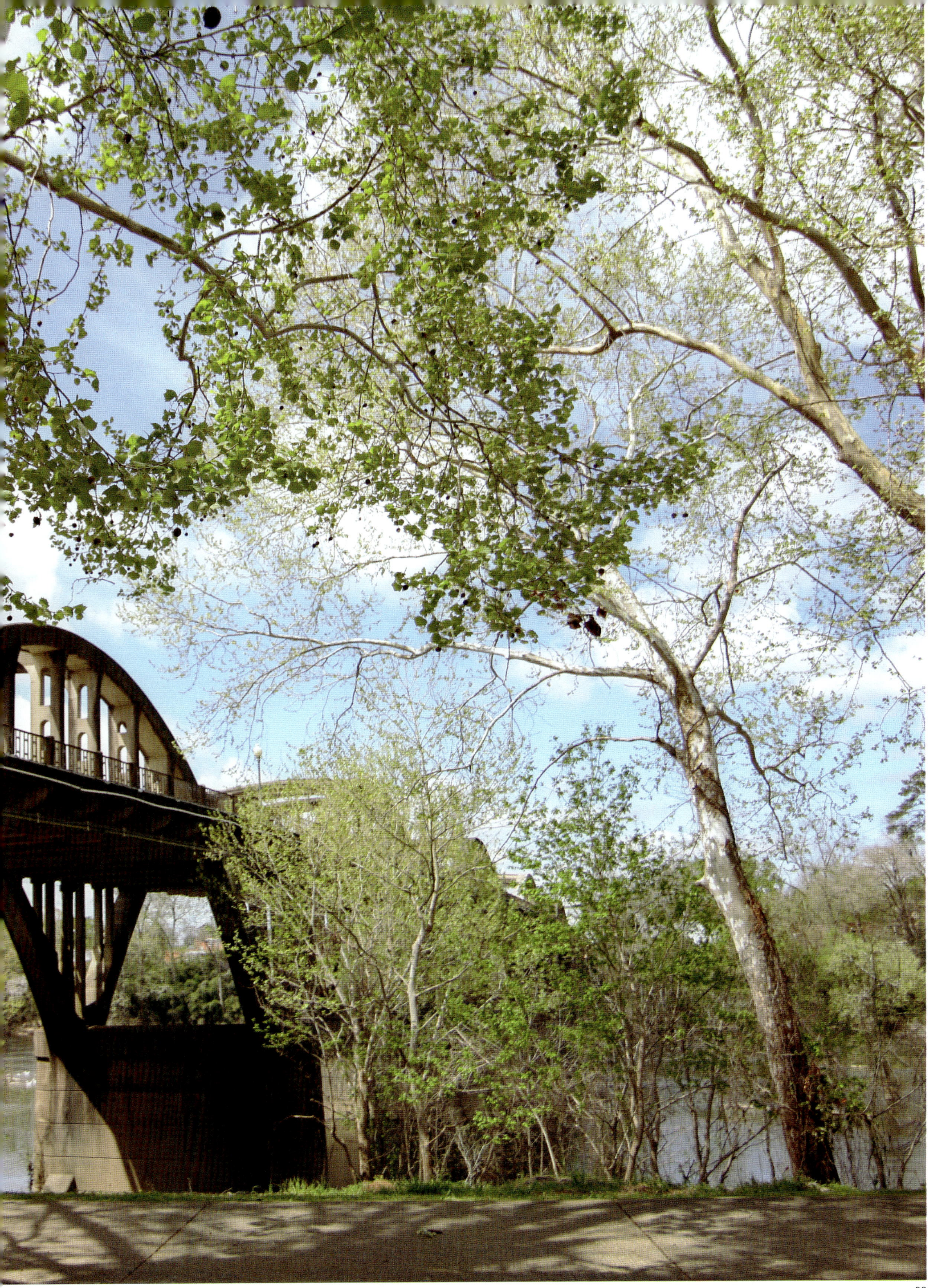

After decades of stagnation, downtown Montgomery is now buzzing with activity, providing a bevy of eating, drinking and entertainment options, places like the pedestrian-only Alley and the industrial chic AlleyBAR, Dreamland's authentic Alabama 'cue, the home-style Italian flavors of SaZa's pizzas, the relaxed but upscale options at Central (housed in an old grocery warehouse), and a truly vintage hot spot, Sous La Terre, a jazz and blues club that's an iconic element of Montgomery's music scene offering smooth grooves with cool attitude.

Photo by Robert Fouts

71

Bringing the Montgomery Biscuits baseball team to the capital city and creating Riverwalk Stadium, a modern ballpark built into a historic railway turn station, was the first pitch that sparked a full-fledged downtown renaissance.

Photo by Eric Salas

Photos by Jonathon Kohn

73

74

Lunch, dinner and special event cruises aboard the Harriott II Riverboat roll on down the Alabama River and offer a unique way to discover the waterway.
Photo by Robert Fouts

Art for All

"The Selma to Montgomery March mural downtown was a public art commission, and I won the proposal to do it. It was so meaningful to me to get to create it because civil rights is a subject I am passionate about, and, of course, I'm passionate about art. To have the opportunity to do a project that combined the two made that mural the most important work I've done to date. And I love seeing more and more public art pop up around downtown; it's an integral piece of reviving the area and telling the story of its many historic sites."

– **Sonny Paulk,
Montgomery artist and
creator of downtown's
Civil Rights March mural**

Courtesy of The Montgomery CVB

Courtesy of The Montgomery CVB

Photo by Robert Fouts

77

Making the Grade
Education

Quality education is paramount for the expansion of economic opportunity and high quality of life. Knowing this well, leaders and parents in Montgomery and the River Region are dedicated to do right by area students. Efforts to enhance education and ensure our schools make the grade and meet our children's academic needs have been and will stay a priority.

From faith-based private schools to The Montgomery Public School system's praised Magnet programs, there's a place for everyone. Montgomery's Loveless Academic Magnet Program, the No. 1 high school in the nation, recently moved into a new 82,250-square-foot facility at its new campus at the One Center. Also located in One Center is the Montgomery Preparatory Academy for Career Technologies, an innovative program established to strengthen the area's skilled workforce pipeline by providing hands-on learning for in-demand careers.

The Autauga County Technology Center in Prattville serves several high schools in the area and operates on a similar concept. By offering skills-based education in automotive technology, health sciences, information technology, engineering and more, it's preparing students for the careers of the future using experiential methods.

When Pike Road got a school system of its own, welcoming its first students in 2015, it was the realization of a long-held dream and the result of years of work for the town's leaders and residents. But they're not resting on their laurels. The town is expanding the system's reach and facilities to better serve its students.

Educating thousands of students in Wetumpka and beyond, Elmore County Schools continue to get top marks, too.

After high school graduation, students don't have to look far to go further, thanks to a long list of colleges and universities right here at home, including Alabama State University, Auburn University Montgomery, Central Alabama Community College, Faulkner University, Huntingdon College, Trenholm State Community College and Troy University Montgomery. For those seeking everything from a classic liberal arts experience or the convenience of online courses to classes teaching practical technical skills, the River Region offers access to all.

Photo by Robert Fouts

AUBURN UNIVERSITY AT MONTGOMERY

Developing Partnerships and Responsive Programs for Community Impact and Student Success

Auburn University at Montgomery provides a high quality education that serves the community as well as prepares students from nearby, across the country or around the world for successful careers of their choosing.

Since 1967, AUM has grown to become one of the River Region's most valuable assets. The respected institution has been ranked among the South's top universities by U.S. News and World Report, was named one of the best colleges in the Southeast by The Princeton Review, is designated as a Military Friendly School, and is consistently chosen as the best university in the area. AUM is accredited by the Southern Association of Colleges and Schools.

"Auburn Montgomery's stakeholders — whether they're students, faculty and staff, alumni and donors, government or business, or individuals in the community — all value three things about the university: our commitment to quality education, our history of strong collaborative and service partnerships with our community, and our vibrant campus where students come first," says Chancellor Carl A. Stockton.

Auburn Montgomery delivers educational programs that mirror the strengths of the area economy and are often developed and fine-tuned through the input of vital community partnerships. AUM's deans and administrators are continually talking with local business leaders about areas of educational focus that would lead to a stronger, better prepared workforce, and they apply this insight in program development.

Through five colleges — the Colleges of Business, Education, Arts and Sciences, Nursing and Health Sciences, and Public Policy and Justice — students can select from more than 90 fields of study in bachelor's, master's and doctoral programs. Class schedules provide the flexibility that active students require — whatever their life stage. Each of the colleges offer undergraduate and graduate classes in traditional, online and hybrid formats, with courses offered during the day, evenings and on weekends. In every program, students receive detailed knowledge and hands-on, practical experience, often from professionals in the field.

The attention to the needs of business, government, industry, health care, information technology and all other facets of the economy has led to a responsiveness in creating academic offerings. Unique programs, unavailable anywhere else in the region, include Geographic Information Systems, Hospitality and Tourism, Homeland Security, and Cybersystems and Information Security. In addition, nursing programs are very highly regarded with great job placement, and AUM offers fully online options for medical laboratory sciences. In fact, through AUM Online, a number of online courses are both more affordable and more convenient for working professionals, traditional students, non-resident students and students taking summer courses.

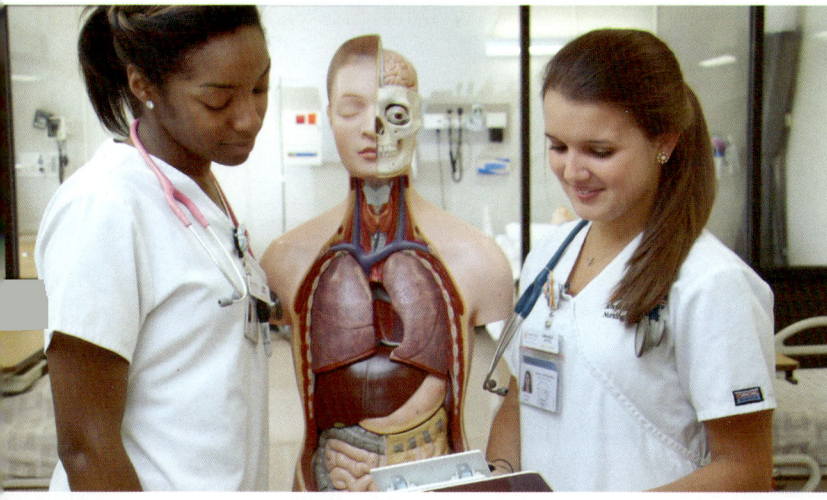

Supporting Student Success

AUM's student body is made up of an interesting mix of traditional and non-traditional students. Some are right out of high school, while others have been working for years. Together, they bring diverse experiences into the classroom that makes for an interesting and dynamic learning environment. Classes are small (on average 16:1 student-to-teacher ratio), allowing for easy interaction with professors.

Student success is a critical part of the mission, especially since 67 percent of AUM students are first-generation college students. Auburn Montgomery prides itself on the attention it gives to each student and has strategically set up programs to help acclimate students to college life.

The Warhawk Academic Success Center (WASC), for example, serves as the one-stop shop for all of AUM students' academic support needs. Here, students can meet with their Student Success Advisor and develop an individualized plan for academic success. Students who are not yet sure of their major can meet with the Undeclared Academic Advisor and begin working on their core classes. The WASC also provides a University Success course for all AUM students to complete in their first year of attendance and offers several other programs that are devoted to providing students the opportunity to reach their goals. Auburn Montgomery also provides critical financial assistance, and each year awards more than $2 million in scholarships to first-time students.

In addition, AUM offers a multifaceted campus life for its students. From Student Government to Greek Life, clubs and organizations, and club and intramural sports, students have plenty of opportunity to pursue their passions or find new ones. Conference sports are a big deal on campus at AUM, as well. AUM fields 11 men's, women's and co-ed sports, including basketball, soccer, baseball, softball, cross country, volleyball and tennis. After bringing home NAIA championships, the university is moving to the NCAA Division II Gulf South Conference.

Supporting Local Businesses

Auburn University at Montgomery is also committed to helping businesses, organizations, and individuals achieve success through consulting services and community professional development events. SummaSource, the consulting division for AUM, provides training, consulting and technology services. Through SummaSource, organizations and individuals are better equipped to become more productive and efficient in reaching their goals.

"Our Mission is to enhance productivity for individuals and organizations," says Dr. Katherine Jackson Webb, Vice Chancellor of the Office of Business & Community Initiatives. "If individuals are more efficient, it creates a better work life."

"Our world is changing very quickly," says Chancellor Stockton. "AUM works to give our students and our partners and neighbors in the region and beyond the tools and skills to change with it and to effect change. AUM's nimble approach and execution are our foundation and our future."

Students from around Alabama visit the capital city each year to learn about the region's rich history at spots like the Museum of Alabama at The Alabama Department of Archives and History.

Photo courtesy of the Alabama Department of Archives and History / Carter Photography & Design, LLC

Athletics play a big role in student life in the River Region. From football to soccer to baseball and track, there's a sport for everyone. Pictured: The Montgomery Academy's cross-country track team.

Photo courtesy of the Montgomery Academy

Saint James students of all ages enjoying the private school's annual Field Day.
Photo courtesy of Saint James School

Photo by Brooke Glassford / Colorbox

A Big Impact

- Ed Castile, Director of AIDT (Alabama Industrial Development Training)

"A workforce is developed in the education systems. At an early age, and all through their education system experience, the worker is learning to communicate, compute and problem-solve, so the education system is the MOST important part of developing our workforce. For the long-term sustainability of the workforce, education systems must endeavor to graduate and educate all their students. And it needs to begin as early as pre-K. Studies clearly indicate that early childhood development and elementary programs are where we have the most impact on the workforce. This is where foundations for learning are formed, work ethic is developed and lives changed. Montgomery's creation of MPACT (Montgomery Preparatory Academy for Career Technologies), by listening to the area employers and immediately responding to their needs by creating specific programs, is a huge and progressive step in developing the local workforce."

83

TRENHOLM STATE COMMUNITY COLLEGE

Shaping the Future

Trenholm State's mission is to provide comprehensive and accessible educational opportunities. These opportunities include courses designed for academic transfer to four-year colleges and universities as well as allied health, service and technical programs designed to promote economic development, enhance workforce development and improve the quality of life for enrolled students and the community as a whole.

Trenholm State Community College, founded in 1966 as H. Councill Trenholm State Technical College, is a multi-campus institution serving the River Region of Alabama with associate degrees, as well as a wide range of certificate and workforce training options. In 2014, Trenholm State was granted accreditation through the Southern Association of Colleges and Schools Commission on Colleges (SACSCOC) and subsequently was authorized to change its status from a technical college to a community college.

Setting New Standards for Workforce Development Training

Trenholm State strives to enrich classroom learning with real-world instructional models and occupational skill development. The college continues to foster innovation in collaboration by reaching out to area employers to offer general and customized training resources provided on campus in classroom labs or on site in the workplace. The college offers both day and evening courses to accommodate working students' employment schedules.

Trenholm State's purpose is to train students effectively to meet the specific expectations of their employers or future employers and continually bridge the skill gap by developing business and industry partnerships that become a transforming catalyst to career pathways for students. Trenholm State aims to promote efficiency and excellence in the ever-changing job market while addressing the need for credentialing and certification.

Trenholm State has a six-county service area—Montgomery, Bullock, Lowndes, Macon, Autauga and Elmore—from which the college attracts students from all walks of life, backgrounds and educational levels. The college provides inclusive and affordable access to higher education, supports the success and achievements of all students, and maintains vibrant partnerships and pathways with educational institutions, community organizations and local businesses and industries.

Trenholm State Community College is helping to combat the coming nursing shortage with its nursing program that uses hands-on learning to train its students.

Photo courtesy of Trenholm State Community College

Montgomery is home to quite a few higher education institutions, like Alabama State University (top), Virginia College (middle; This student started her own hair salon thanks to her degree), and (bottom) Auburn University Montgomery.

Invest in Education

"There are three factors that act as pillars for economic development.

First is proximity to an interstate. Second is the presence of state or federal establishments. The third is access to a comprehensive university for workforce training and enhancement of quality of life. Montgomery's strategic advantages, like access to roads and highways, being a state capital with a military base and the presence of universities like AUM, along with its rich culture mean we have all the necessary attributes for economic growth and continued prosperity. Our history is our wealth. We've just got to make sure we invest in opportunities — like education — that are conducive for long-term economic growth."

- Dr. Keivan Deravi, Dean of Auburn University Montgomery's College of Public Policy & Justice

TROY UNIVERSITY

Troy University has a long history of serving students from the River Region and, today, is uniquely positioned to serve as the area's center for graduate education.

Through its partnerships with state and city government and the business community, TROY Montgomery provides working professionals the opportunity to advance their careers while also advancing the city and the region.

Day, night and weekend classes structured in five nine-week terms throughout the year provide convenient academic opportunities for students who are often balancing work, family and pursuing their career goals and dreams. Troy Montgomery strives to prepare students to take their careers and, by result, our city to the next level.

Students at Troy Montgomery find degree programs in high-demand fields such as social work, human resource management, computer science, psychology, counseling, nursing and adult education. The dedicated faculty and staff at Troy Montgomery are committed to equipping students with the tools necessary for success.

Nursing, Service to Military Give Rise to Montgomery Campus

TROY first offered classes in Montgomery in 1957, teaching nursing at St. Margaret's Hospital. The initiative would eventually develop into the University's School of Nursing.

In 1965, at the request of the U.S. Air Force, Troy State College—as it was then known—began offering classes at Maxwell Air Force Base. The following year, classes were initiated at Gunter Air Force Base as well. Those relationships with the Air Force in Montgomery were among the initial steps in TROY's journey to becoming the military-friendly institution it is today.

In 1966, TROY's Montgomery Campus was designated as a branch campus and was authorized to offer degree programs at both undergraduate and the graduate levels. The first graduates of TROY's Montgomery Campus received their diplomas in 1968.

TROY Plays Key Role in Downtown Revitalization

TROY's impact in downtown Montgomery began in the early 1970s with the purchase of the former Whitley Hotel, and the University has played a key role in revitalization of the downtown area ever since. The University's first Montgomery-based classes were offered in the historic Whitley in 1974 with students studying in the same building that housed such notable guests as Eleanor Roosevelt, Katharine Hepburn, Duke Ellington, Gene Autry, Spiro Agnew, Clark Gable and Hank Williams.

The building later went through a series of renovations and, today, serves as the campus' main building, including classrooms, administrative offices, meeting rooms, the Barnes & Noble College Bookstore and the Trojan Café.

In 1976, the former Paramount Theatre, built in 1929, became the University's next renovation project and would become known as Troy University's Davis Theatre for the Performing Arts in honor of Tine Davis. Today, the Davis Theatre plays host to numerous performing groups from the University and the region and serves as home to the campus' commencement ceremonies.

In 1998, TROY broke ground for the Rosa Parks Library and Museum on the site of the former Empire Theatre near the spot of Mrs. Parks' historic 1955 arrest for her refusal to relinquish her seat on a Montgomery city bus to a white male. Mrs. Parks' arrest sparked the 381-day Montgomery Bus Boycott, which would lead to the desegregation of public transportation in Montgomery. Mrs. Parks was on hand to turn the first shovel of dirt during the ground-breaking ceremony and would return with members of her family on Dec. 1, 2000, as the museum opened its doors for the first time—45 years to the day following her arrest.

Since its opening, the museum has seen visitors from around the world and is a frequent destination for school children throughout the state who come to learn about Mrs. Parks' legacy as the "Mother of the Civil Rights Movement."

The Children's Wing of the Rosa Parks Museum was opened in 2006 and features the Cleveland Avenue Time Machine. Within the Children's Wing, visitors can take a 20-minute, virtual journey covering historical events leading them through the Jim Crow Era and up to the modern-day Civil Rights Movement.

Today, the museum continues to educate thousands of visitors annually through its permanent exhibits, special events and forums, and traveling displays within its galleries.

In addition to being a stage-setter in downtown revitalization, Troy Montgomery's dedication to serving the community is evident through its operation of the W.A. Gayle Planetarium, the region's premier astronomy education facility. Each year, countless school children attend shows at the planetarium learning about astronomy, the universe and weather.

Through its quality academic offerings in high-demand fields and a dedicated faculty and staff committed to helping students realize their educational and career aspirations, Troy Montgomery is committed to serving the educational needs of the city and the region. That's the Trojan Warrior Spirit, and in Montgomery, that spirit is moving our city forward.

Learning a Trade

"Investments in education help to reduce crime and poverty while increasing the overall quality of life in the River Region. Educational opportunities, such as those that MPACT offers to students, have a massive impact on the community as a whole. MPACT offers high school students an opportunity to learn highly skilled trades that provide a pathway to a successful future. They are trained by business and industry certified instructors in programs that meet the demands of the River Region. Students have the best of both worlds, earning core course credits at their zone school, while focusing on specific skills at the career tech center that will enhance their earning potential and future opportunities. I love seeing the excitement of young adults who have mastered a skill set that they see will open more doors for them than they ever thought possible."

-**Marsha Baugh, MPACT principal**

Photo by Robert Fouts

Innovative ideas are propelling education in the River Region to new heights. One example is The Montgomery Preparatory Academy for Career Technologies (MPACT), a new high school focused on experiential, job-specific skills training and that's repurposing an abandoned mall as its home.

Photo courtesy of MPACT

CENTRAL ALABAMA COMMUNITY COLLEGE

With a strong history as one of Alabama's five original community colleges, Central Alabama Community College (CACC) provides a comprehensive and diverse academic and career-learning environment for its students throughout the region. The two-year institution is located in Alexander City and has three campuses: the Alexander City Campus, the Childersburg Campus and the Talladega Center. The college began teaching evening classes at the Millbrook Instructional site, which is currently housed at Stanhope Elmore High School, in the Spring of 2015. This expansion gives citizens in the River Region the opportunity to take college courses online or on-site at Stanhope Elmore High School.

CACC traces its history to the Alabama State Legislature Act No. 93, passed in 1963, which provided for the establishment of several institutions of higher learning in Alabama. The college opened its doors as Alexander City State Junior College (ACJC) in 1965 in the old Russell Hospital in Alexander City. In 1966 the college moved to its current campus and Nunnelley State Technical College in Childersburg, Alabama opened as part of the No. 93 Act of 1963. In 1989 the Alabama State Board of Education merged ACJC and Nunnelly to form the present day community college.

Historically one of the top programs at ACJC, Nunnelley and CACC has been nursing. The Coosa Valley School of Nursing began as the Sylacauga School of Nursing in 1921 as a hospital diploma program. The school was reorganized in 1951 and continued to operate as a hospital diploma program until 1994, when CVSN introduced an associate degree of nursing program. Academic courses for the program were offered by the ACSJC, and then CACC, since 1972. Coosa Valley School of Nursing merged with Central Alabama Community College in a three-phase program that was completed on November 21, 1996.

With the new millennium also came a time of tremendous growth for CACC. First, the college completed the construction of the The Jim Preuitt Nursing and Allied Health Building on the Childersburg campus in 2001. The Coosa Valley School of Nursing would eventually move into the brand new facility where it remains today.

Soon after the completion of the nursing building in Childersburg, the college broke ground on The Betty Carol Graham Technology Center on the Alexander City campus. That facility opened its doors in 2004 and has since been dedicated to increasing the competitiveness of companies, improving the effectiveness of the workforce throughout Alabama and enhancing the State's economic development efforts through a flexible and responsive combination of education, technical assistance and technology transfer. Rockwell International has made the center one of only a few training sites for Allen Bradley controls, the worldwide standard control in the robotics industry.

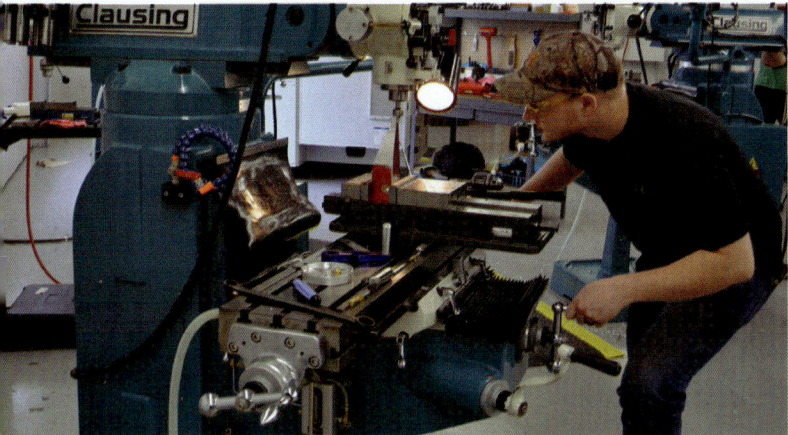

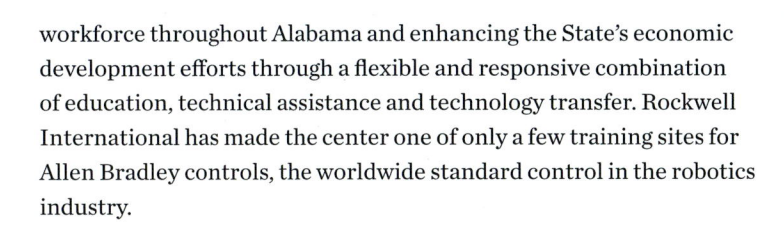

In addition to the expansion in both Alexander City and Childersburg, in 2004 the college broke ground on a new center in Talladega. The goal of the Talladega Center was to expand course offerings to students in the northern part of the service area. The center opened its doors in 2006 with an opening enrollment of 130 students. The 28,500-square-foot facility is a result of donated land from the city of Talladega. The Center is a combined partnership with a number of state agencies including the Career Link, Employment Services, Vocational Rehabilitation Services, Adult Education, and Veterans Affairs.

In addition to strong academic and technical programs, the college offers a vast array of clubs and organizations, performing arts, and state and national championship athletic teams in baseball, softball and golf.

CACC has long enjoyed success in athletics but 2013 was truly the year of the Trojans. The Central Alabama baseball and men's golf teams won the Division 1 National Championships in their respective sports. This was the sixth national championship for the Trojan golf program and the first national championship for the baseball program, as well as the first baseball championship for the state of Alabama at the junior college level.

In true heart-stopping fashion, the Trojan golf team battled back from a 20-stroke deficit after the first two rounds to claim a one-stroke victory over Odessa Community College out of Texas.

In addition to the national title, Coach Jennings was named the National Coach of the Year and golfer John Michael O'Toole was named the Alabama Sportswriter's Association JUCO Athlete of the Year.

Not to be outdone, the baseball team had a similar run to the championship. Down 13-9 to Cochise Community College out of Arizona in the bottom of the ninth, the Trojans battled back to tie the game at 13-13 and eventually win 14-13 in extra innings in the eleventh to set up a winner-take-all national championship game against Palm Beach State out of Florida. The Trojans would defeat Palm Beach 7-3 to win the first national title in school and state history.

Today, the Alexander City and Childersburg campuses along with the Talladega Center and Millbrook site offer resources and expertise that address the education and training needs of central Alabama.

93

In fall 2018 Troy Montgomery partnered with Valiant Cross Academy to host VCA's high school classes. Valiant Cross students gain access to expanded resources, and Troy Montgomery College of Education students are learning from leaders and faculty at VCA.

Photos by Brooke Glassford / Colorbox

> "We have an opportunity to help Montgomery impact the world again."

Creating Future Leaders

- Fred and Anthony Brock,
Founders of Valiant Cross Academy

"Being from Montgomery, we wanted to come back home and do some meaningful work in the city that raised and nurtured us. We believe that by setting high expectations and sharing a lot of love, all students can achieve a level of success, so we founded Valiant Cross Academy for young men in our city. Our ultimate goal is to create leaders who can come back and impact their communities, and education is the key. It is important that we create quality citizens who are ready to join the workforce after graduation. A quality education can also create opportunities to change the trajectory in the lives of so many families. We get so excited seeing our students grow and mature physically, mentally and spiritually, and we're excited to do it here. Montgomery is a special and unique place, the 'Birthplace of the Civil Rights Movement and the Cradle of Confederacy.' At Valiant Cross Academy, we have an opportunity to help Montgomery impact the world again."

AIDT *Alabama's Number One Incentive*

When an industry announces that it will locate or expand within the state of Alabama, AIDT's mission is to prepare Alabama workers for the jobs these industry investments will create. Within the state government organizational structure, AIDT is an independent agency under the oversight of the Alabama Department of Commerce.

The Department of Commerce is considered the "sales arm" for luring new industry and its jobs to Alabama. Through that process, the state's economic developers have a big selling tool as they create incentive packages: AIDT.

Providing quality worker training at no cost to new or expanding businesses has long been seen as "Alabama's Number One Incentive." These services and resources are coordinated through the AIDT Total Workforce Delivery System, which has provided thousands of skilled, motivated employees to Alabama industries since the agency was established in 1971.

AIDT's services include employee recruitment and screening, pre-employment training and assessments, and post-employment or on-the-job training, as well as many others. As a company commits to creating new jobs in Alabama and turns to AIDT to help make that happen, a Project Manager begins to assess the company's training needs.

If a pre-employment program is to be done, AIDT develops a training program that defines the staffing schedule and skills needed, selects and prepares instructors, secures a training location and develops training materials. The agency then recruits applicants, who are screened and scheduled for an interview if they meet certain criteria. After their training is completed and their performance assessed satisfactorily, they may receive a job offer and begin employment.

Training is customized for each company. For example, if an international corporation is opening a new location in Alabama, AIDT's team will visit the current plant to study, document and film the company's processes. From there, they create a training video, work instructions and CAD design, and develop training environments that simulate the actual work environment.

For larger companies, such as Hyundai Motor Manufacturing Alabama, the training continues to backfill production jobs as existing workers are

"At AIDT our job is to build a high quality workforce and to help prepare the citizens of Alabama for gainful employment opportunities."

— Ed Castile, AIDT Executive Director

promoted or seek other opportunities. In any case, as long as an industry keeps adding jobs – perhaps with a new shift or additional product – it enjoys the benefit of AIDT's services.

AIDT will also provide post-employment on-the-job training for these companies. Or as an alternative, the company may choose to recruit and hire its workers and ask AIDT to provide on-the-job training. Other services include maintenance assessments, industrial safety assessments and training, leadership development, and process improvement assessments – all specific to the company's needs. Notably, AIDT's unique workforce selection and training processes have achieved the nation's first ISO certified state-funded workforce training program. AIDT's pre-employment program currently holds a ISO 9001:2015 certification.

AIDT also operates centers of excellence around the state that provide training for high-demand careers in that area. In North Alabama, for example, AIDT partnered with robotics and automation industry leaders around the nation to establish the Robotics Technology Park to provide a technically trained, highly skilled, and educated workforce for automation and robotics. Farther south, AIDT launched a maritime training program in Mobile to provide job seekers with qualifications and skills needed to join the growing maritime industry.

In Montgomery, AIDT opened the Montgomery Regional Workforce Development Center in partnership with several entities including the Montgomery Public Schools, Alabama Community College System, ATN, AUM, the Department of Education, and the Montgomery Area Chamber of Commerce. Located at the OneCenter on East South Boulevard in the former Montgomery Mall, the goal of MRWDC is to provide entry-level training, existing employee upgrade training, two-year technical college level training, and K-12 career training to adequately supply businesses with a trained workforce for the Montgomery region. The training is focused on three categories – Information Technology, Manufacturing Fundamentals and Workforce Skills training – which are areas that have been identified as critical and in demand in the region.

The Information Technology program provides certification training from entry-level operator to highly skilled technician in the areas of industrial information technology, networking, security, and data management. Manufacturing Technology courses are designed for companies within the manufacturing industry that desire additional training for their employees. Workforce Skills Training consists of soft skills training for non-management employees and Leadership Development courses for management-level employees.

AIDT established these centers and other similar collaborations by seeking input from businesses and industries through seven regional workforce councils. Ed Castile, AIDT's executive director, also serves as a deputy director of the Department of Commerce. The DOC's Workforce Development Division is under his purview, as well as the workforce councils which provide a direct link to the workforce needs of business and industry at the local level.

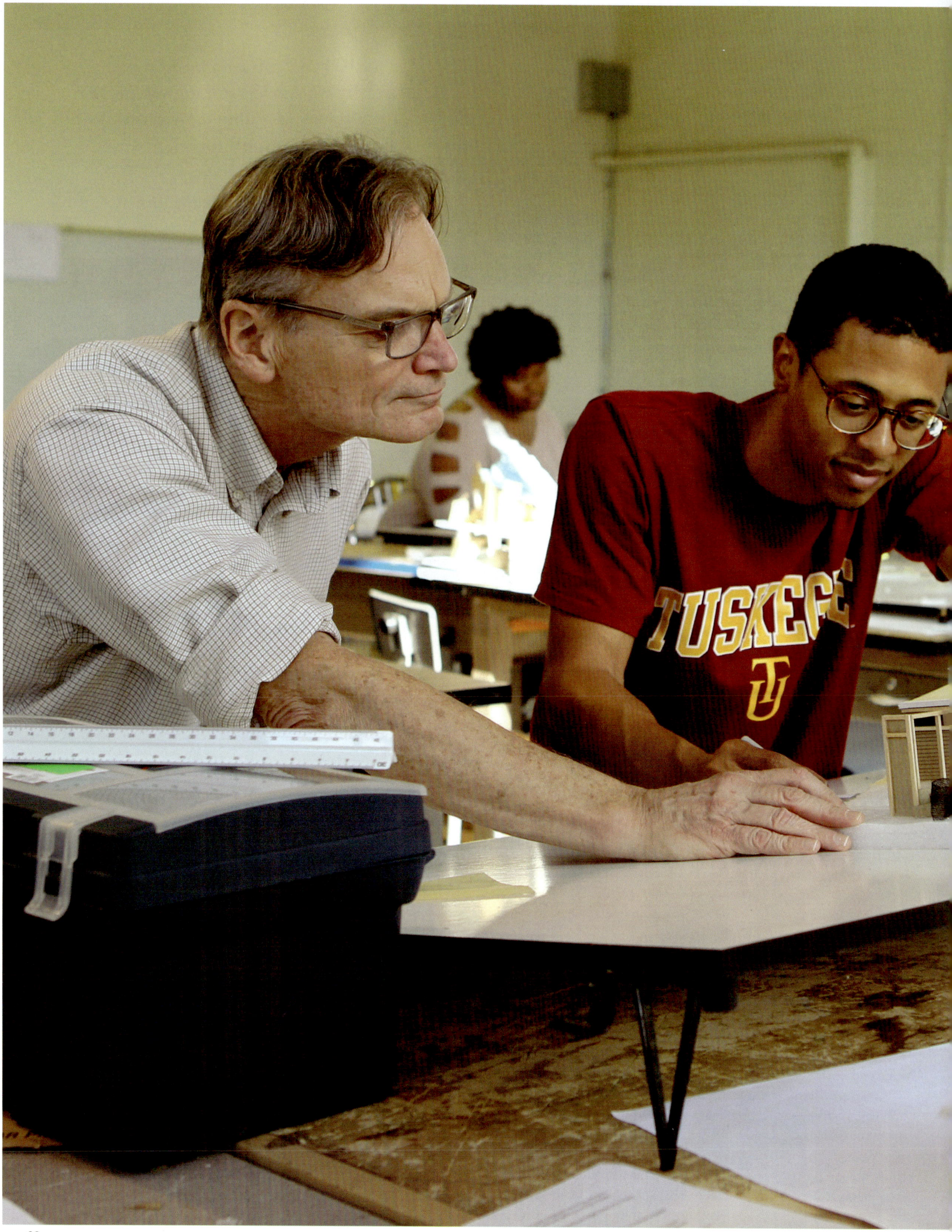
TUSKEGEE

History Lives Here

For more than 137 years, Tuskegee University has prepared tomorrow's leaders for success. As "the Pride of the Swift-growing South," its nationally ranked degree programs, historic Alabama campus, vibrant student life programs and robust research initiatives make it a destination of choice for students seeking a supportive academic environment — and a future of endless possibilities!

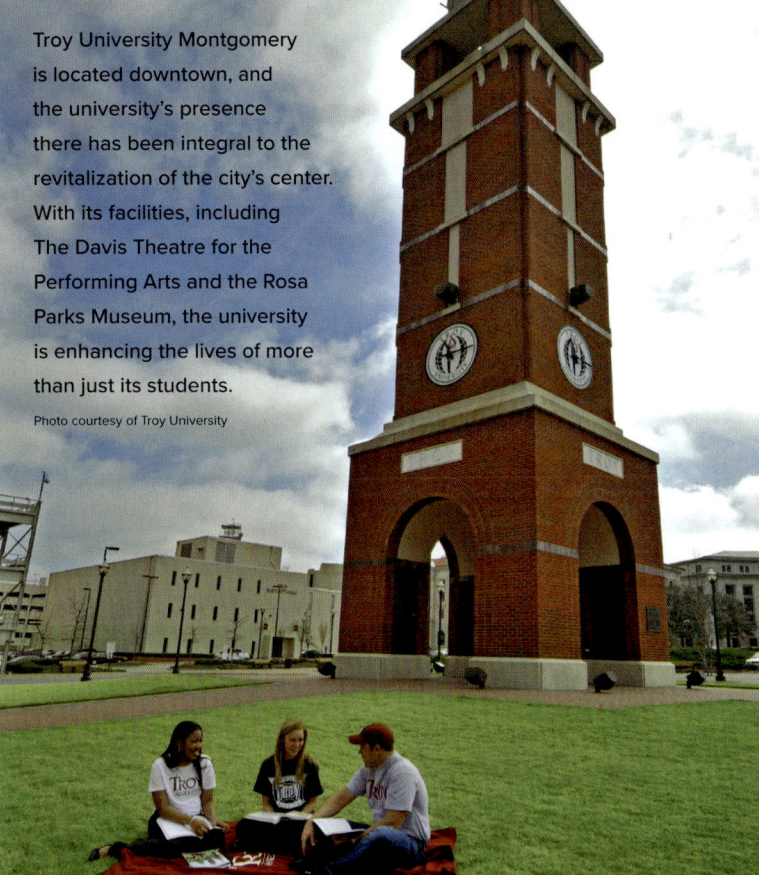

River Region education goes beyond reading, writing and arithmetic. The arts are emphasized, too.
Photo courtesy of ASU

Troy University Montgomery is located downtown, and the university's presence there has been integral to the revitalization of the city's center. With its facilities, including The Davis Theatre for the Performing Arts and the Rosa Parks Museum, the university is enhancing the lives of more than just its students.
Photo courtesy of Troy University

Photo courtesy of Tuskegee University

Photo courtesy of Huntingdon College

SAINT JAMES SCHOOL

Developing Knowledge, Values, Character and Creativity

Known as the premier independent school in Central Alabama, Saint James School is well respected as the beacon for innovation and educational excellence. "Our teachers provide the strongest and most complete college preparatory curriculum within a caring and supportive learning community," said Dr. Larry McLemore, Saint James Head of School. "Our commitment to caring for and inspiring the best in each Saint James student has guided us for over 60 years, and that will continue to illuminate our path as we look ahead to the future."

A focus on content and skill acquisition in STEAM (Science, Technology, Engineering, Arts, and Math) disciplines, as well as other essential areas such as English, history, and world languages, has long been part of the college preparatory mission at Saint James School. As visitors walk the beautiful collegiate-style 68-acre campus and pass through the halls of students and teachers engaged in a vibrant learning community, it is evident why Saint James has been recognized as the top private school in Montgomery.

The Early Years

Preschool and kindergarten teachers encourage children to learn through hands-on instruction in math, science, English language arts, social studies and physical education. Students also participate in art, music, world language, and technology classes weekly and work with the science lab coordinator to develop and practice essential lab skills. The elementary counselor conducts classroom guidance lessons assisting students as they develop the maturity, self-confidence, skills and knowledge base necessary to navigate the school's college preparatory curriculum.

True Middle School

Saint James was the first independent school in the area to establish a true middle school for students sixth through eighth grade. Recognized nationally for its innovation and emphasis on the adolescent student, the Saint James Middle School has served as a model for other independent schools for many years. While focused on strong core academic instruction, the middle school program promotes the intellectual, social, emotional, physical and cultural well-being of students during these important transitional years. Through core academic courses, advisory periods, exploratory courses and electives, students strengthen their abilities, explore their individual talents, and develop important character traits including empathy and perseverance.

Educating the Whole Child

The high school college preparatory curriculum at Saint James is challenging and intellectually rigorous to meet the needs of its college-bound student population. Students are nurtured by a caring, dedicated and talented faculty committed to providing the finest educational opportunities. Students benefit from a well-rounded program that prioritizes academics, embraces the arts and athletics, and fosters a sense of personal confidence and integrity.

Students and teachers at all levels have access to the most current technology tools as well as a controlled, wireless campus infrastructure. All faculty members have their own technology tools; SmartBoards, AppleTV, and/or Clear Touch Panels are available in each classroom; students in grades five through 12 participate in the school's 1:1 program with iPads or MacBooks; and Pre-School through fourth grade students regularly use the school's iPad, iPod, and MacBook carts in their classrooms.

FAULKNER UNIVERSITY

Faulkner University is celebrating more than 75 years of serving the River Region as a private, Christian, liberal arts university based in Montgomery. Serving both traditional and non-traditional students, Faulkner is home to five colleges: The Alabama Christian College of Arts and Sciences, the Harris College of Business and Executive Education, the V.P. Black College of Biblical Studies, the College of Education, and the Thomas Goode Jones School of Law. Faulkner also operates extension campuses in Birmingham, Huntsville and Mobile, as well as partnership programs across the southeast all while providing a myriad of online degree programs.

With a mission to provide an education anchored by not only intellect but also character and service, the Faulkner experience aims to educate the whole person. Faulkner seeks to join academic excellence, spiritual development, and service to our fellow man and remain steadfast in its spiritual heritage by providing Bible courses for all majors and daily chapel services for students. The university has a student public service program in place and has also partnered with the City of Montgomery through its school partnership program. Faulkner is proud to have started an annual day of city-wide service as well as playing host to the Alabama Special Olympics and the National Down Syndrome Society's Buddy Walk.

Faulkner was founded by Dr. Rex Turner, Dr. Leonard Johnson and Joe Greer in 1942 as Montgomery Bible School on a few acres of land on Ann Street. Originally seeking to provide preaching education, the school grew into a four-year institution and was renamed Alabama Christian College. In 1964, the school moved to its current location on the Atlanta Highway. In 1975, the college opened extension campuses in Birmingham, Huntsville and Mobile. The Thomas Goode Jones School of Law was acquired in 1983, and a year later the college was accredited as a four-year university. In 1985 the school was renamed Faulkner University after longtime trustee and benefactor Dr. James Faulkner.

Since becoming Faulkner University, the school has experienced rapid growth including new buildings for classrooms and administration, new residence halls and apartments, a student multiplex, and modern facilities for the football, soccer, baseball and softball programs. A new entrance for the university was constructed for the 2017-2018 academic year.

As the school looks to the future, plans for the opening of its Center for Health Sciences are moving forward. Proposals for physical therapy, speech and language pathology and an autism center are already underway.

The campus of Auburn University Montgomery
Photo courtesy of AUM

A Legacy of Learning: First AUM Taylor Road campus student still learning at AUM

Pam Taylor was the first student to register for classes at Auburn University at Montgomery's Taylor Road campus.

Almost half a century later, the grandmother is still learning at AUM, delightfully studying alongside her granddaughters, thanks to AUM's Osher Lifelong Learning Institute (OLLI). In the pages of Taylor's home scrapbook is a picture of her that was published in the *Montgomery Advertiser* on September 17, 1971, in which the paper records Taylor as "First to Register" at AUM's campus, which then was in its infancy. "One of the memories that stands out, during my four years at AUM, is the growth of the school that I saw firsthand. I am very proud to see that my alma mater has continued to grow and I am proud to be a graduate of a truly great university," Taylor said. This summer, Taylor enrolled in an experimental course — Fruitcakes and Kites — taught by Nancy Anderson, distinguished OutReach fellow at AUM, a class for which grandparents and grandchildren were invited to enroll. The two generations of each family read and talked about Truman Capote's "A Christmas Memory," watched a film version of the short story, then wrote versions of memorable Christmases in their own lives with the goal of publishing each family's narratives. "The experience of being in a class with my granddaughters has been priceless," Taylor said. "I don't know who enjoyed it the most, and I would not be surprised if they follow in my footsteps and attend AUM some day."

Story courtesy of AUM

AMRIDGE UNIVERSITY

A Pioneer in Distance Learning

Founded in 1967 and located on a stately nine-acre campus off Taylor Road in Montgomery, Amridge University is a non-profit, independent, coeducational institution dedicated to the spirit of its Christian ideals and heritage. Amridge is unique among other area institutions in that it was a pioneer in online education. The university has taught in the online arena since 1993, and in 1999, Amridge was one of 15 institutions chosen by the U.S. Department of Education to serve in a groundbreaking pilot Distance Education Demonstration project. During that period, the educational sector was seeking proof that distance education was a solid way of teaching. Amridge not only began to deliver education online effectively, but distance learning became its primary instructional delivery system.

Today, Amridge is a distance learning institution with all courses available via the Internet. Students can take their courses in real time at home, seeing and hearing the professor and interacting with the other students. The courses are not restricted to time or place. The university has a sizeable national and international influence and serves students in 50 states and 20 countries.

Instructional faculty members total approximately 100 – with around 65 percent of full-time faculty members holding doctoral degrees. Faculty members specialize in their area, and in some cases work in their fields. All have exceptional training in distance learning delivery. They are selected for expertise rather than geography and can deliver courses from anywhere.

Amridge University is accredited by the Southern Association of Colleges and Schools Commission on Colleges (SACS-COC) to award bachelor's, master's and doctoral degree programs in business, counseling, Biblical studies, and many more. The university offers a variety of curricula with more than 36 degree programs. Degrees awarded include the Associate of Arts, Bachelor of Arts, Bachelor of Science, Master of Arts, Master of Science, Master of Divinity, Doctor of Ministry and Doctor of Philosophy.

Tuition costs are also competitive with in-state tuition for public universities. More than 90 percent of all Amridge students receive financial aid in the form of grants, scholarships and other sources. Amridge is very student-services driven. Staff members are prepared to answer student questions ranging from degree planning to technology support. Amridge University's mission is to prepare men and women, through a commitment to academic excellence and spiritual vitality at the undergraduate and graduate levels for a lifetime of learning, leadership and service to their professions, society church and family.

THE MONTGOMERY ACADEMY

The Pursuit of Excellence

At The Montgomery Academy, the pursuit of excellence is a schoolwide commitment that is carried out in each student's experience. In a welcoming K-12 environment where all children are known, students learn and grow through academics, athletics, arts and activities that best fit their own goals and desires. The mission of The Montgomery Academy is to develop leaders committed to honor, scholarship, service and the pursuit of excellence.

In the Lower School, the curriculum is designed to educate the whole child by focusing not only on each child's academic development but also on his or her physical and social-emotional development. Students receive daily instruction in either art, music or Spanish. Physical education classes and recess are also held daily. In addition, students attend STEM (science, technology, engineering and math) class and visit the library on a weekly basis, and technology is incorporated into the curriculum in meaningful ways.

In Middle School, the curriculum gives students the opportunity to explore a range of content areas. Art, music, drama, Speech & Debate, STEM and World Languages offer outlets for curiosity, creativity and a wide view of learning. Students also learn important life skills, such as resilience, responsibility, hard work, problem solving and collaboration, and they take in experiences beyond the classroom with field trips and educational travel. The opportunity to participate on one of the many athletic teams begins in seventh grade.

In the Upper School, students are challenged with a strong college preparatory curriculum, and 100 percent of MA graduates go on to attend a college or university.

As Upper School students, they engage in a wide variety of courses in all academic areas, including diverse offerings in STEM and in the visual and performing arts. Numerous Advanced Placement courses offered in many subject areas help students earn early college credits. Co-curricular activities in community service, the arts, clubs and athletics also play an integral role in developing character and leadership abilities. Signature programs such as Speech & Debate and Chorus provide the opportunity to compete on a national level. The athletics program is notably strong as well. MA has won more state championships than any other school in the River Region.

Enrollment is open at any time for any level for students who qualify. The school offers a mentor program where a new student is paired up with a student mentor, and students find that it's easy to adjust at whatever stage they enter.

Most importantly, The Montgomery Academy's carefully crafted program is designed to develop the unique potential of each student while it also seeks to build strong moral character and a foundation for students to become leaders in society and in the community.

Studies have shown that beginning education early goes a long way in assuring future success in school. It's why the River Region has made providing quality Pre-K education a priority.

Photo courtesy of ClefWorks / Bryce Carter

Photo by Grace O'Connoer

MONTGOMERY CATHOLIC PREPARATORY SCHOOL

Faith. Service. Excellence.

A K4-12 college preparatory school whose Catholic mission calls for an inclusive admission process, Montgomery Catholic Preparatory School welcomes students of all faiths to apply to the school.

Since 1873, Montgomery Catholic Preparatory School has provided an exceptional education program. As the oldest continuously running non-public K-12 school in Alabama, our history is rich.

In 1873, the Sisters of Loretto arrived in Montgomery and founded the St. Mary of Loretto School for Girls at the Gerald Mansion in downtown Montgomery. However, a yellow fever epidemic delayed the school's opening as the sisters cared for the sick and earned the admiration of citizens. The school officially opened in October. In 1929, at the request of St. Peter Parish, St. Mary of Loretto became a coeducational institution. In 1952, grades 9-12 moved into a new building behind St. Peter Parish funded by St. Peter, St. Andrew, and St. Bede parishes and was renamed Catholic High School of Montgomery.

The "Baby Boom" years saw St. Bede Elementary open its doors in 1958. In 1962, Our Lady Queen of Mercy School opened to accommodate the growing community, since the Gerald Mansion no longer suited the needs of the school. In 1965, the Sisters of Loretto led a move to the new Montgomery Catholic High School site on Vaughn Road, which was little more than a cow pasture.

Over the next 35 years, the school grew tremendously:
- In 1999, a science/library building was built and dedicated to Sr. Martha Belke, the last of the 117 Loretto Sisters to have served the school.
- The millennium ushered in the addition of the new athletic complex in 2003 and the opening of the Middle School for grades 7-8 in the fall of 2004.
- In 2006, Archbishop Oscar H. Lipscomb approved the final merger of St. Bede, Montgomery Catholic Middle School and Montgomery Catholic High School to form Montgomery Catholic Preparatory School.
- In 2012, Montgomery Catholic, in conjunction with Holy Spirit Catholic Church, opened an elementary campus in east Montgomery to accommodate the increasing need for Catholic education.
- In 2014, the construction of a gym at the Holy Spirit campus (Phase II) was completed to enhance Montgomery Catholic's athletic program, as well as serve the needs of the Holy Spirit Parish.
- In 2017, Montgomery Catholic's Middle/High School campus was granted permission by Archbishop Thomas J. Rodi to expand again, and construction began to build a new state-of-the-art gymnasium and refurbish the current gym to accommodate the school's growing music, choral, and drama departments.

Montgomery Catholic is proud to serve students of various academic skill levels, helping them reach their God-given potential. In partnership with parents, the school strives to develop students' talents so they graduate ready for college. A lasting legacy from the Sisters of Loretto, one of hard work and commitment to Catholic education, leads Montgomery Catholic into the future. While keeping the core values of the Christian faith at the center, the school will continue to teach students to serve and love as Christ taught. This future continues a devotion to providing a modern and rigorous academic program, one that offers introduction to engineering, computer science, foreign language and arts curriculum options and extra-curricular options including athletics, service organizations, leadership groups, honor societies and robotics to serve a diverse student body.

TRINITY SCHOOL

Academic Excellence in a Family Atmosphere

Trinity School holds itself to a higher standard as it guides students to do the same within a setting that embraces Christian values.

Academic excellence is nurtured in an attentive atmosphere where highly qualified teachers and administrative staff provide outstanding instruction. The single location in a state-of-the-art facility fosters a family environment where siblings across many grades attend the same school. Notably, for the 2018-19 academic year, the school added K3 to grades K4-12, further setting it apart as a one-school destination for the Montgomery community.

The challenging college-preparatory education, which includes 27 advanced placement (AP) and honor courses, provides a solid foundation. One hundred percent of Trinity students are accepted to postsecondary institutions, with many attending some of the finest colleges in the nation. Graduates have received more than $40 million in merit-based scholarships over the last five years.

Trinity is also the ideal size to allow every student to participate in visual and performing arts. For example, exposure to music and song begins at the earliest ages with the Kindergarten Christmas Play. Expression through vocal and instrumental music extends through Middle and Upper School in formal choral and band performances. The theater department produces a full-scale musical each spring with a cast of more than 100 Upper School students.

Arts students exhibit locally and win major state and national awards. Trinity is also the only independent school in Montgomery to offer a full-time dance program.

The Athletic Program is equally essential to Trinity's well-balanced educational experience. From the Lower School to the Upper School, opportunities are available for boys and girls to reach their potential through performance and to further their experiences in teamwork, physical well-being and positive citizenship. Trinity fields 39 interscholastic sport teams, and the 32-acre campus provides a 3,000-seat football stadium, two regulation gyms, beautifully manicured football/soccer, baseball and softball fields, a weight room and tennis courts.

Service is also viewed as an integral component of a Trinity student's education. For example, students bring change each Friday for the school's Change 4 Change mission project, which has donated tens of thousands of dollars to charitable organizations in recent years. Junior and Senior classes provide more than 1,100 community service hours annually to local organizations. In addition, a wide variety of extracurricular activities helps students develop personal gifts and talents.

Altogether, Trinity offers an unparalleled academic experience with an emphasis on scholarship, citizenship and Christ-like service as it prepares students to have an impact in the world.

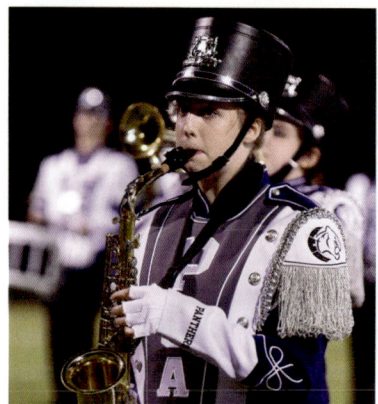

PRATTVILLE CHRISTIAN ACADEMY

Prattville Christian Academy is a K3-12 independent school dedicated to providing academic excellence, with an emphasis on life readiness skills, in a caring, Christian environment.

PCA seeks to create a meaningful difference by preparing Christian leaders for life. The children of today will be the leaders of tomorrow, and we aim to make the world of tomorrow a place that is full of hope and security. We believe that everyone has the ability to change the world through the use of God-given talents so students are led to discover their purpose within this life through the cultivation of their spiritual, academic, physical and emotional development. Through personal example and individual relationships, we develop confident, independent thinkers that find purpose in the pursuit of life.

Founded in 1997 with just 13 students, as a vision of Don and Marilyn Greer, PCA has grown into one of the premier educational institutions in the River Region. Prattville Christian Academy remains committed to building faith in God, love of His Word, and respect for His creation while providing a Bible-based education with an emphasis on the individual and the importance of the family.

Art stirs the soul and engages the mind. The Montgomery Museum of Fine Arts Education Department is dedicated to providing unique learning experiences focused on visual arts.
Photo courtesy of MMFA

Photo by BrookeGlassford / Colorbox

ALABAMA CHRISTIAN ACADEMY

Since 1942, Alabama Christian Academy has helped to prepare students for a successful, faithful life. Alabama Christian Academy is a K4-12th grade school committed to offering a challenging, Christ-centered education to its students, while keeping in mind their individual needs.

Along with advanced academics, ACA provides a comprehensive AHSAA athletics program, an award-winning fine arts department and other enrichment opportunities.

Students at ACA are also encouraged to grow spiritually. All ACA students attend a daily Bible class as well as school-level chapel assemblies. Because it is important to extend what students learn beyond the classroom, a life lab is vitally important for a full understanding of being Christ-like. For this reason, we encourage our faculty and students to get involved in service to the community.

Soar into excellence at ACA and ensure your child will thrive in wisdom and serve in spirit.

Living Well in the River Region
Health & Wellness

The River Region's hospitals provide myriad functions; one of the most important (and heartwarming) is helping families welcome tiny new arrivals in safe, caring environments thanks to state-of-the-art birthing centers.
Photo by Aubrie Moates

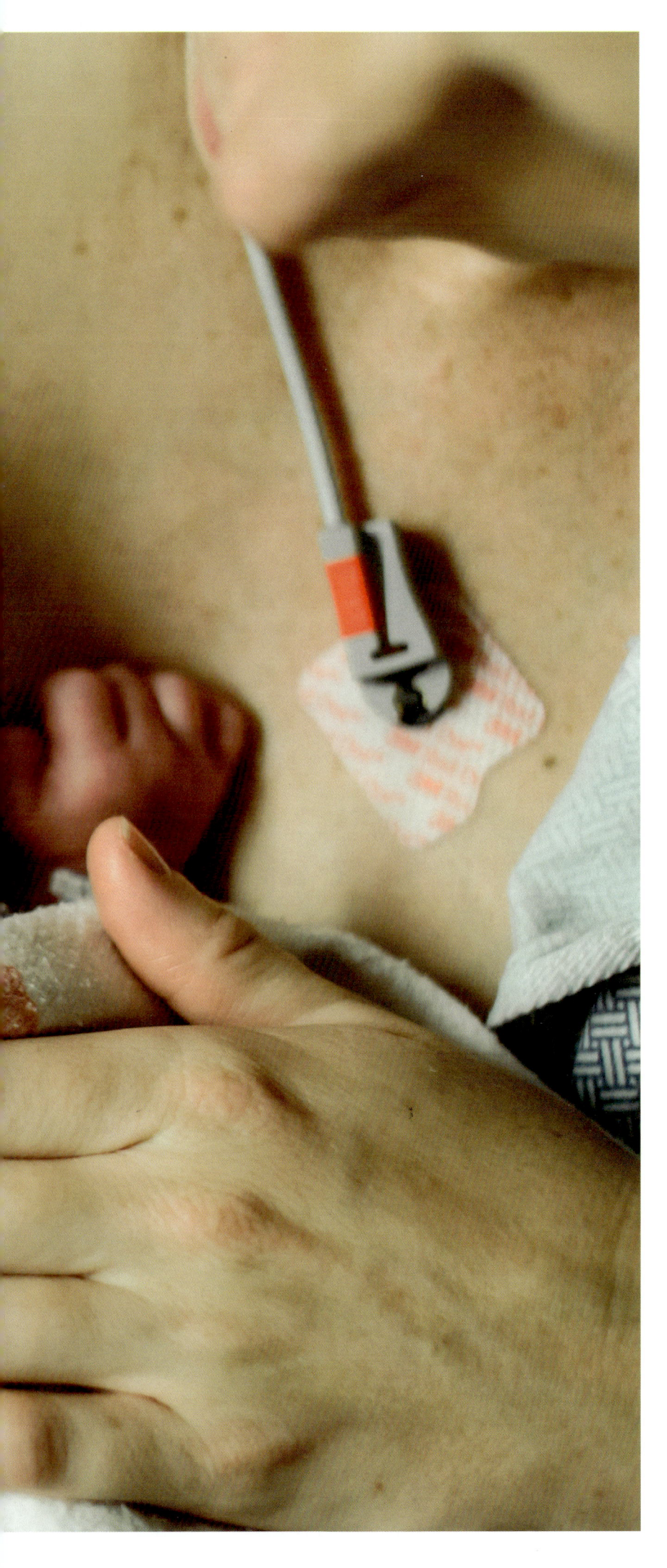

The health of the River Region is in good hands. With three full-service hospitals, specialty clinics, imaging centers, urgent care offerings and a long list of trusted physicians, area residents now have more options than ever to help them achieve a sense of well being.

Baptist Health System is a dominant force in the tri-counties, and its facilities — outfitted with the latest cutting-edge advancements in medical technology — combined with the hard, benevolent work of its administrators, doctors and nurses has earned it recognition as a Thomson Reuters 15 Top Health Systems in the country. Its two hospitals in Montgomery have garnered awards from the American Heart Association and the American Stroke Association, and their staff continually strive to meet the physical, emotional and spiritual needs of their fellow residents.

Baptist Health's partnership with the University of Alabama at Birmingham's lauded medical school led to the formation of the UAB School of Medicine Montgomery, bringing smart, eager students to the city to learn and contribute to our community.

Since its founding in 1946, Jackson Hospital's commitment to its mission to provide high-quality, cost-effective care that's focused on each individual patient and delivered in a safe, compassionate environment has led to it being named a Blue Cross and Blue Shield Tier 1 Hospital, becoming the first hospital in Alabama to be certified in spinal surgery and receiving a Medal of Honor for organ donation.

All of our area hospitals are doing more than attending to current patients; both Jackson Hospital and Baptist Health are stepping up and finding solutions to ongoing medical challenges, particularly the quest to bring the best and brightest health care professionals here.

Ensuring that no one is left behind or denied access to quality care, there are programs in place, including clinics like Medical Outreach Ministries (MOM), a faith-based initiative, that provide free health care to the un- and under-insured in the River Region. In the last 20 years, MOM alone has delivered more than $30 million in medical services.

There's no question that River Region residents are blessed with quality health care, but equally important is the fuel the health care industry pumps into our area's economic engine. Baptist Health System is one of the largest private employers in the River Region and, combined with Jackson Hospital, they represent approximately 5,800 jobs, making their contribution a significant part of the area's prescription for robust progress.

BAPTIST HEALTH

Guided by a Faith-Based Mission, Baptist Health Grows Its Healing Impact in Central Alabama

Baptist Health's mission to promote and improve the physical, emotional and spiritual well-being of the communities it serves through the delivery of quality health care services began with the opening of its first facility, Baptist Medical Center South, in 1963. In the decades since, the system's services and facilities have grown and expanded many times over even as that foundational faith-based mission continues to guide every action.

"Our mission guides everything that we do, every decision we make," said W. Russell Tyner, Baptist Health's President and CEO. "Caring for patients in literal life and death situations requires the utmost accountability among our caregivers and we take this role very seriously," Tyner said. "The patient must always come first."

Baptist Health is the largest health care system serving central Alabama and, with more than 4,500 employees, it is also the largest non-governmental employer within this area. The three-hospital system includes Baptist Medical Center South (BMCS), a 514-licensed-bed regional acute care referral center and the tertiary care flagship facility. Baptist Medical Center East (BMCE) is a 150-bed acute care hospital providing a broad range of health care services, specializing in obstetrics, women's and children's services. Prattville Baptist Hospital is an acute care, community hospital with 85 licensed beds, offering a full range of health services to residents of Autauga and Elmore counties.

In addition to comprehensive hospital-based services with 24/7 emergency care, Baptist Health also offers in- and outpatient specialty services including orthopedics, cardiology, oncology, primary care, general surgery, neurosciences, imaging, lab, breast health, wound care, sports medicine, diabetes and nutrition education, home health, hospice, sleep disorders, speech and hearing, mental health and physical rehabilitation. The system serves nearly 600,000 people in Central Alabama.

"Health care has changed quite a bit in the 50-plus years since Baptist Health's inception," Tyner said. "We deliver it differently now, but not without the same empathy and compassion and perseverance that Baptist Health was founded upon. That's how we grow. Identifying the community's needs one at a time and meeting them where they are differentiates Baptist Health from other health care providers," Tyner said.

Partnerships Increase Services

Baptist Health meticulously manages the role of delivering health care through the compassionate, skilled care of attentive physicians and clinical staff while strategically reinforcing its mission with advancements in medical technology and continued expansions in services and facilities.

For example, in 2016, Baptist Health partnered with UAB Health System to open the UAB Medicine Multispecialty Clinic at Baptist Medical Center South. The clinic, which is owned and operated by Baptist Health, offers much-needed specialties, including urology, gastroenterology, endocrinology, rheumatology, cardiothoracic surgery and breast health. The 12 UAB physicians housed at the clinic were recruited by Baptist Health and employed

"Identifying the community's needs one at a time and meeting them where they are differentiates Baptist Health from other health care providers."

— W. Russell Tyner, President & CEO of Baptist Health

by UAB Health Services Foundation. All are highly trained medical specialists and offer cutting-edge services along with surgical procedures and treatments that had not been offered in our area

Thanks to the addition of the UAB Multispecialty Clinic, residents of central Alabama no longer have to travel outside the area for medical services that had been limited by a shortage of specialists amid an increasing need for specialty care. The physicians provide added access to specialty care in a convenient, centralized location close to home, which will help lead to earlier diagnosis and treatment of disease. In addition, patients have access to clinical trials and research activities being performed at UAB.

Baptist Health has been an affiliate of the UAB Health System since 2005 and has partnered with UAB throughout the past four decades to support the UAB Internal Medicine Residency Program and, most recently, the addition of the UAB School of Medicine Montgomery Regional Campus at Baptist South.

These highly sought-after programs, along with the Baptist Health Family Medicine Residency Program, enable Baptist Health hospitals to improve ongoing quality of care by serving as teaching academic facilities and producing future generations of highly skilled, competent, compassionate physicians.

In 2014, Baptist Health and American Family Care (AFC) partnered to provide primary and urgent care services throughout Central Alabama. AFC is the largest urgent care provider in the state of Alabama and one of the largest in the United States with more than 126 clinics in operation. Together, the health care providers operate eight facilities in Montgomery, Wetumpka, Prattville and Greenville that are co-branded as AFC PriMed. All of the clinics are designed, equipped and staffed to provide accessible primary care, urgent care, minor emergency treatment and occupational medicine. They use a high-tech, high-touch approach, with digital x-rays, on-site lab testing, state-of-the-art diagnostics, and electronic medical records. The clinics are staffed by board certified physicians and kind, caring and compassionate health care professionals. They are open daily, with extended hours, and no appointments are necessary.

In another milestone, in 2011, Baptist Health partnered with the Montgomery Cancer Center, which also includes the Montgomery Breast Center and Carmichael Imaging, to add the health care providers to the Baptist Health family of services. For more than 20 years, Montgomery Cancer Center has been recognized as one of the largest comprehensive freestanding cancer centers in the United States. Its team of eight physicians and health professionals provide understanding, compassionate, one-on-one attention with state-of-the-art technology and treatment. The center's radiation-oncology practice is an independent entity on the Montgomery Cancer Center campus as well as a valued partner in the delivery of comprehensive cancer care services.

In March 2017, Baptist Health and the Montgomery

Cancer Center opened a newly renovated cancer clinic in Prattville. The 15,000-square-foot space at Prattville Medical Park enables area residents to benefit from cutting-edge cancer care, a team of board-certified oncologists and highly trained oncology nurses. The clinic holds 24 infusion bays for patients undergoing chemotherapy and immunotherapy along with 10 exam rooms, conference areas and support facilities.

Expanding the Mission

Altogether Baptist Health has 30 facilities across a three-county area, and continued expansions of the mission continue to bring advancements to the communities it serves.

For example, at the end of 2015, Baptist Medical Center East expanded with the addition of a new wing. The $5.5 million dollar project added 26 patient rooms to the postpartum area of women's services and a four-bed intensive care step-down unit. The expansion allows for improved patient and staff flow to and from labor and delivery as well as to the nursery, neonatal intensive care unit, pediatrics and the postpartum areas. The rooms are twice the size of the former postpartum rooms and feature high-quality amenities for comfort of mother and baby, along with the latest medical technology.

The 65-bed Level 3 Regional Neonatal Intensive Care Unit (R-NICU) of Baptist Health – with 25 beds at Baptist Medical Center East and 40 beds at Baptist Medical Center South – is one of five regional units in the state. In 2015, BMCE unveiled a newly remodeled NICU featuring a $2 million in improvements. In 1998, BMCS increased its bed capacity from 26 to 40 beds in order to accommodate distressed infants and has a remodel project in the works. A Level 3 NICU is capable of caring for the smallest and sickest of newborn babies.

Improving the Quality of Care

Since 2006, Baptist Health's Institute for Patient Safety and Medical Simulation (IPSMS) has pursued a mission of reducing the likelihood of medical error and improving the quality of health care. The IPSMS has been in its current 22,500-square-foot facility since October 2008. The IPSMS facility houses fully equipped and realistic clinical space, simulated operating rooms, emergency/trauma rooms, a neonatal intensive care unit, pre-hospital settings and other training areas.

As the first freestanding surgery center in the state of Alabama, Montgomery Surgical Center provides advanced procedures and cutting-edge medical technology, allowing patients to go home on the same day as their procedure. It has eight state-of-the-art, integrated operating rooms and two expanded endoscopy suites. Taylor Medical Complex provides much needed space for growing clinical services and is an attractive addition to the East campus.

Baptist Health has been named a Thomson Reuters Top 15 Health System, a distinction that recognizes the nation's top 15 health systems for setting industry benchmarks for excellence across the health care spectrum. BMCE has been recognized four times as one of the top 100 hospitals, BMCS recognized for cardiovascular care, and Prattville Baptist recognized as a distinguished hospital by J.D. Power & Associates based on quality metrics.

In 1963, the Montgomery Baptist Association along with community leaders saw a need for a hospital that serves as a witness to its faith-based mission, and that vision continues to be realized today. "Our mission provides all of our staff, physicians and volunteers an environment that allows them to grow personally, professionally and spiritually within their individual job responsibilities," Tyner said. "Those who work here don't just have a job; they're able to seek their role as a calling."

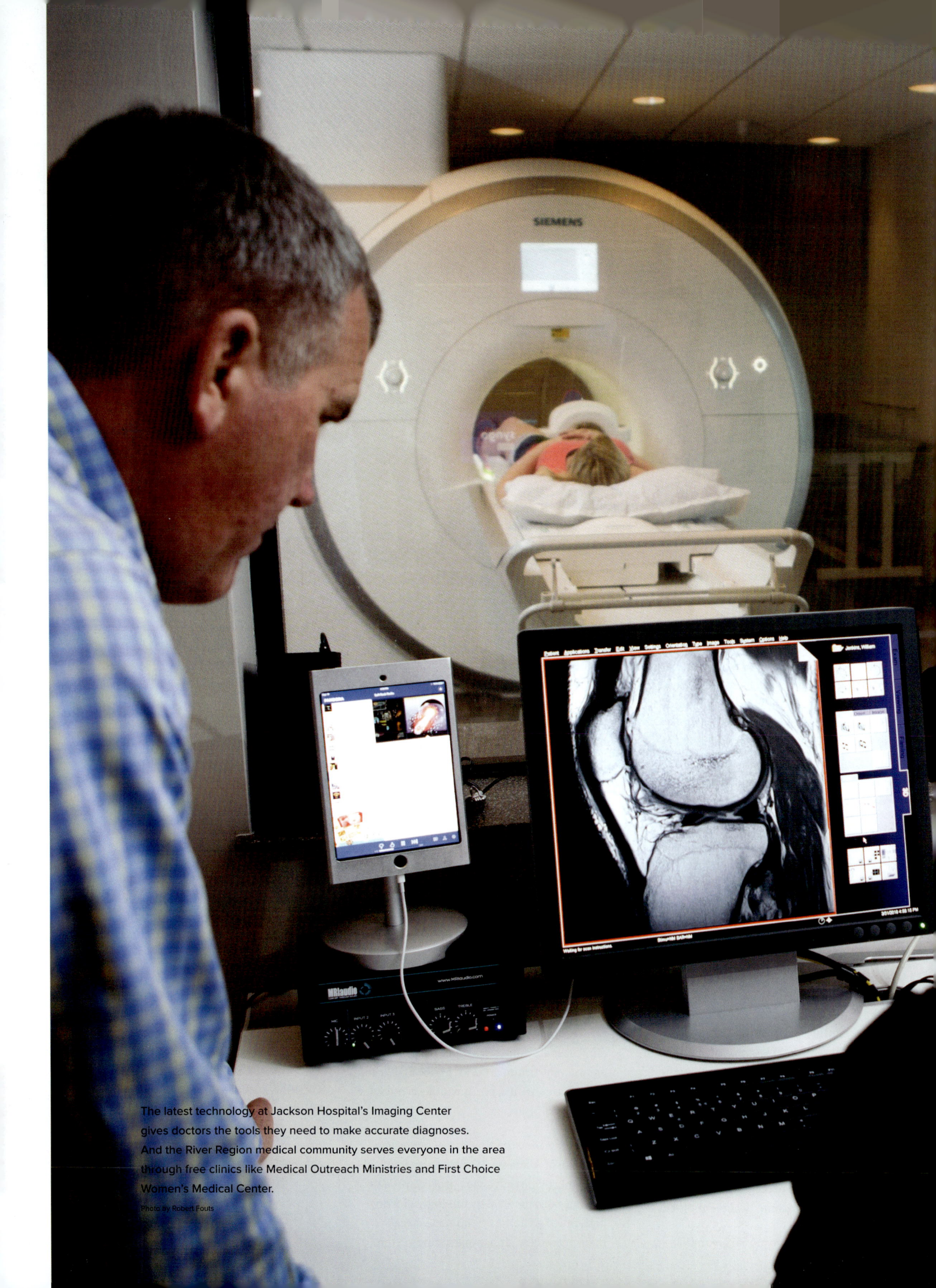

The latest technology at Jackson Hospital's Imaging Center gives doctors the tools they need to make accurate diagnoses. And the River Region medical community serves everyone in the area through free clinics like Medical Outreach Ministries and First Choice Women's Medical Center.

Photo by Robert Fouts

The Jackson Clinic is the area's largest multi-specialty clinic. With more providers and specialties, it provides care that's both exceptional and accessible. The Jackson Clinic offers everything from family medicine to cardiology to obstetrics and gynecology and everything in between. And with a single electronic medical record, care is better coordinated at every step.

Photo courtesy of Jackson Hospital

An Incubator of Service

"At Jackson Hospital, we work daily to ensure we are meeting the area's health care needs. With 344 beds, Jackson Hospital ranks among the largest in the state and is nationally recognized for its excellent care. To help meet the demand for medical professionals in our area, we expanded our medical school campus and added a nurse residency program. We also have robust recruiting efforts and continue to invest in the upgrades and expansions for our facilities and stay on the cutting edge of medical technology to improve patient care."

– Joe Riley, Jackson Hospital Chief Operating Officer

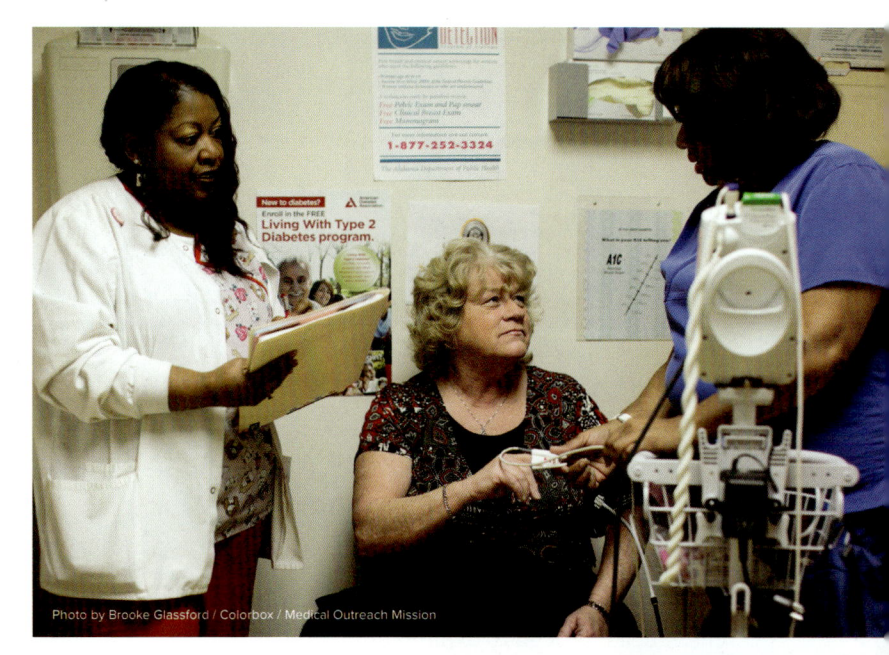

Photo by Brooke Glassford / Colorbox / Medical Outreach Mission

Photo courtesy of First Choice Women's Clinic

Photo by Brooke Glassford / Colorbox

"I am very positive about all that the River Region has to offer in health care. Services, technology and capacity continue to expand in our region. Our biggest challenge has been to expand our medical staff, as some of our physicians retire and as we face the growing need for services, especially as Baby Boomers require greater access. But, we have been highly successful at this; in the past three years alone, Baptist Health has recruited more than 50 physicians to our community. I have lived all over the country but have really loved calling Montgomery my home for the past 15 years. I have found it to be a warm and welcoming city that is large enough to provide everything needed in daily life but also small enough that you can quickly make friends, become involved in community service and have many opportunities for cultural, historical and recreational activities. I have seen such positive growth in our community. I tell my friends from afar that I think Montgomery is the best-kept secret of a great place to live and work."

-Robin Barca, Chief Operating Officer of Baptist Health

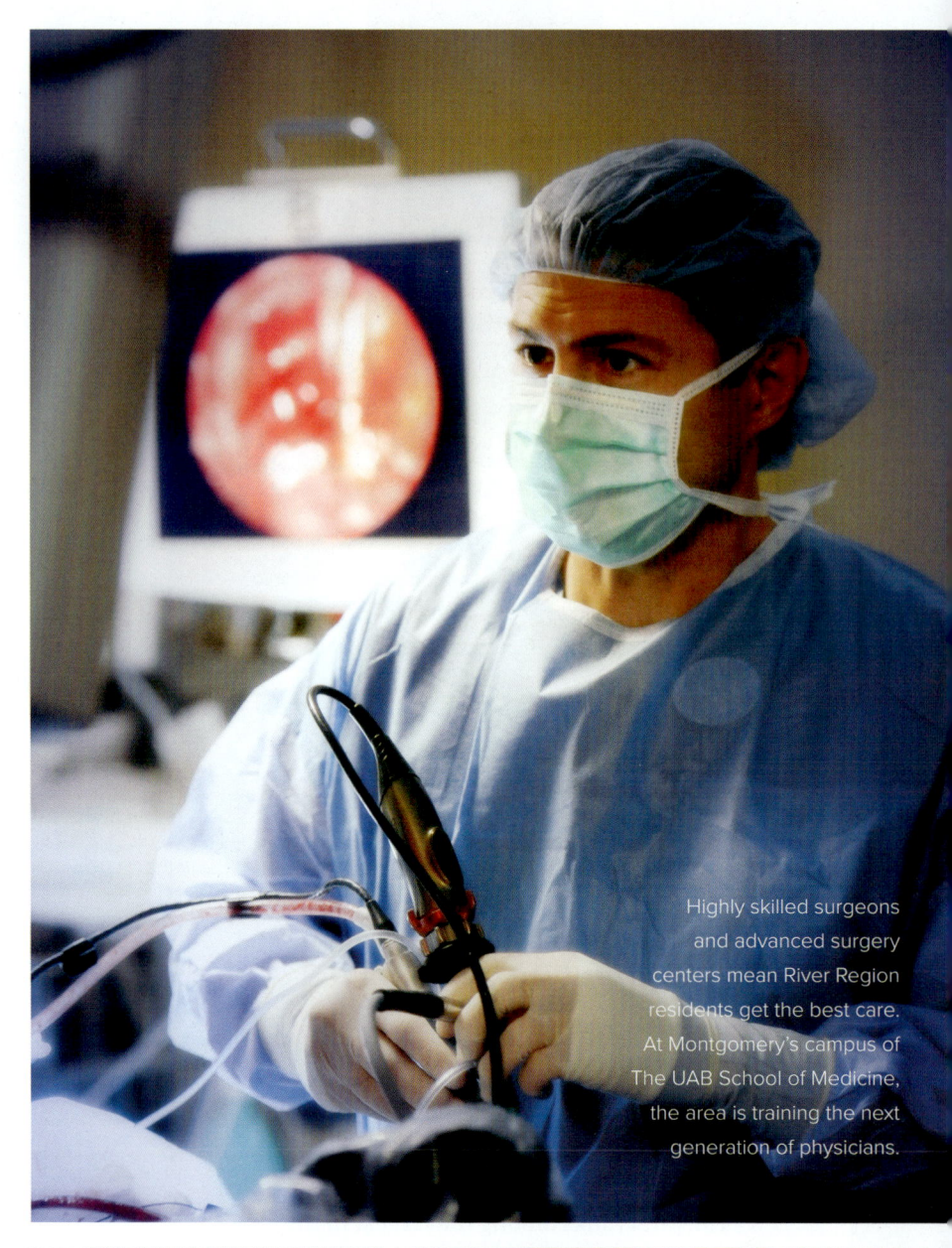

Highly skilled surgeons and advanced surgery centers mean River Region residents get the best care. At Montgomery's campus of The UAB School of Medicine, the area is training the next generation of physicians.

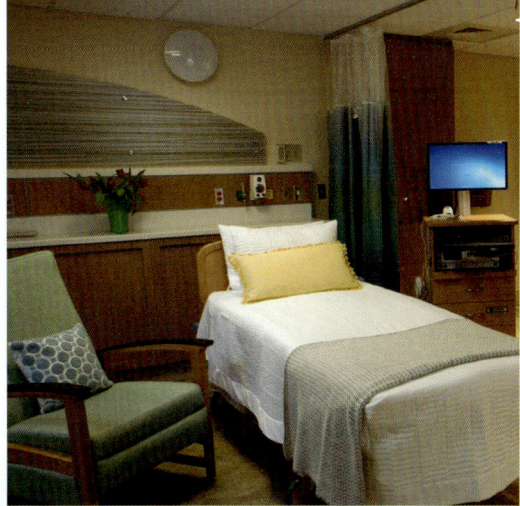

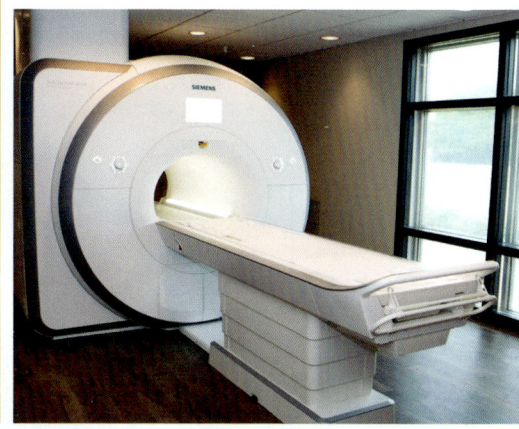

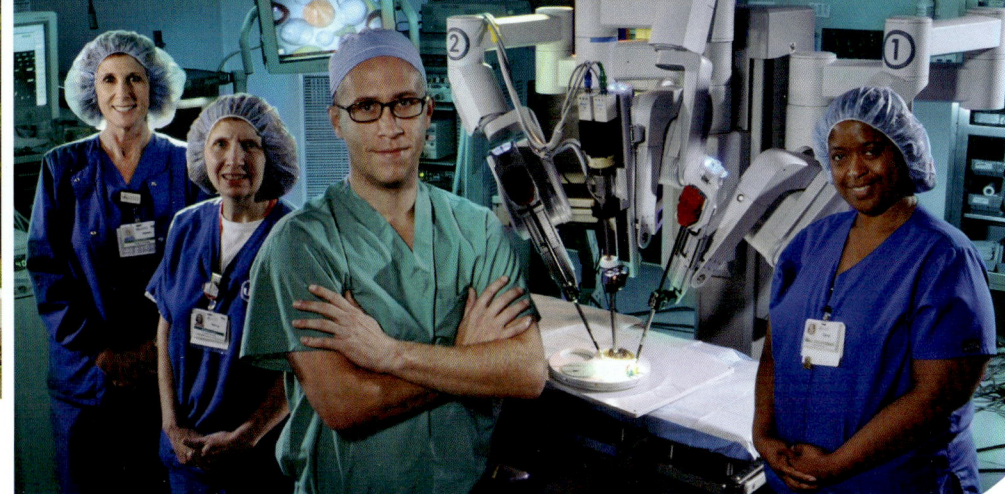

JACKSON HOSPITAL

Leader in Innovation and Expansion of Services

Jackson Hospital has served the communities in the River Region for more than 70 years and continues to lead the way in innovation and quality of care. A community not-for-profit hospital licensed for 344 beds, Jackson provides comprehensive health care services that include cardiac, cancer, neurosciences, orthopedics, urology, and women's and children's care, along with 24-hour Level III trauma services.

The hospital's growth is strategically aligned with the health care needs of River Region communities. The Jackson Clinic, established in 2006, has become the area's largest multi-specialty clinic. Whether patients are seeking a routine checkup with a primary care physician or additional care from a specialist, a single medical record for each patient enables their care to be coordinated at every step. In 2016, the hospital opened its completely renovated Family Birth Center, a $3 million project funded through donations to the Jackson Foundation. More recently, the hospital completed a renovation of its 6 North patient care unit, which consists of 25 private inpatient rooms for urology and medical/surgical patients.

Jackson also offers a fully integrated MR-to-ultrasound fusion prostate biopsy solution. The hospital owns the 3 Tesla MRI, the most powerful MRI system on the market, proven to be effective in identifying suspicious lesions in the prostate. Added to this capability, Jackson is the first urology group in Alabama to offer bkFusion™, a groundbreaking solution for improving biopsy targeting for assistance in diagnosing prostate cancer.

Jackson has also established one of the Southeast's most advanced robotic surgery centers. When advanced robotic equipment is placed in the hands of skilled Jackson physicians, patients benefit from smaller incisions and less invasive tools, while the surgery is more precise with fewer risks. Robotic surgery may be used for a number of different procedures, including urology, gynecology, and general surgery.

Jackson ranks among the largest hospitals in Alabama and is widely recognized for providing excellence in care. Among its prestigious designations, Jackson was the first hospital in Alabama to receive the Joint Commission's Gold Seal of Approval for three centers of excellence: heart attack care, spine surgery, and abdominal aortic aneurysm surgical repair. The Joint Commission has also certified Jackson as an Advanced Primary Stroke Center, and the hospital has received the Blue Cross Distinction Center Plus designation in knee and hip replacement, and spine surgery. Jackson is also ranked as a Blue Cross Blue Shield Tier 1 provider, offering exceptional and quality care to every member of the River Region community.

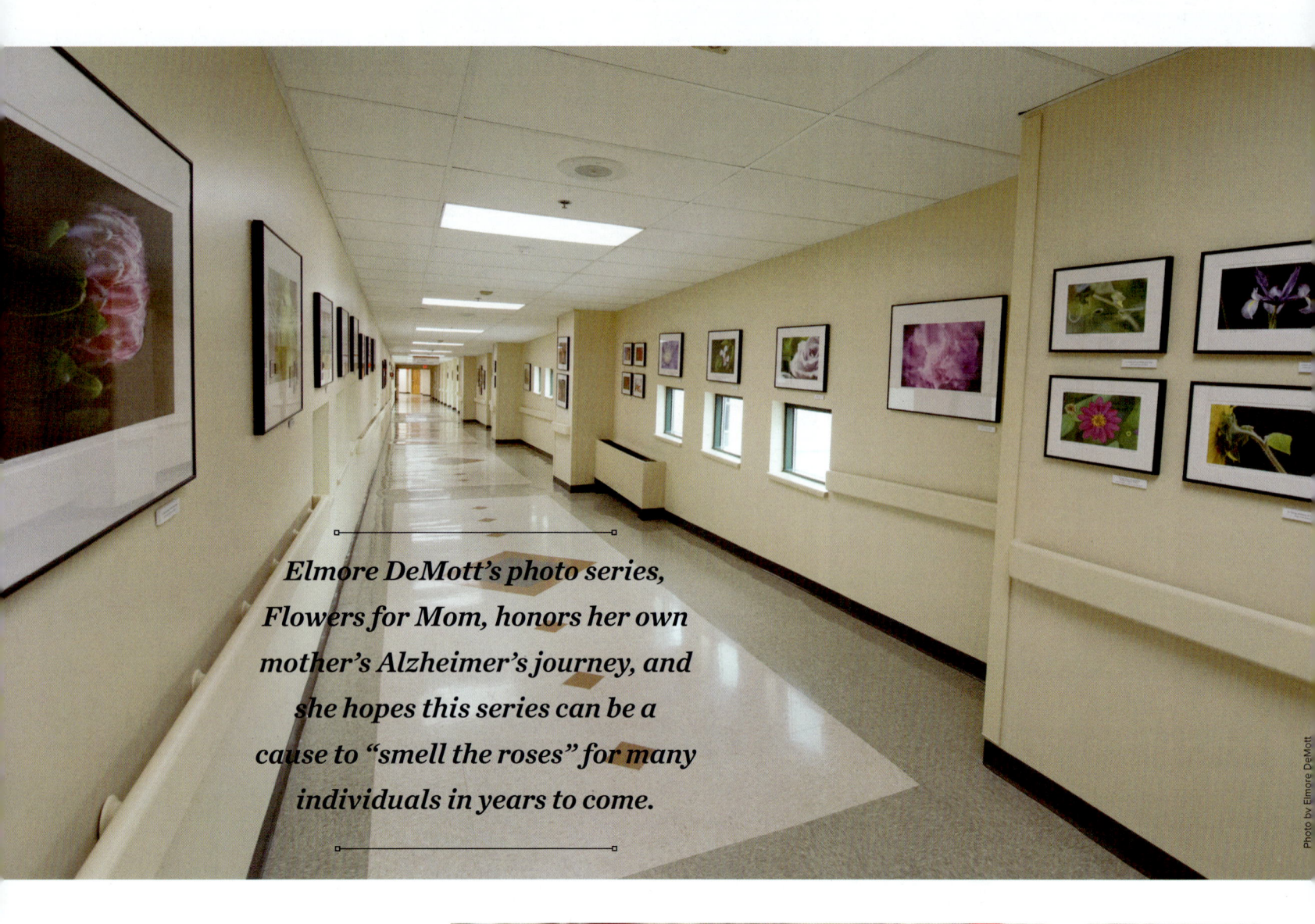

Elmore DeMott's photo series, Flowers for Mom, honors her own mother's Alzheimer's journey, and she hopes this series can be a cause to "smell the roses" for many individuals in years to come.

Compassionate doctors, nurses and many volunteers come together at Medical Outreach Ministries to ensure that the region's medically underserved always have access to quality health care no matter who they are.

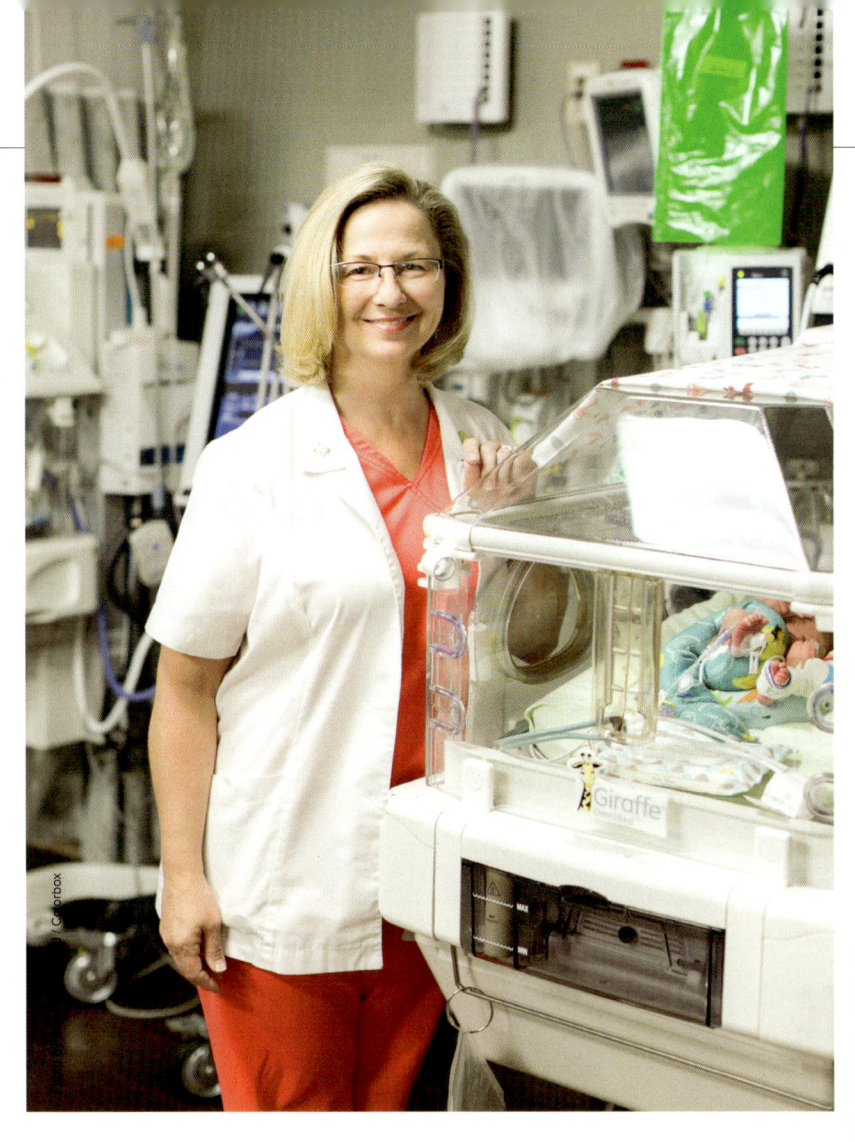

Loving Care:

Yvonne Willis, Nurse Manager at Baptist Health's Neonatal Intensive Care Unit, has been a nurse for 31 years, with 29 of those years in Montgomery. With a heart for her work with newborns and their families that is obvious in her words and actions, she personifies the commitment and spirit of service found in so many of the River Region's thousands of health care workers.

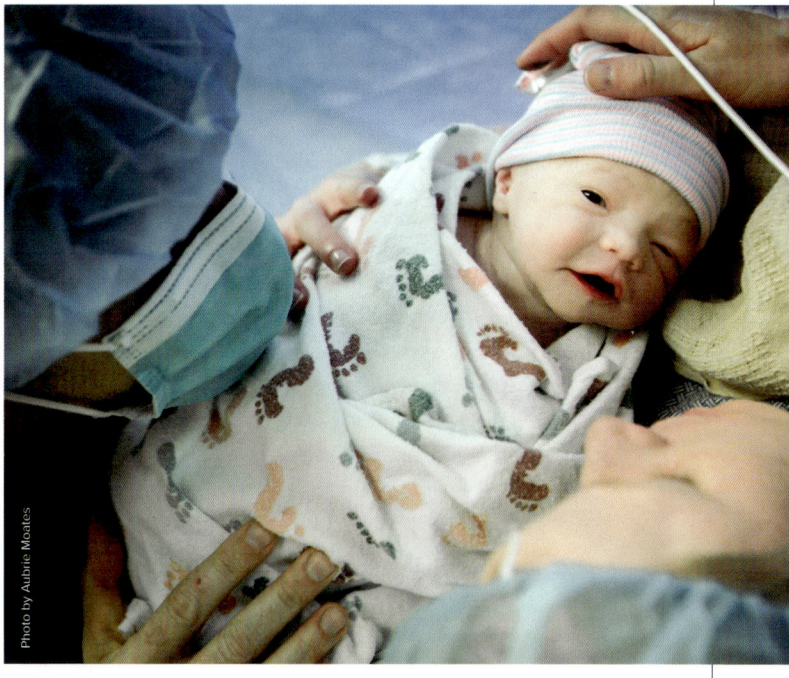

"In the NICU, our vision is to provide a healing environment for our infants and their families. To guide a family with education and compassion from helplessness and anxiety to confidence and competence in caring for their newborn is incredibly challenging and deeply rewarding. The bond one develops with the NICU families is like none other.

The majority of the patients we care for are born prematurely, so are likely to be with us for a significant period of time. This allows the staff to create special relationships. The 'NICU experience' is one that parents will tell you they will never forget.

Very recently, I had a parent say to me after their daughter's 70-plus day stay, 'I used to think of the NICU as a scary, stressful place, but now it just feels sacred.' THAT is the power of neonatal nursing, and it feeds our souls every day. For me and the staff, it truly feels like a privilege to do what we do and see what we see. I love that I am entrusted to care for these wee ones. I love the teamwork and camaraderie. I love seeing the tears that flow from the eyes of the parents (yes, even dads) when they have the opportunity to hold their fragile babies for the first time. I love seeing them progress from so sick and unstable, to being passed around for one more cuddle from the nurses on their day of discharge. The blessings are just endless."

RENAL ASSOCIATES OF MONTGOMERY, PC

Renal Associates of Montgomery, PC was established in 1976 (under the original name of Nephrology Associates) with the primary focus of care in dialysis and chronic kidney disease. Our practice has seven physicians and two nurse practitioners. All of our physicians are board certified in Nephrology. We serve as medical directors of the nine dialysis facilities where we see patients. These facilities are owned and operated by Fresenius Medical Care, N.A., the largest dialysis provider in the United States and worldwide with more than 2,300 dialysis facilities and over 180,000 dialysis patients in the U.S. alone. In addition, our physicians are consultants to eight hospitals in the region, and we see patients in four clinical settings in Montgomery, Prattville, Troy and Greenville.

According to the National Kidney Foundation, 30 million American adults have chronic kidney disease (CKD) and millions of others are at increased risk. Diabetes and high blood pressure are the two main causes of CKD and represent about two thirds of the cases. If kidney disease progresses, it may eventually lead to kidney failure, which requires dialysis or a kidney transplant to maintain life.

Renal Associates physicians include **Dr. William L. McGuffin, Jr.,** who received an undergraduate degree from Georgia Tech, earned his MD from Duke University, completed Internal Medicine residency at Massachusetts General and completed a Nephrology fellowship at Duke.

Dr. Robert B. Hoit, Jr., completed undergraduate studies at Valdosta State College, earned his MD at Medical College of Georgia, and completed Internal Medicine residency and Nephrology fellowship while in the U.S. Air Force.

Dr. Gerald V. Jones received an undergraduate degree from Auburn University Montgomery, earned his MD from UAB School of Medicine, and completed Internal Medicine residency and Nephrology fellowship at University of Tennessee College of Medicine in Memphis.

Dr. Melanie H. Halvorson graduated from Auburn University, earned her MD at UAB School of Medicine, completed Internal Medicine residency at University of Virginia and completed a Nephrology fellowship at the Medical College of Georgia.

Dr. Rodney T. Smith graduated from the University of Alabama, earned his MD at University of South Alabama College of Medicine, completed Internal Medicine residency at the UAB Montgomery Internal Medicine Residency Program and completed a Nephrology fellowship at UAB.

Dr. Kim R. McGlothan completed both undergraduate and medical studies at UAB before completing Internal Medicine residency and Nephrology fellowship at University of Tennessee in Memphis.

Dr. Sumeet Munjal earned his MD in India. He completed an internal medicine residency at University of Buffalo in New York and completed a fellowship in Nephrology at UAB. He joined Renal Associates the summer of 2017.

RIVER REGION DERMATOLOGY AND LASER

Comprehensive Services in Skin Care

River Region Dermatology and Laser is a Dermatology practice providing the most comprehensive services in skin care in Central Alabama. The practice is dedicated to consistently providing high patient satisfaction by rendering excellent service, quality medical care and cutting-edge technology. River Region Dermatology and Laser provides services in Medical Dermatology, Cosmetic Dermatology, and Laser Surgery.

Dr. Porcia Bradford Love is a board-certified Dermatologist and the founder of River Region Dermatology and Laser. She is also a Clinical Assistant Professor at the University of Alabama School of Medicine, where she enjoys precepting and mentoring resident physicians and medical students.

A native of Montgomery, Dr. Love graduated from the LAMP Program at Sidney Lanier High School, where she has since been inducted into the LAMP Hall of Fame. She attended the University of Alabama, where she graduated magna cum laude with a degree in biology. During her undergraduate years, she was the recipient of prestigious student awards, including her recognition as the University of Alabama's National Alumni Association Student of the Year.

Dr. Love received her medical degree from Duke University School of Medicine, where she was named the Student National Medical Association Member of the Year. She completed an Internship in General Surgery at Vanderbilt Medical Center and her Dermatology residency at Duke University Hospital, where she held the honor of serving as Chief Resident. Dr. Love also completed a clinical research fellowship at the National Institutes of Health, where her research focused on skin cancer in young women and minority populations. She received the National Medical Fellowship's David Rogers Memorial Prize and the National Cancer Institute Fellowship Achievement Award for her research

Dr. Love's specialty interests include acne, cosmetic dermatology, hair loss, melasma, laser surgery, and skin cancer prevention and treatment. Dr. Love is a Fellow of the American Academy of Dermatology, the American Society of Dermatologic Surgery, the Skin of Color Society, and the Women's Dermatologic Society. She also serves on the University of Alabama's Community Affairs Board of Advisors, the Leadership Advisory Board of the American Cancer Society, President of the Capital City Medical Society, Leadership Montgomery, and Medical Outreach Ministries.

In addition to the treatment of common skin conditions such as acne, hair loss, mole evaluation, psoriasis, pediatric dermatology, and skin cancer treatment and prevention, the practice provides a variety of cosmetic and laser services. Cosmetic services include BOTOX®, chemical peels, dermal fillers, microneedling and platelet rich plasma therapy for hair loss. The practice also has a variety of lasers and light devices available for hair removal, rosacea, skin tightening, psoriasis, vitiligo, and more. Details on all services are available at rrdermatologylaser.com

LIVING LIFE TO THE FULLEST

Montgomery and the River Region are blessed with a bevy of natural beauty. From multiple rivers (that earned the area its name) and broad pine forests to manicured gardens and parks, there are plenty of outdoor spaces begging to be explored and enjoyed. Mix in the area's mild climate, and you've got a recipe for recreation that encourages the fresh-air activities that are essential to a healthy lifestyle.

CAPITAL CITY GASTROENTEROLOGY

Pictured left to right: Dr. Nina P. Nelson-Garrett, Dr. William P. (Penn) White III, Dr. Heather Echols and Dr. Mark M. Anderson.

Sensitivity. Compassion. Professionalism.

Capital City Gastroenterology was founded in 2004 with a vision to provide patients with the highest quality health care in a compassionate and professional atmosphere. The practice evaluates and treats gastrointestinal disorders with sensitivity, compassion, professionalism and complete confidentiality. Along with a dedicated support staff, Capital City Gastroenterology has four board-certified gastroenterologist physicians.

Dr. Mark M. Anderson, a native of Tuscaloosa, Alabama, received a bachelor's degree from the University of Alabama and then attended UAB School of Medicine. From there he completed a Residency in Internal Medicine and Fellowship in Gastroenterology at the Medical University of South Carolina. Dr. Anderson has been practicing Gastroenterology in Montgomery since 1988. Interestingly, he once performed a colonoscopy on a cheetah at the Montgomery Zoo. Dr. Anderson enjoys his family, teaching Sunday school at First Baptist Church, traveling, reading and golf.

Dr. William P. (Penn) White III is an Atlanta native and a son of a physician. He earned his BS degree and subsequently went to medical school at Emory University in Atlanta. He then completed a Residency, and was Chief Resident in Internal Medicine at the Medical University of South Carolina. For Gastroenterology Fellowship training he went to the University of Kentucky in Lexington. He has been practicing Gastroenterology in Montgomery since 1994. Dr. White enjoys hiking, camping, and painting.

Dr. Nina P. Nelson-Garrett spent her formative years in Jackson, Mississippi. She completed a double major in Molecular Biology and Classical Studies at Vanderbilt University and attended medical school at the University of Texas Health Sciences Center at Houston. She then completed a Residency in Internal Medicine and Fellowship in Gastroenterology at Emory University in Atlanta in 1995. Following training Dr. Garrett practiced in Little Rock, Arkansas, Jackson, Mississippi and Baltimore, Maryland. She joined Capital City Gastroenterology in 2007. Dr. Garrett enjoys traveling, spending time with family and painting.

Dr. Heather Echols, a second-generation gastroenterologist from Houston, Texas, earned a Bachelor of Arts degree from Trinity University (San Antonio, Texas) and a Masters of Public Health from Boston University. After serving as a Peace Corps Volunteer in Guatemala, she received her Doctorate of Medicine from Robert Wood Johnson School of Medicine in New Jersey. She completed her internship and residency at Tulane University Health Sciences Center and affiliated hospitals in Internal Medicine. She further trained in Hepatology and Gastroenterology/Hepatology fellowship programs at Loyola University Medical Center in Chicago, Illinois and the University of Arkansas for Medical Science in Little Rock, Arkansas. Dr. Echols joined the practice in 2016. She enjoys spending time with family, traveling, photography and reading.

The River Region boasts an abundance of outdoor activity and adventure opportunities.

Photo by Nancy Fields

Photo by Scooter Painter

Photo by Robert Fouts

Take a Hike
The Alabama Nature Center (ANC) on the grounds of the Alabama Wildlife Federation's headquarters in Millbrook shows off Alabama's biodiversity with a good sampling of several different ecosystems all in one place. This 350-acre outdoor education facility's five miles of boardwalks and trails that traverse forests, fields, streams, wetlands and ponds invite visitors to hike through the region's natural wonders. The ANC offers several special events each year for the public (guided hikes, kids' fishing rodeos, nature photography classes), especially in the summer.

Park It
Located in Montgomery, Lagoon Park's 432 acres include 176 acres of open space. A great way to explore it is using the park's five-mile multi-purpose loop trail designed for biking, walking and running. A mix of paved and dirt track sections, the trail runs through forest, meadows and beside water. The park also boasts a single-track mountain bike trail and a 1-mile nature walk that runs alongside the park's large pond as well as around a few small wetland areas.

At Jasmine Hill Gardens in Wetumpka, guests leisurely wander through acres of flowers, shrubs and trees as well as classical statuary representing mythical Greek heroes and gods. This oasis of natural calm was planned and planted to ensure that there's something beautiful and colorful in bloom almost all year long.

Walk, run, fly a kite or just feed some feathered friends by the lake at Montgomery's Blount Cultural Park, the massive wide-open green space modeled after English moors. The property also houses the Alabama Shakespeare Festival and The Montgomery Museum of Fine Arts.

Pedal Pushing
Mountain bikers find lots to love in the River Region. The Swayback Bridge Trail in Wetumpka travels through shady woodlands and is a favorite ride thanks to its natural beauty, some tight turns, fun switchbacks and the "roller coaster" ride up and down the rolling hills along the banks of Lake Jordan. The 12-mile loop trail hosts the Attack on Swayback race each summer and is also open to hikers.

You can also pedal your way through some of the area's most striking scenery with a ride along the cycling road route that links Wetumpka to Tallassee on Rifle Range Road. Or experience the picturesque rural landscape of the Town of Pike Road via its Nature Trail system, featuring several miles of paved trail designed for biking as well as walking or running.

WESLEY GARDENS RETIREMENT COMMUNITY

Enriching the Lives of Older Adults

Wesley Gardens provides a warm and caring home for seniors who still enjoy an active life. The gathering places, mealtimes and events are filled with friendly faces and lively activities, and there's always help nearby whenever it's needed. Located on Taylor Road near the entrance to EastChase, the comfortable and comforting retirement community was the first of its kind when it opened in the 1980s as Halcyon Terrace. "We were the first free-standing domiciliary in the U.S.," said administrator Randy Allen, ALA.

In 1989, Wesley Gardens became part of the Methodist Homes Corporation, which operates a dozen communities in Alabama and Northwest Florida. The Montgomery location fully incorporates the mission, "to enrich the lives of older adults and all those who serve them in faith-based communities where life is celebrated, relationships are valued, teamwork is embraced, service excellence is expected, and the touch of God's love is ever-present and ageless."

As a need arises in a person's life, perhaps after a fall or illness, families look for a place that can reduce the burden of managing a household. Allen acknowledged that often "the ones who come here didn't want to come here." Yet very quickly their attitude changes, and they wonder, "Why didn't I do this sooner?!" Wesley Gardens welcomes a wide range of individuals aged 62 and older, and residents currently range from 68 to 99 years old.

In fact, about a half dozen residents will celebrate their 100th birthday in the next year!

Assisted Living arrangements provides just the right balance of independence and support. Nurses and care staff are available around the clock to assist with medications, grooming and other personal care services. In addition, a memory care section adds security features for those with mild to moderate dementia.

Wesley Gardens also offers a full dietary department and serves three meals a day in a well-appointed dining room. During mealtime, residents order from a menu of daily selections and are served by friendly waiters and waitresses.

But Wesley Gardens isn't just about security and convenience. It's also about fun! The staff includes a life enrichment director who provides a full roster of social opportunities and activities to help make each resident's days more enjoyable. In addition, church groups and volunteers sponsor events and offer a range of entertainment, speakers and presentations to pique their interests. Transportation is also available so residents can go out and about in the community to visit a museum, dine at a local restaurant or enjoy a play or movie. With all this and more, Wesley Gardens offers the perfect combination of care and comfort for River Region seniors.

JONES DRUGS

A Family Pharmacy Serving You

As a pharmacy founded on superior customer service and family-friendly prescription fulfillment, it's no wonder customers choose Jones Drugs.

After establishing several pharmacies in the area, James Jones, RPh, opened his pharmacy to serve downtown Montgomery and residents living in close proximity to Fairview Avenue. The Fairview location opened in 2016 in a former bank building and was applauded for being part of the revitalization taking place along the thoroughfare. In addition, Jones Drugs has one location in Prattville and one in Greenville to better serve the region.

The caring, friendly and sincere approach of Jones and his entire team has earned the pharmacy the reputation of fulfilling prescriptions fast and at the same price as the box stores with outstanding friendly service. They also offer convenient pharmacy services from free consultations to prescription refills.

Jones says he wants to make the local community better by providing a more convenient, accessible pharmacy with an emphasis on personal service. Jones Drugs looks forward to serving its customers every day and being a part of helping people not only feel better, but live a healthy life!

The Alabama River that flows alongside downtown Montgomery is part of The Alabama Scenic River Trail that traverses the entire state and is the longest designated river trail in America.
Photo by Charles Seifried

River Runs

The Alabama River rolls right alongside the edge of downtown Montgomery and is the backdrop to Riverfront Park and Amphitheater. It is also part of Alabama's Scenic River Trail, which showcases some of our state's abundant natural wonders. This network of rivers is the longest such trail contained in a single state in the country, and it begins at the Georgia state line on the Coosa River. One favorite way to enjoy this liquid asset is sliding across the river's surface on a stand-up paddleboard.

In Wetumpka, the Coosa River offers the thrill and rush of whitewater. Rent a canoe, kayak or sit-a-top kayak for the day and spend three to four hours paddling through some amazing scenery and relaxing calm waters leading to Class I and II rapids. Several nearby outfitters rent everything needed for a day of fun on the water.

Active Events

The River Region has a calendar full of annual events that get bodies moving and hearts pumping, including multiple runs and walks, often benefiting local charities, and the Montgomery Half Marathon. Its course leads runners of all skill levels through the heart of the city and into lovely Old Cloverdale before finishing in Riverwalk Stadium. The 13.1-mile race began in 2009 and has grown to become one of the premier active events in the Southeast.

ANSWERED PRAYER HOME CARE SERVICES

John and Sherry White have the passion to help people lead a happier and healthier life. After 20 years in the long-term care industry, the couple decided to pour their purpose into a new venture: Answered Prayer Home Care Services.

With offices in Montgomery and Foley, Answered Prayer provides private home care services helping their clients lead dignified, independent lifestyles in the comfort and safety of their own homes.

As a nurse-owned agency, they go beyond to provide personal and customized programs to fit each individual's needs. Whether it's housekeeping, running errands, managing medications, meal preparation or going with a client to a doctor's appointment, their highly trained team strives to turn a stressful situation into an opportunity for ease and comfort for the client and their family. "We are passionate and believe that by being involved with our clients' care and having open communication between our clients and family members, we can provide a higher level of service."

Sustaining Mind, Body and Spirit
Community Organizations & Non-Profits

ClefWorks, an innovative Montgomery arts organization, offers our area a fresh approach to chamber music with performances and educational events in unique venues with unexpected additions. Photo courtesy of ClefWorks / Carter Photography & Design, LLC

Montgomery and the River Region are full of people who collectively make up the soul of the city and define its character with their charitable and philanthropic spirits. Evidence of this can be found in the area's multiple community organizations and non-profits. Each group is dedicated to ensuring Montgomery is a great city for all by giving back and providing opportunities for everyday citizens to be a part of the change they're making.

Our region's people are known for warm welcomes and for their generosity, sharing their financial blessings along with their time and talents. This generosity shines brightest through their support of large organizations like United Way, the Montgomery Area Food Bank, Red Cross and Salvation Army as well as grassroots groups like Common Ground, an inner-city ministry, and the Joy to Life Foundation, a local breast cancer charity that raises funds to provide mammograms to medically underserved women throughout Alabama. We help animals through the Montgomery Humane Society and care for our most valuable and vulnerable, our children, through organizations like Brantwood Children's Home.

From providing food and health care for the poor and protecting the environment to promoting race relations, strengthening families and fighting domestic violence, Montgomery and the River Region have an organization in place to spread the word, engage the community, rally needed resources and do the good work.

Feet on the Ground

"I have come to believe that CGM is a place where all kinds of people come to both give and receive mercy. For some kids from the neighborhood, this looks like not being in a gang, not carrying a pistol, not dying on a front porch, not dropping out of school or not starting kindergarten with a developmental deficit. They escape gangs, teenage pregnancy, lack of education and fatherlessness to be developed into producers who love others well, who begin a legacy of an intact family and can creatively change the world. And, they will do it better because they aren't racially, politically and socially isolated. On the flip side, those who come from outside the neighborhood to help and get involved see what their time and financial resources would be spent on without being connected to their purpose. They see how their own lives and the lives of their children can be impoverished or damaged by being in spiritual isolation, despite having great material affluence and influence. They experience God in ways they never thought available to them, and find their story in His story. And the line between mercy giver and mercy receiver becomes blurred as we find kinship, together, in this place. This is what we get to see over and over again here."

-Bryan Kelly, Founder of Common Ground Montgomery

For more than a decade Common Ground Ministries has taken its good news and good works straight to the people it serves. Founded by Bryan Kelly and located in Montgomery's Washington Park neighborhood, this inner-city ministry's mission is transforming its community by focusing on youth development and leadership.

Photos courtesy of Common Ground Montgomery / Matt Wolfe

135

JOY TO LIFE FOUNDATION

#liveheregivehere

Every journey, no matter how epic it becomes, begins with a single step. That's how things began for the Joy to Life Foundation. After she battled breast cancer and won, Joy Blondheim and her husband Dickie stepped into a new world, creating the Joy to Life Foundation in 2001 as a way to arm women all over Alabama with the resources and information to be survivors too.

The non-profit raises funds to ensure that un- and under-insured women in Alabama have access to mammograms and other screenings to detect breast cancer earlier and therefore, greatly increase their chances of survival. It also raises awareness about breast cancer in general and has become a shining symbol of hope and support for people of all ages and walks of life who are facing and fighting breast cancer.

Joy shared the Foundation's impetus. "After I made it through breast cancer, I was just so thankful for my recovery," she said. "But Dickie and I started to think about how we could help others going through the same thing. As a show of gratitude for my health, we wanted to give back, and the Foundation seemed like the right way to do that."

There are multiple wonderful ways to support Joy to Life and its mission. People can order a pink curbside trashcan to display on their street. They can participate in the annual "Walk of Life," the Foundation's initial fundraising effort and still a highly successful 5k walk/run that traverses downtown Montgomery and gives people a chance to honor a breast cancer survivor or remember someone who lost their fight with the disease, all while raising money for JTL. Of course, donations are a major way for people to help, but equally important is people spreading awareness and benefitting the Foundation by "pinking their ride" with JTL's pink breast cancer car tags, motorcycle tags and boat tags. A large portion of the proceeds from all tag sales go directly to the Foundation.

The Blondheims have been blown away by the support they've received through the years from corporate sponsors, from individuals and from thousands of volunteers. "It's inspiring and so gratifying to see others get behind our vision and to help us help so many people around Alabama," Dickie said.

The vehicle through which JTL Foundation provides mammograms is The Alabama Department of Public Health and its Breast and Cervical Cancer Early Detection and Prevention program (ABCCEDP). Money that the Foundation brings in from sales of its car tags, registration for and sponsorships of the Walk of Life and other avenues are given to ADPH, which in turn "pays" for mammograms for at-risk women who could not afford them. With Foundation funds, ADPH screens at-risk women 40-49, but the Foundation goes even farther, independently paying for screening services for women under the age of 40. "No matter what the age, we want to provide screenings for all at-risk women," Joy said.

Joy to Life   Walk of Life

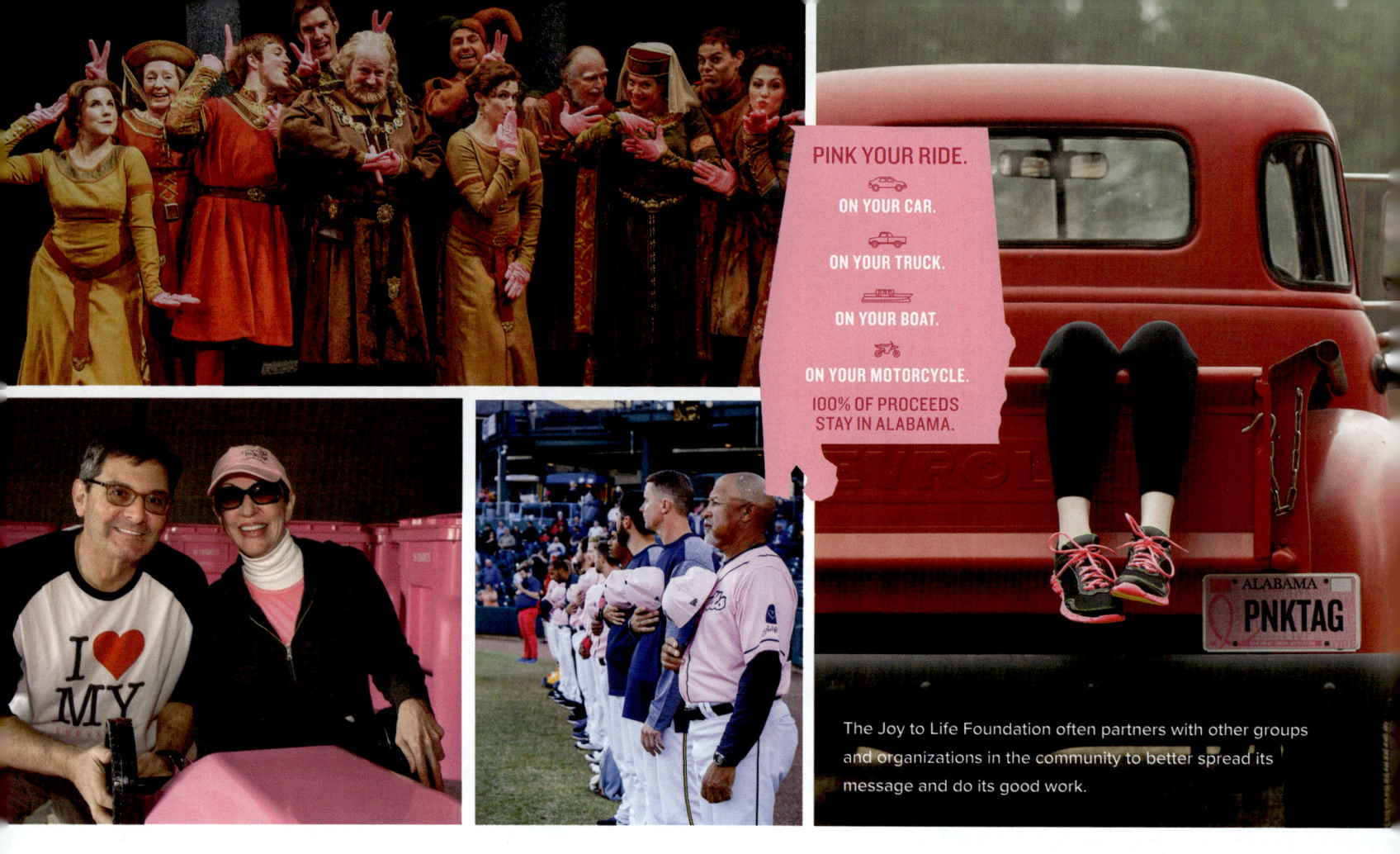

PINK YOUR RIDE.
ON YOUR CAR.
ON YOUR TRUCK.
ON YOUR BOAT.
ON YOUR MOTORCYCLE.
100% OF PROCEEDS STAY IN ALABAMA.

The Joy to Life Foundation often partners with other groups and organizations in the community to better spread its message and do its good work.

The Foundation was not only the first and largest private provider for the ABCCEDP, it has now provided more than $1.4 million to the Alabama Department of Public Health.

In 2001, the ADPH was providing approximately 1,500 mammograms per year. Today, they provide more than 15,000 per year, in large part due to the Foundation's consistent financial support and its leadership promoting breast cancer awareness. Since 2007 and as of 2018, the Foundation has directly and indirectly been responsible for more than 95,000 mammograms and screenings, meaning more than 1,100 women have been diagnosed and treated because of its work. And since its inception, JTL has raised in excess of $7 million in the fight against breast cancer.

The impressive numbers proving JTL's massive positive impact on our state continue to grow every year, yet the reach of the Foundation goes so far beyond these figures and statistics. Every digit represents a life, someone's mother, wife, sister, daughter and friend. Joy explained her and Dickie's motivation in creating Joy to Life. "We wanted to see something positive come from my personal experience with breast cancer, and we saw a need in our community for better access to preventative care," she said. "Now, almost two decades later, we feel that our impact has been monumental."

And it's not just the screenings that JTL makes possible that are making a major difference. Dickie believes that the Foundation's general breast cancer awareness efforts are just as important. "Our pink breast cancer car tag, which is the sixth most popular car tag out of more than 120 different specialty tags in the state, plus our motorcycle tags and boat tags, all act as a moving billboard in every county in Alabama that reminds everyone to pay attention to their breast health and to always get their mammograms," he said. "It has been a key marketing tool for early detection and saving lives."

JTL is always looking forward and moving ahead, and in 2013, the Foundation took a bold leap with a new venture that both strengthened its mission and furthered its scope: the launch of Joy to Life magazine. In recognition of the powerful role that proactive, healthy lifestyles play in breast cancer prevention and survival, the Foundation decided to create and distribute a health resource in the form of an inspirational and informative magazine and website. "We couldn't be more proud of this publication," Joy said. "The goal is simple: to empower and encourage individuals of all genders, ages and walks of life to take care of themselves. Living healthier lives helps prevent not just breast cancer, but all types of cancer, heart disease, diabetes and more. Plus it makes us feel better, with more energy to expend on the things and ones we love."

Dickie pointed to the magazine as just one more avenue for spreading JTL's message, including its goal of keeping breast cancer a top-of-mind issue. "In addition to our efforts like the Walk, our vehicle tags, the trashcans and our billboards, the magazine and its website are great ways to increase breast cancer awareness and education," he said.

While the Blondheims are proud of what the Joy to Life Foundation has accomplished and thrilled that it has provided access to needed resources that save lives, they know they have not done any of it alone. "If there is one thing I want people to know, it is that we always so appreciate their support," Joy said. "We never take a single sponsorship, donation, Walk sign-up or volunteer for granted. We know we could never have come so far or done our important work without them, and we can never thank our supporters enough. They are Joy to Life!"

joytolife.org

Montgomery's Court Square Fountain bathed in pink light to celebrate Joy to Life's annual Walk of Life event.

Photo courtesy of Joy to Life Foundation / Nancy Fields

Building Community

"Our mission at the YMCA is to put Judeo-Christian principles into practice through programs that build a healthy spirit, mind and body for all, and I'm proud of the way we do that here. When I took the helm as President and CEO of the YMCA of Greater Montgomery, I was no stranger to the Y. I began my career in Nashville, as the director of teen programs. God has given me a purpose in life and that's to serve others. The Y allows me to do that. Through my gift of leading people and the opportunity to share that gift with the community through the Y, I am so thankful that I was able to play such a vital role in the lives of so many. I am equally thankful for and proud of how well our community collaborates to affect positive change and build a wonderful quality of life for all. We work so well together to produce positive results through our many active civic clubs and other many diverse partnerships that keep working together in so many different ways to push our community forward."

- Gary Cobb, CEO, Montgomery Area YMCA

Refreshing fun at a Montgomery Area YMCA.

Photo courtesy of the Montgomery YMCA

The Junior League of Montgomery is an organization committed to promoting voluntarism, developing the potential of women and improving the community through the effective action and leadership of trained volunteers. Its purpose is exclusively educational and charitable. Founded in 1926, the Junior League of Montgomery is one of over 290 leagues across four countries representing almost 150,000 women. The Montgomery league is composed of nearly 800 members who donate approximately 20,000 hours of volunteer services annually. The JLM reaches out to all women regardless of race, religion, color or national origin.

The dramatic success of the league's annual fundraisers has made possible a financial commitment to the Montgomery area that has totaled well over $1 million in the last 10 years alone. Proceeds raised by the Junior League of Montgomery support its work in the community through projects that improve the quality of life for families and children.

Helping Hands

"Families have chosen to live and work in the River Region, returning their time, talent, treasure and trust to the area. People working together will continue to make Montgomery and the River Region special and one of America's best communities for years to come.

For more than 30 years, the Central Alabama Community Foundation has been a part of what makes Montgomery and the River Region special. We are committed to being a strong community partner in the years to come."

- Burton Ward, Executive Director of the Central Alabama Community Foundation, a nonprofit foundation that brings area donors together with charitable interests and nonprofits

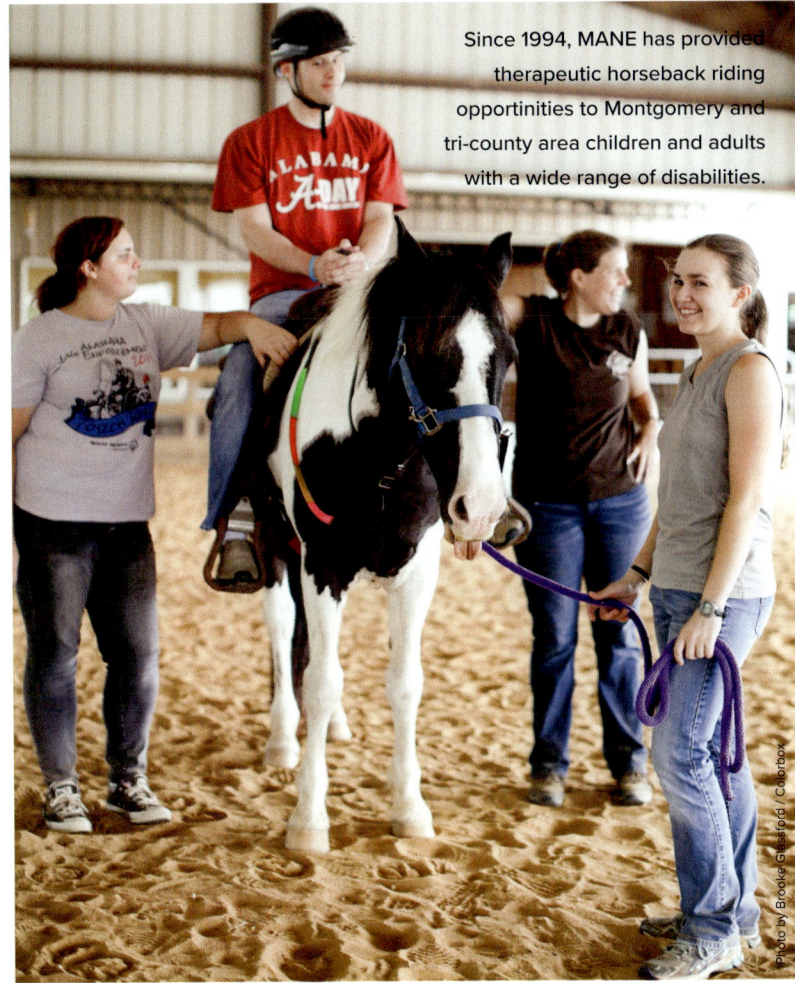

Since 1994, MANE has provided therapeutic horseback riding opportunities to Montgomery and tri-county area children and adults with a wide range of disabilities.

The Montgomery Humane Shelter helps furry friends find a home throughout the River Region.

Sharing Hope

"Employers are in such need for qualified workers, but many unemployed men and women simply do not possess the basic life skills that are necessary. Employers have fully embraced our efforts to improve the pool of individuals they have to choose from. Others have valued our approach to dealing with poverty, which is to provide a viable means for people to take control of their lives and become self-sufficient. The willingness of the citizens of our communities to share their resources with those they do not know is amazing. Our residents have a strong desire to see people succeed and are willing to roll up their sleeves and work to bring real solutions."

- Michael Coleman, Founder of Hope Inspired Ministries, a non-profit that serves low-skilled, poorly educated and chronically unemployed men and women by preparing them to obtain and maintain employment

Photos courtesy of Hope Inspired / Lori Mercer

PRATTVILLE YMCA

A Small-Town YMCA with a Big Impact on the Community

"When I think of the Prattville YMCA, I think of it as part of the fabric of the community," said David Lewis, who has served as CEO since 2012. "Our community is what it is, in large part, because of the Y. They've grown hand in hand."

In 1963, Prattville was a small town of 5,000 and some said too small to have its own YMCA. Yet community leaders connected with a young man from Georgia named Willis Bradford and hired him to develop the Y programs. Bradford served a 49-year tenure at the helm as Prattville grew to a city of almost 40,000.

The first facility, the Don M. Smith Branch on East Main Street, was built in 1966. Today it houses administrative offices and serves as a specialty branch, providing a prestigious gymnastics program and competitive swim team, along with an indoor pool for year-round water exercise and aquatic activities for kids and adults. The adjacent Fitness Center Branch, added in 1988, provides equipment and classes for cardio, group exercise, strength training and even ballroom dancing.

The youth athletic fields, located on McQueen Smith Road since the early 1980s, evolved into the larger Willis Bradford Branch and opened in 2000. This branch includes two basketball gyms, fitness area, multi-purpose room, child care area, play center and two outdoor pools. Programs are offered for all ages, infant through senior adult. The adjacent Child Care Branch houses a licensed pre-school and provides leadership for Y after-school programs and summer day camps. The Bradford Branch is also home to The Field of Dreams, an ADA accessible baseball field, which opened in 2014 and offers physically and developmentally challenged young people and adults the opportunity to participate in a baseball league specifically designed for them. For many, it's their first opportunity to play a team sport.

The Wellness Branch on Hwy 82, which opened in 2008, offers group exercise classes and fitness equipment. The Prattville YMCA also offers after-school care and summer day camps at schools in the community and operates many programs for youth and adults throughout the year.

"The Y has added tremendous quality of life to this community," Lewis said. "The Y is more than a gym or a pool. It's a movement. The Y is committed to strengthening our community through youth development, healthy living and social responsibility. Every day, we work side-by-side with our neighbors to make sure that everyone, regardless of age, income or background has the opportunity to grow and thrive."

At any location, the Y provides a year-round gathering place for everyone in the community. "We put Christian principles into practice through programs that build a healthy spirit, mind and body for all," Lewis said. "More than a facility or child care center, the Y is a deeply rooted nonprofit organization committed to changing lives in our community."

Doing More

Michelle Browder can be spotted sporting her signature red glasses while guiding tourists from all over the county (and world) around historic Montgomery on her MORE THAN tours that have garnered the attention of *The New York Times*. "I started my non-profit to empower young people to see their worth and to rise above negative stereotypes and generalizations. We're also teaching the community how to look past tattoos, piercings and dreadlocks and see the kid, who they really are. The tour portion of I AM MORE THAN is the business that funds our other work, and we have received great support from the city and other groups. I am not from here, but Montgomery is such an amazing education destination. There is so much history here. People all over the world know our civil rights history, and that is so powerful, and it makes Montgomery unique. I'm proud to be a Montgomerian now."

- Michelle Browder, Founder and Executive Director of I AM MORE THAN

RIVER REGION UNITED WAY
Making Life Better for Everyone

The River Region United Way is making life better for everyone. For more than 95 years, United Way has been making an impact by addressing the most acute needs in the communities it serves.

United Way fights for the health, education, financial stability and basic needs of every person in every community. Every year, the River Region United Way directly impacts the lives of nearly 135,000 people in Autauga, Elmore, Lowndes, Macon and Montgomery counties. In 2017, United Way invested nearly $4.25 million in the River Region through its support of 40 plus agencies and nearly 90 programs.

What sets the River Region United Way apart from so many other nonprofit organizations in this area is its work to create lasting change. With the help of hundreds of volunteers, United Way assesses community needs, acquires the resources necessary to meet those needs, allocates funds to effective programs, and accounts for donations to ensure they are used efficiently for maximum impact.

By helping to build strong families and strengthen communities, the River Region United Way is deeply invested in the future of Montgomery and the River Region. To learn more about the United Way and how you can get involved, visit www.RRUW.org.

147

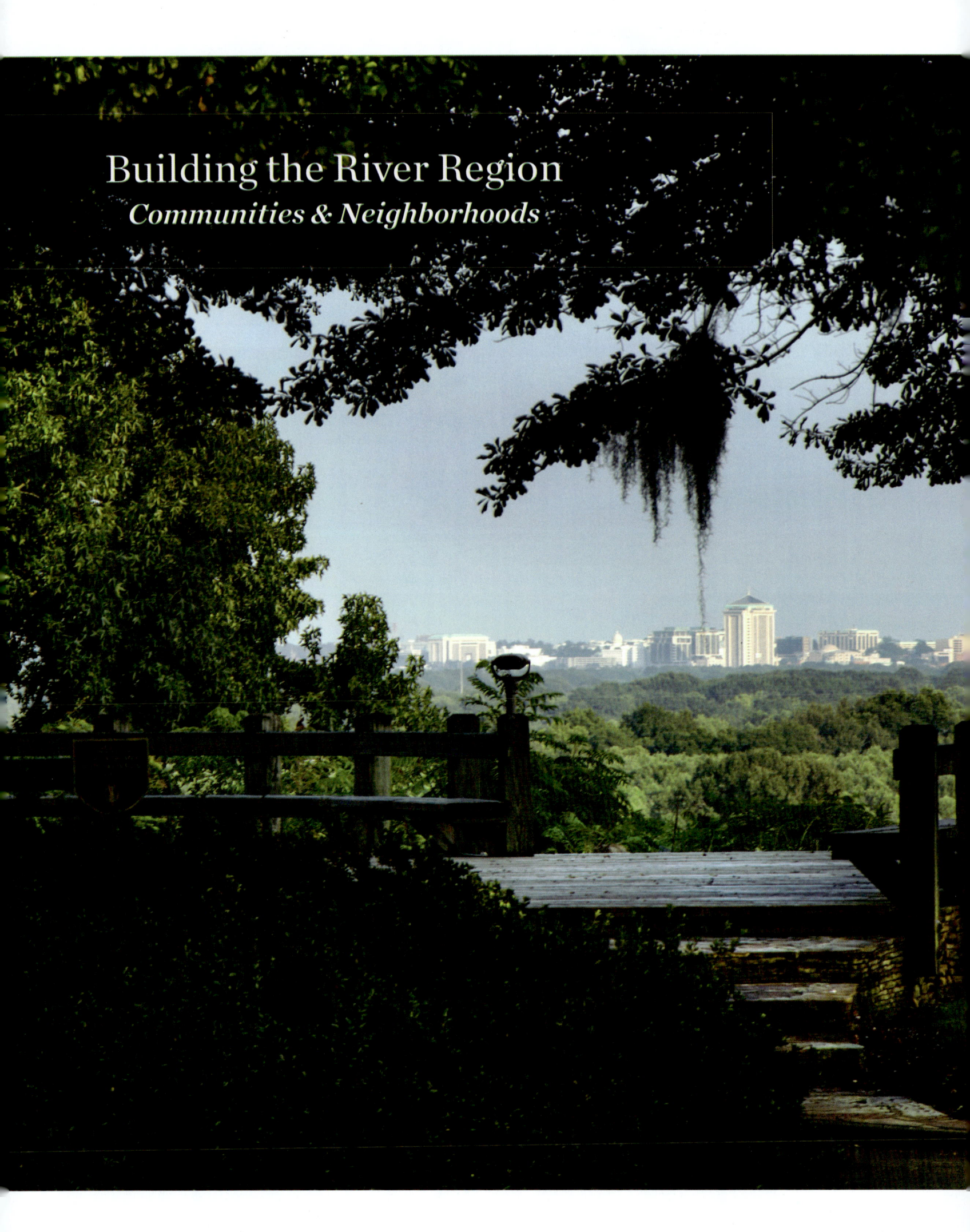

Building the River Region
Communities & Neighborhoods

A postcard-perfect view of Montgomery from Capitol Hill, the Prattville stop on the Robert Trent Jones Golf Trail.

Photo by Robert Fouts

From the magnificent mansions and cozy cottages nestled along the tree-lined streets of historic neighborhoods like Old Cloverdale in Montgomery and the Daniel Pratt Historic District in Prattville, to the amenity-packed options in convenient communities that have sprung up across the area, the capital city and River Region are filled with unique neighborhoods and myriad selections to fit any lifestyle.

There's a palpable energy pulsating through the housing options in the heart of the capital city. From lofts built into industrial spaces in the middle of downtown, to full-scale renovations of once-abandoned homes on the area's perimeter, people are investing and living in Montgomery's historic urban center again.

At the other end of the city's limits, the Southern Living community of Hampstead is making its own history. By utilizing smart-growth principles to beautiful effect and offering multiple sized homes and mixed-use spaces, Hampstead is more than just a neighborhood. It's a place to discover a true sense of connectivity and the chance to live a more sustainable life.

In between, Midtown is thriving. Homes in this mid-century neighborhood are getting facelifts and housing everyone from retired empty-nesters to young families.

The surrounding River Region offers a diverse range of places to call home too. From the quaint charm of the Town of Pike Road and natural beauty of Wetumpka and its well-loved Jasmine Hill neighborhood, to the bustling growth in Prattville where the historic gin shop is being transformed into luxury apartments, the area has something for everyone.

But the area offers more than multiple choices for finding the right physical home. With spiritual growth and fellowship occupying a meaningful place in many residents' lives, the River Region's faith communities are just as varied and vibrant. The congregations of the many local churches and synagogues include some of our most engaged citizens, and they welcome any and all to join their ecclesiastical families.

A Story to Tell

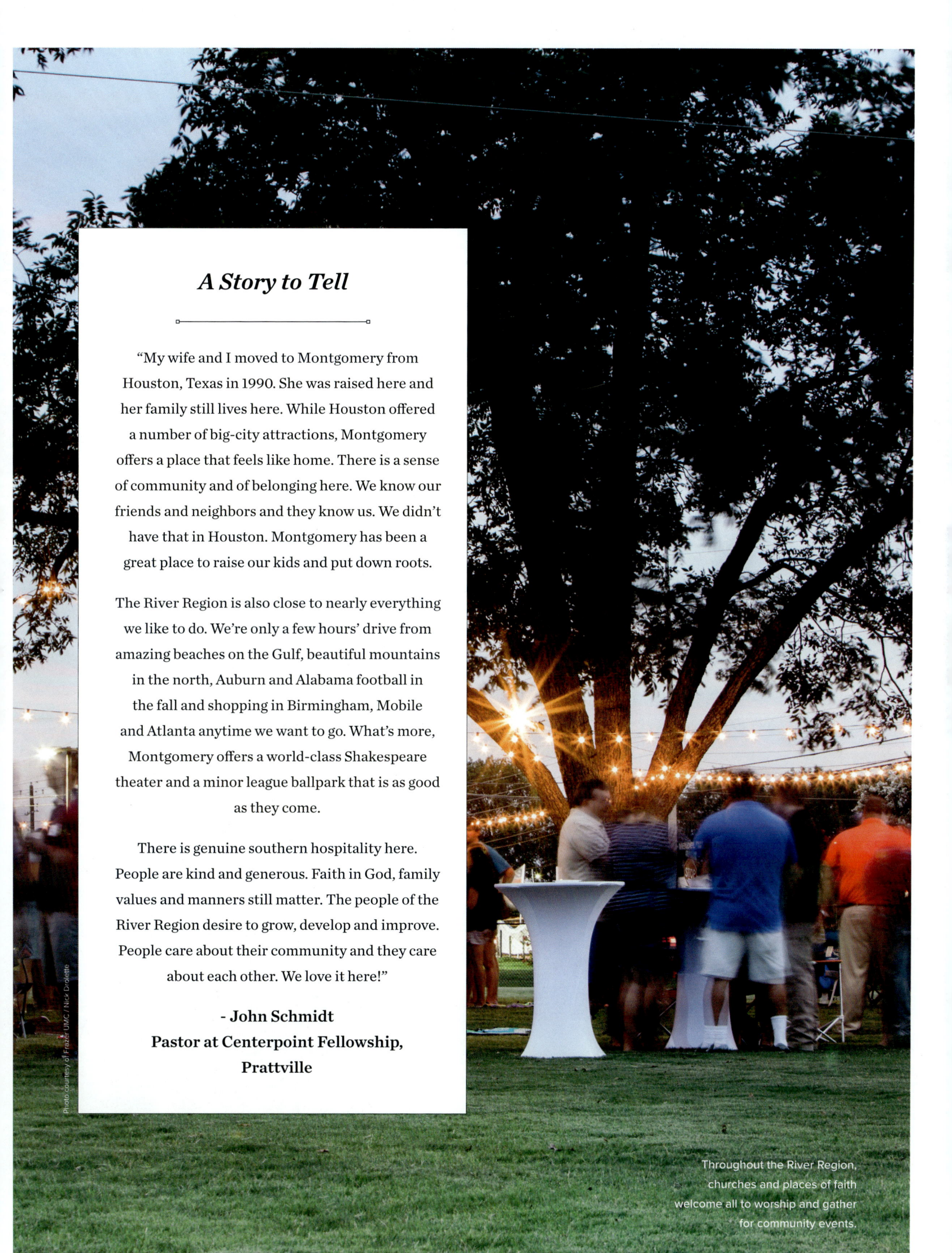

"My wife and I moved to Montgomery from Houston, Texas in 1990. She was raised here and her family still lives here. While Houston offered a number of big-city attractions, Montgomery offers a place that feels like home. There is a sense of community and of belonging here. We know our friends and neighbors and they know us. We didn't have that in Houston. Montgomery has been a great place to raise our kids and put down roots.

The River Region is also close to nearly everything we like to do. We're only a few hours' drive from amazing beaches on the Gulf, beautiful mountains in the north, Auburn and Alabama football in the fall and shopping in Birmingham, Mobile and Atlanta anytime we want to go. What's more, Montgomery offers a world-class Shakespeare theater and a minor league ballpark that is as good as they come.

There is genuine southern hospitality here. People are kind and generous. Faith in God, family values and manners still matter. The people of the River Region desire to grow, develop and improve. People care about their community and they care about each other. We love it here!"

- John Schmidt
Pastor at Centerpoint Fellowship, Prattville

Throughout the River Region, churches and places of faith welcome all to worship and gather for community events.

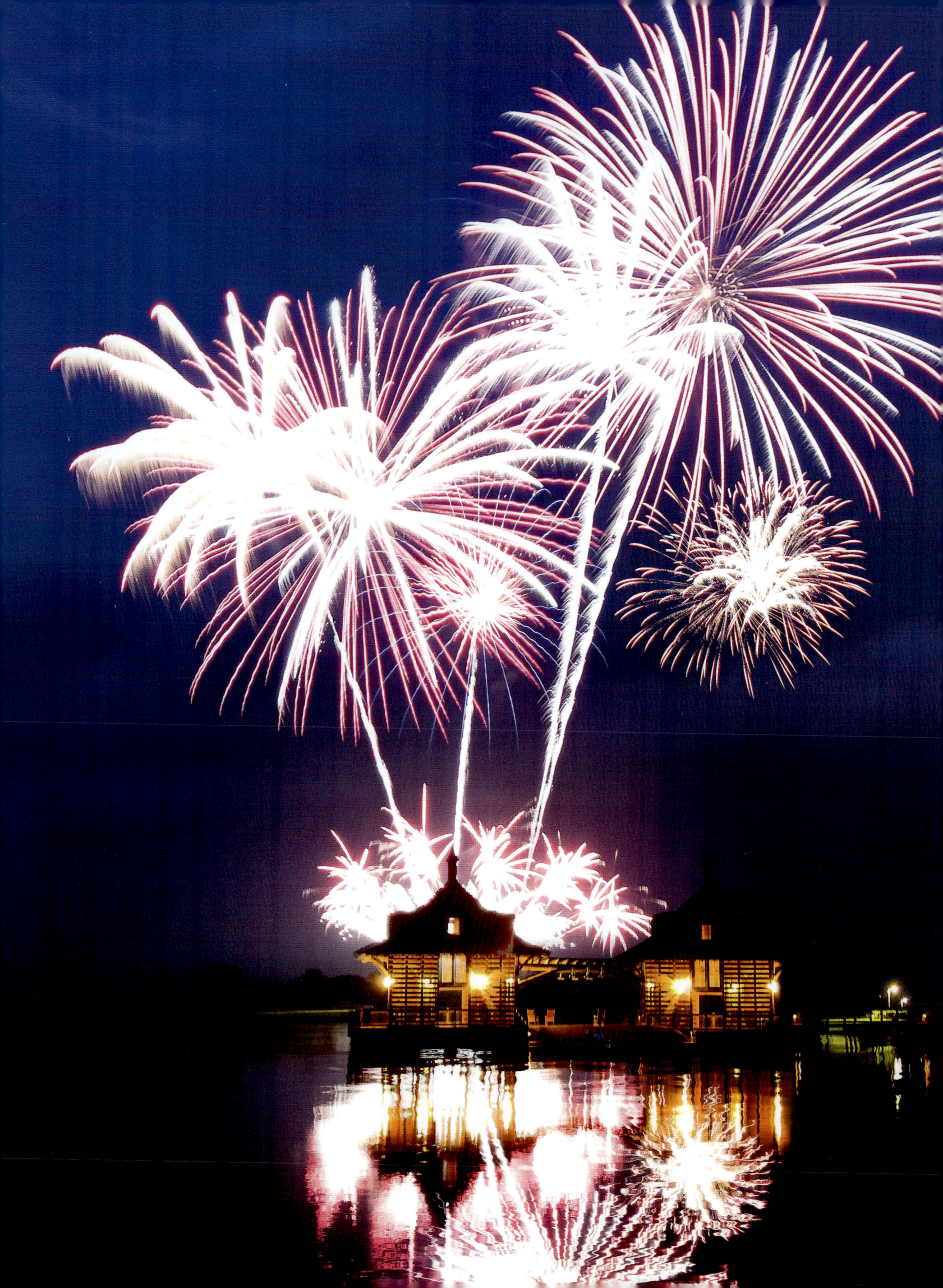

THE TOWN OF PIKE ROAD

Welcome Home

"Our people make The Town of Pike Road special," said the town's Mayor Gordon Stone. He praises the town's residents and their passion for their home every chance he gets, pointing to their level of engagement as a driving force behind its recent growth and prosperity. "We've seen so much progress in such a short time and that's due to our citizens getting involved in our town, participating in our planning and supporting the schools, churches, businesses and each other," he said. It's evidence of The Town of Pike Road's true and deep sense of community that's personified in its motto "Welcome Home." Add its pastoral scenery, relaxed pace and friendly vibe, and the town is an almost perfect snapshot of idyllic small-town life.

Yesterday

Incorporated as a municipality in 1997, The Town of Pike Road is still quite young, yet people have chosen to make a life in the Pike Road area for more than 175 years. It all began with the arrival of three families in 1815, the Marks, Mathews and the Meriwethers, who settled in the area just east and south of Montgomery. They farmed the fertile land and were soon joined by other families. A small but thriving town took root at the intersection of Pike and Meriwether Roads, both major thoroughfares with heavy traffic. Pike Road earned its name from the toll or "pike" that travelers desiring to travel it had to pay. The community that formed near the crossroads borrowed its name and was known simply as Pike Road until the Town of Pike Road was officially established.

Today

The town's sprawling meadows and woodland glens are dotted with more than 70 unique neighborhoods, each with its own personality and including some of the region's oldest settlements. The population of approximately 9,500 residents is diverse, with citizens across the demographic spectrum calling the Town of Pike Road home. Now, as the area draws new families, those looking for both the tranquil appeal of days gone by and the excitement and fresh ideas of a modern town, a happy marriage of old and new anchors The Town of Pike Road and every decision made.

The town and its residents honor their heritage and preserve the past while planning for continued prosperity. It is this detailed planning that has allowed the town to grow, but grow in the right way. From its founding, leaders and residents have focused on four primary priorities and consistently evaluate how new goals and actions will affect them. Protecting and promoting these four pillars — quality of life, public services, community planning and education — always guides their steps. "The people of Pike Road started this town from scratch, and I am thankful that we have remained visionary while also making the practical daily decisions to get us to our goals," Mayor Stone said. "Our four pillars are critical to the mission to maintain our character while realizing progress. It is a delicate balance, but we look to the four pillars every day to maintain that balance. It has been the people of Pike Road who have engaged and supported this process that has made it work. The unique working relationships between citizens, business, and town leaders have been amazing!"

Fireworks fly high each summer over Lake Cameron during Summerfest, the Town of Pike Road's annual 4th of July celebration.

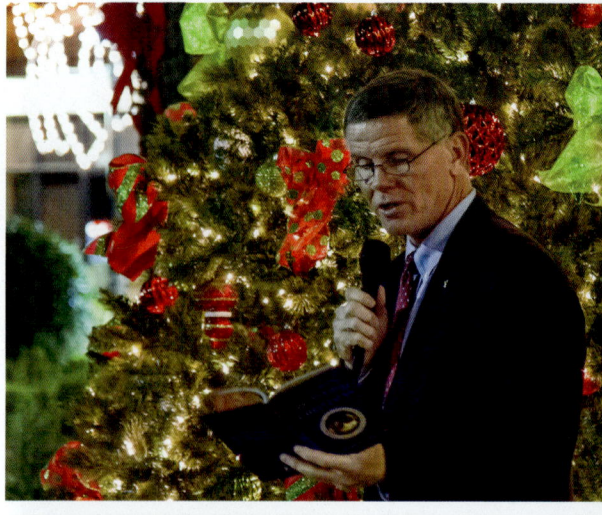

This page: In addition to providing stellar service, the Pike Road Volunteer Fire Department is very engaged in the Town of Pike Road Community. Right: Mayor Stone reads a Christmas story at the annual Town of Pike Road Christmas Tree Lighting. Bottom right: Zinnias are a tradition at Veterans Park in the Historic Town Center along Pike Road.

And it's not just the mayor and other leaders who have had a say and played a role in the town's direction. Over time, several planning sessions have hosted open discourse and exchanges of ideas, with many residents adding their thoughts to the conversation and helping set the zoning regulations and construction standards that govern continued development. After 3 years of assertive work from internal and external professionals, as well as multiple citizen groups, the town has also wisely created a comprehensive growth plan, meaning it is ready to respond to citizens' needs as the area continues to move forward. "It's great to see how our development has been nurtured by our process to ensure that everything meets the standards put in place by our community members," Mayor Stone said. "Preserving the character of our community is of the utmost importance."

Providing top-notch essential services at a low cost has been a part of the town's plan from day one. To achieve this, the town founders built relationships with public and private entities for public services and can boast accomplishments including continued support of several stellar volunteer fire departments, spreading sewer and water services as well as garbage and recycling services. This partner-provider model allows the town to continually evaluate services, collect citizen feedback, and revisit relationships when necessary to ensure citizens receive the best possible outcome.

To fuel the town's booming economy, an economic development director works closely with the area's existing businesses to meet their needs while also spearheading efforts to bring even more jobs to the town.

In 2012, an initiative called ENHANCE was put in place to ensure an exceptional quality of life in the town. Standing for Exercise, Nutrition, Health, Agriculture, Nature, Community and Education, the program is led by volunteer committees who create innovative ways to conserve the area's agricultural heritage, expand recreation and broaden artistic offerings. More than 80 events each year contribute to the initiative. ENHANCE also led to the creation of the town's Natural Trails System, a group of beautiful multi-use trails that crisscross the town's rural landscapes and connect neighbors, family and friends. Eight miles of trails are currently complete, and six more are soon to follow. Patriot Park, an Innovation Campus for Agriculture, Life Sciences and Wellness, began construction in 2017. Once completed, this education and recreation complex will provide flexible learning spaces for local students, sports facilities including football, softball, baseball, and more.

The multitude of community activities and events in the town also highlight its close-knit character. "It's exciting to see so many people of all ages participating in so many different events," said

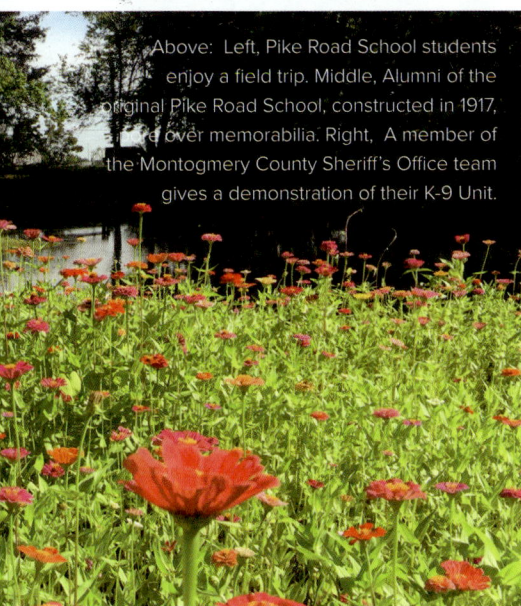

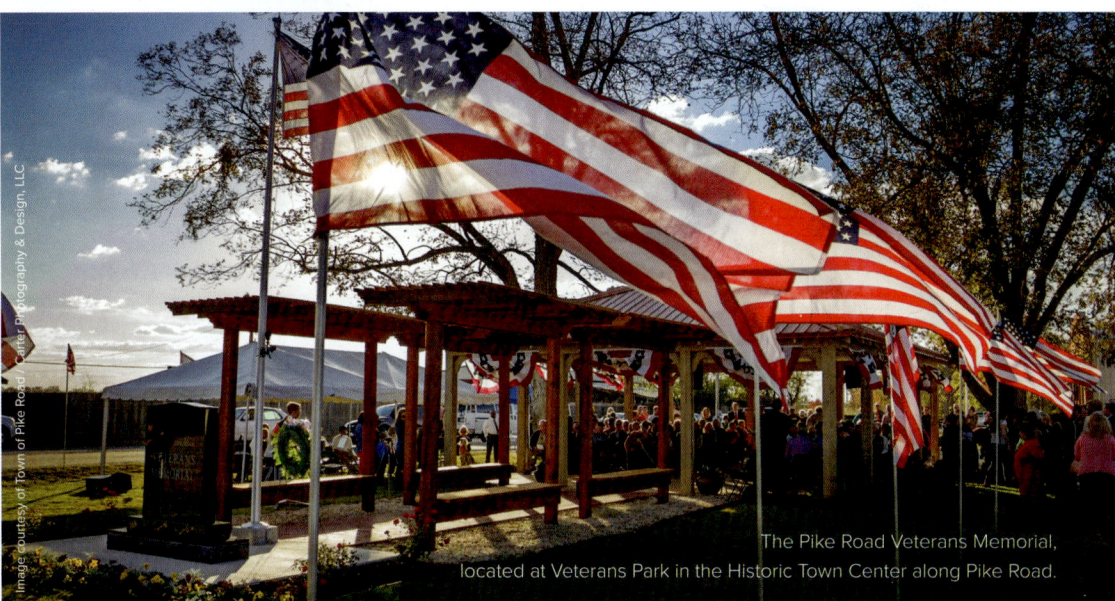

Above: Left, Pike Road School students enjoy a field trip. Middle, Alumni of the original Pike Road School, constructed in 1917, pore over memorabilia. Right, A member of the Montogmery County Sheriff's Office team gives a demonstration of their K-9 Unit.

The Pike Road Veterans Memorial, located at Veterans Park in the Historic Town Center along Pike Road.

Mayor Stone. "From our Summer Fest celebration and our annual Art Market, to our Veteran's Day Ceremony and our Christmas Tree Lighting each December, they draw diverse crowds. The best part about these activities is that they are led by citizens and held by citizens."

Perhaps the town's most visible success has been the Pike Road School System and its first completed campus, which welcomed students in the fall of 2015. This milestone was the culmination of a vision shared by countless community members for decades. Parents and students have the opportunity to experience a unique and creative quality public education system in their hometown, and it's just one more tool in the Town of Pike Road's efforts to offer a promising future for all of its residents. When the first group of students graduate, the school will be serving more than 1900 students. "It gives me great joy to visit the school and see so many young people proudly wearing their Patriot t-shirts. It also warms my heart thinking about the hundreds and hundreds of people who put thousands of hours into making the school happen, and we are also thankful for those who are continuing the hard work that it takes," said Mayor Stone. In the fall of 2018, the Town of Pike Road school system experienced 100 percent participation in its parent teacher organization across both campuses, one housed in a remodeled, century-old community school building that connects generations of learning in the Pike Road community.

As there are more and more announcements to share, town leaders work diligently to keep residents abreast of town news and aware of upcoming events and opportunities. Using emails, social media, its website, newsletters, and more, the town pursues constant and transparent communication.

In its short lifespan, The Town of Pike Road has accomplished so much, and it has done it all with exemplary fiscal efficiency. By carefully managing its financial resources since its founding, the town earned an AA+ credit rating, a ranking not often received for a city just two decades old. It has also kept a 10 percent operating reserve at all times; this is the largest reserve of any municipality in the state and will prove a vital safeguard if difficulties arise in the future.

Tomorrow

In the 20 years since its incorporation, The Town of Pike Road has expanded into a flourishing town and one of the fastest growing areas in the state. But it has never lost sight of what makes it distinct. "We have such great people, and the town's leadership has listened to them and stayed true to what is important to them," Mayor Stone said. "Now, seeing our citizens coming together and investing both their prayers and passions in their hometown is very exciting. It is special to live and work in a place that has so many engaged people!"

More and more River Region residents are choosing to live downtown. Historic neighborhoods like Cottage Hill are being revived as people of all ages and walks of life are drawn to its shady streets, friendly vibe and proximity to all the city's center offers.

Photo by Johnathon Kohn

Photo by Johnathon Kohn

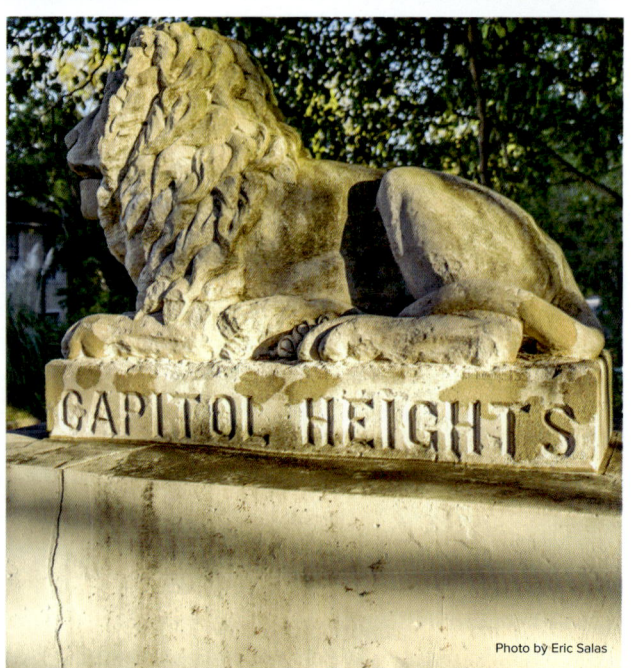

Photo by Eric Salas

Growing Together

Chase Fisher is the founder and serves on the board of The Five Points Cultural Commission, an organization that started in 2015 to help ensure that downtown Montgomery's redevelopment included neighborhoods in close proximity, areas like the Cottage Hill and Five Points neighborhoods just west of the city center. He explained the group's work and vision. "These spots provided a perfect opportunity to bring life back to a place where vacant buildings and overgrown lots frame a racially diverse, mixed-income neighborhood," Fisher said. With grants and the support of individual donors, FPCC is using creative and arts-based strategies to develop multiple properties with limited resources. "Our board of directors is a racially diverse collection of neighborhood residents who are small business owners, artists, set designers, real-estate developers and musicians, and we are finishing nine commercial and community spaces in the heart of Five Points to spur revitalization in the neighborhood." FPCC's work is vital to the continued progress of the city, a progress that is inclusive. "Everyone has a vested interest in this project. We have hosted several neighborhood events and focus groups where people from the community have come together to give their suggestions and let us know what they would love to see to make this neighborhood one of the best places to live in Montgomery," Fisher said. "City officials have been supportive and helped us in various ways too." Fisher's dedication to this work (which is a volunteer position on top of his day job) stems from his belief in Montgomery's still untapped potential. "Montgomery has a reputation as this sleepy Southern city, and that gives us the opportunity to really surprise people as we continue to develop. I think we are doing that now," Fisher said. "Our historical tension and diversity offers us a really incredible chance to come together in a way that sets us apart as a city that owns and accepts its rough parts in order to be truly great."

-Chase Fisher,
The Five Points Cultural Commission

As a pioneer of retail development in the South, Aronov shopping centers provide a solid mix of national, regional and local retailers. Top right: Aronov has created business parks and office buildings that are home to Fortune 500 companies as well as leading regional and local businesses. Bottom right: With a history of residential success, Aronov has consistently delivered great places to live – from master planned neighborhoods to apartment communities.

ARONOV REALTY MANAGEMENT

Founded in 1952 by Aaron Aronov to develop housing for returning WW II veterans and to provide residential and commercial real estate services, Aronov Realty Management has grown to be one of the largest privately owned real estate companies in the Southeast.

Over its accomplished history the company has developed and managed properties in more than 84 communities in 17 states – from as far north as Illinois and as far south as Florida, and from New Mexico in the west to Charleston, South Carolina on the Atlantic. The Aronov portfolio has contained a variety of multi-family properties including garden apartments, high-rise condominiums and vacation homes. The company has developed and managed more than 12,000 multi-family units. As part of its community development efforts, the company has successfully marketed more than 31,000 single-family home sites. Other developments and investments include hotels, office buildings and warehouse facilities. The company also has acquired, developed and managed a wide variety of shopping centers – from enclosed malls with exciting collections of retailers to community and specialty centers. Since its founding, the company has developed over 20,467,400 square feet of real estate. But since the beginning, the heartbeat of its operations has been in Montgomery.

For more than 63 years Aronov has played an active role in the economic growth and community development of the central Alabama region with residential communities and apartments in Montgomery and Prattville that house tens of thousands of residents; shopping centers including Eastdale Mall, Cornerstone, Taylor Crossing, Zelda Place, and the new Chase Corner that introduced Whole Foods Market to Montgomery, in addition to many others that offer a variety of appealing goods and services and generate the largest cumulative volume of retail sales of any group of retail properties in the region.

Aronov also offers area businesses attractive and efficient office space and warehouse space in buildings including Carmichael Center, One Commerce Center, Executive Park, Montgomery East Industrial Park and the Bailey Building, among many others. The company continues its decades-

Aronov brings communities to life with the latest and most innovative retail concepts.

In vacation home development and management, Aronov's reputation has been built by upholding the highest standards of design and construction excellence, along with the utmost respect for nature.

long tradition of providing expert real estate advice and services through its residential and commercial property brokerage divisions. A related company, Aronov Insurance, Inc. prides itself on its sensitive evaluation of risks and on its ability to tailor cost effective insurance packages to help provide a secure future for businesses, institutions and families.

Aronov's active role in the River Region extends to its community involvement as a committed supporter of many educational, cultural, business and community service organizations. In 2009, through its homebuilding division, Aronov Homes, the company had the privilege of coordinating the volunteer efforts of thousands of participants to build a home for a deserving family in connection with the ABC program, Extreme Makeover-Home Edition.

Under the leadership of Jake and Owen Aronov the company continues to employ the skills honed over six decades to develop, acquire and manage commercial and residential properties and to provide real estate and insurance services in the River Region and beyond.

Aronov develops iconic destinations that provide the perfect mix of shopping, dining and entertainment — all in one convenient location.

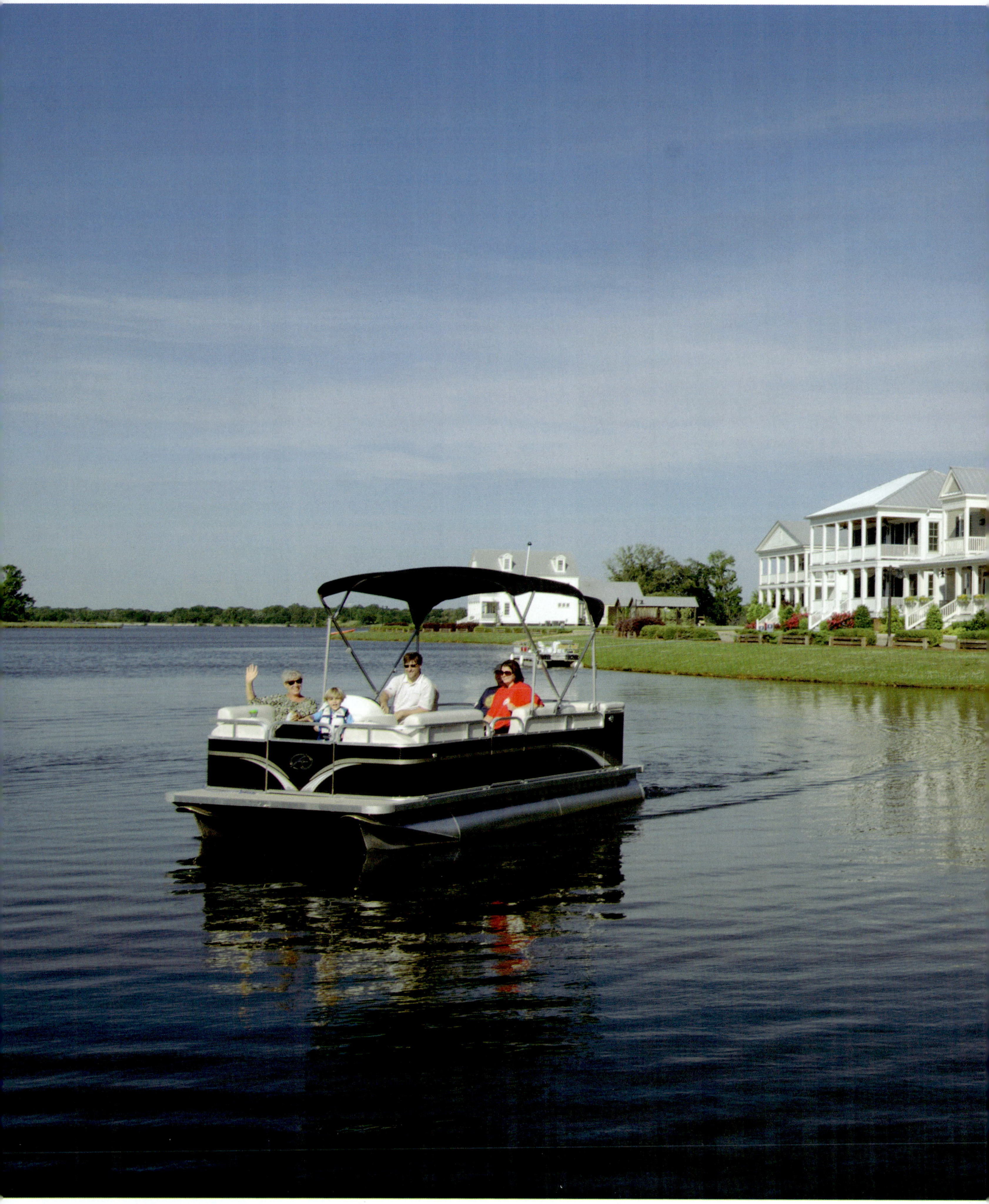

At The Waters in Pike Road and Hampstead in east Montgomery, a true sense of community is a key part of the appeal. Green spaces for gathering, lakes and pools for relaxing and playing, and multiple neighborhood events for catching-up foster close-knit feelings.

Photo by Robert Fouts

Photos courtesy of Montgomery CVB / Hampstead

THE LILLY BAPTIST CHURCH

From its organization in 1900 to its rejuvenation at the turn of the millennia as the largest predominantly black congregation in Montgomery, The Lilly Baptist Church continues to foster a rich, historic, socio-economic and cultural legacy.

The congregation of 3,500 members has come a long way from its humble beginnings as everyday people meeting on Winifred Street. Today, the congregation gathers on a 9-acre campus and 1,500 seat sanctuary in the Western Hills community near Maxwell AFB. Worshippers encompass a broad spectrum of professionals, physicians, nurses, professors, business owners, retired military, office workers, clerks and domestics, young and old who have joined together to turn the ordinary into the extraordinary.

Under the 48-year leadership of Pastor Thomas E. Jordan, the church has moved from a time when it could not pay its bills from an $85 weekly offering to one that operates on a $600,000 annual budget. The church has transitioned from staging fish fries and chicken dinners to regular tithing commitments. "In the process we've amassed a physical plant valued at $2.5 million, with programs and ministries reaching all age groups," says Jordan.

In a time when movements of social change are on the rise, "The Lilly" (as she is affectionately known) is proud to have been on the forefront of pivotal times in history. From their involvement in the Montgomery Bus Boycott to presidential elections, the congregation also hosts nationally recognized speakers. In 1990, nearly 500 members played a role in the production of the internationally acclaimed film, *The Long Walk Home*, starring Whoopi Goldberg and Sissy Spacek.

But the church's work does not stop at home. "The Lilly's" alignment with the National Baptist and American Baptist conventions allows the church to extend its reach to the world through missions. Its local community outreach serves as a catalyst for other churches, inspires others to undertake building programs and reaches out for interfaith and racial reconciliation efforts. One of their most notable involvements is with the Metro-Montgomery Baptist Minister's Conference.

Pastor Jordan, baptized by then Dexter Avenue Baptist Church pastor, Dr. Martin Luther King, Jr., has been a guiding spiritual influence since 1969 – more than a third of the church's history. He describes worship at The Lilly as "an old-fashioned service with up-to-date people." Pastor Jordan constantly reminds his beloved congregation and Montgomery's River Region "to watch God change things!"

Over the next decades, Pastor Jordan hopes the membership will continue to proclaim the Gospel of Jesus Christ, radiate the community with a positive spirit, and transform the River Region for a better world.

Lilly Baptist Church has come through periods of segregation, degradation, and humiliation to become a church whose members have lifted themselves up and reached out to help others. Lilly is a congregation that will continue to demonstrate great faith in God as they go into the world to make a difference.

REALTY CONNECTION

Finding a Home in the River Region

Broker Robin Davies has lived in Prattville for more than 25 years and has seen how much it has evolved as a flourishing economic community.

"Prattville is good to their businesses," Davies said. "When I acquired my REALTOR® license, I never foresaw opening my own brokerage. This was an opportunity I never saw coming. It has to do with the support I've received. This is a community that promotes the people that are part of the community."

In 2011, Davies established Realty Connection in her adopted hometown, and today the company is a multi-million dollar producer year after year.

"Prattville has a lot of new home growth," Davies said. "Vacant property in the area has been turned into really nice residential homes." In the same neighborhood, for example, buyers can choose from patio homes from the $180s, and options go up to larger homes in the $300s. "Combined with that, preexisting homes have been able to hold their value," Davies added.

"We continue to have the growth and resilience that is keeping Prattville safe and prospering." The school systems are a selling point, plus the increase in retail options and a re-energized downtown area brings more interest. "It seems like the city never stops growing," she said. "That helps people want to continue to move to the area."

Realty Connection's market extends much farther than "The Preferred Community," however. The company has nine other agents in addition to Davies and serves the wider River Region area with properties in Autauga, Elmore and Montgomery counties.

"We also manage rental properties," Davies said. The team handles leasing and arranges for upkeep and repairs for the homeowner. "We have properties from North Prattville into Montgomery and all the way to Eclectic."

In addition to personal local service, the Realty Connection team has a strong Internet presence, and they work with prospective buyers out of state or even out of the country – especially military families – to find the right home in the River Region area. "When they find a home online, we'll do a Skype walk-through for them," Davies said. "We have clients from everywhere."

Clients also include local people in starter homes who are moving up and other people who are downsizing.

As Realty Connection enjoys the success of helping individuals and families buy and sell homes, it continues to demonstrate its commitment to the community it serves. "We put a lot back into our community. We make a point to give back," Davies said.

Meet the Lowry Family: Christian, Korie, Carson & Max

A key piece of creating a vibrant city center is enticing people not to just work and play there, but to live there too. The Lowry family was drawn to downtown's Cottage Hill neighborhood in 2013. Korie and Christian Lowry and their two boys, Max and Carson, bought one of the oldest homes in the neighborhood – one that had been sitting empty for decades. The McBryde-Screws-Tyson house is a stunning, pre-Civil War home completed in 1832 with its Greek Revival facade added in 1855. In 1980, in recognition of its significant heritage, it was added to the National Register of Historic Places. Former owners Diane and Fred Bush did massive amounts of work to save the home, restoring it to its former glory, and the Lowrys are proud to continue to make improvements. They chose the downtown house as home for their family for several reasons. "It is simply an amazing house," Korie said. "In fact, each house in the neighborhood has its own personality and story, not the cookie-cutter structures you see in some newer developments." They also want to make a real investment in their community and forge long-term connections. "We love our neighbors who are as diverse as the architecture of our neighborhood. Additionally, having a historic home is a great way to meet people; we can't spend time in the front yard without meeting at least one or two people who are interested in the house and area." Korie grew up in Prattville, but Christian, a Major in the Air Force, had only lived in Montgomery off and on during his service until they came back to the capital city to make it their permanent home. "We have traveled around the world, and while we have loved every place we lived or visited, we have always felt the ties of home are strongest in Montgomery. We cannot think of a better place to raise our family. We love the history of the area and the amenities of living downtown while still having a neighborhood with a sense of community," he said. "Additionally, new developments downtown are creating exciting opportunities that will have lasting benefits for the city overall and our family. We love being a part of those efforts."

Winter Place, one of the capital city's loveliest old homes, is being revitalized. The two-house complex featuring both Italianate and Second Empire styles built from the 1850s to the 1870s is being carefully restored to its former glory.

Photo by Becca Beers

The Cloverdale Playhouse and the Capri Theatre are two performing arts venues nestled in the historic Old Cloverdale neighborhood. The Playhouse, a community-based and volunteer-driven community theatre, is known for its lively productions and musical events.

Across the street, the Capri Theatre has been entertaining Montgomery since opening in 1941. Today, it's the longest continually running theatre in Alabama and has developed a reputation for its eclectic blend of independent, foreign, popular and classic films.

Sandra Nickel has been selling real estate in Montgomery for almost 40 years and loves getting to help area residents achieve the dream of home ownership, especially when that home is in one of the Montgomery's long-established neighborhoods. "That feeds my preservationist's soul!" she said. "Montgomery's older neighborhoods—particularly her historic districts—are so walkable with sidewalks on both sides of the street, multiple neighborhood parks and shopping and entertainment venues in their midst. Local historic designation assures the architectural integrity of these neighborhoods and protects property values and quality of life." She also loves the options our region offers. "There really is something for every taste and every budget. We have urban properties, then rural properties. Love a low-maintenance, tiny yard? We've got it. Prefer a home on acreage? Got that, too!" And all of these different choices sit in a region Nickel calls "special." "Montgomery truly sits at the intersection of Civil War and Civil Rights history. Race relations are amazingly good when considering this. And Southern hospitality is real: People here are truly friendly, caring and welcoming. Plus, we're not stuck in our past. We are on the cusp of an immense influx of tech-based businesses and 'techie' young people. Our downtown is vibrant and offers the lifestyle they value. Perhaps most importantly, we—our leadership and our people—are committed to creating and maintaining a Montgomery that all people can be proud to call home."

Many of Montgomery's older neighborhoods like the garden-inspired Old Cloverdale and charming Capitol Heights have recently undergone resurgences, with multiple home renovations and an influx of young families.

Photo by Becca Beers

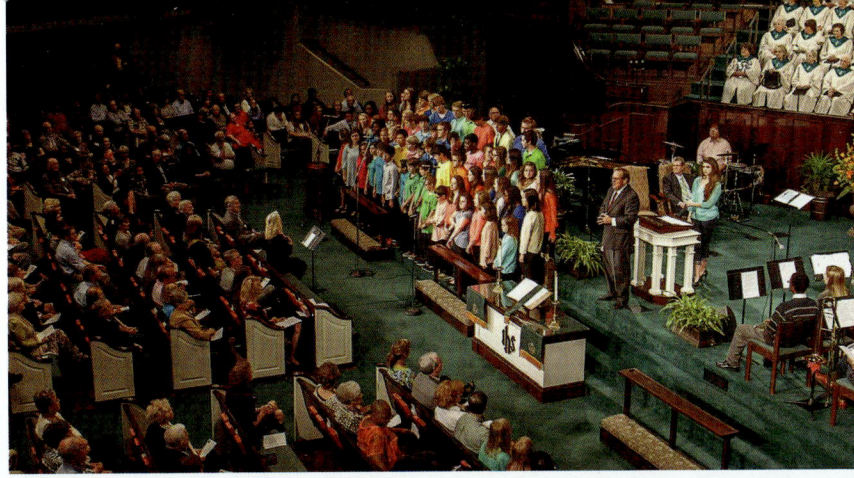

FRAZER UNITED METHODIST CHURCH

Over the years, Frazer Church has developed many nicknames among Montgomerians. Some refer to it as "the church with the big tower and the cross." Lifting up the cross of Jesus Christ has been central to Frazer's mission from its founding in 1892 right up to the present. Frazer's Methodist heritage emphasizes a dynamic, living relationship with God through Jesus rather than formal religion. In fact, Frazer's No. 1 core value statement is, "Jesus is first."

Others have jokingly referred to Frazer as "Six Flags Over Jesus." As Montgomery's first mega-church, Frazer's eight Sunday morning worship services (including three Contemporary and three Traditional-style services along with Hispanic and Chinese worship) can seem overwhelming. However, those who visit the church find a friendly, welcoming congregation where they can quickly feel at home.

Moreover, a thriving Small Group ministry makes this large church feel more like a close-knit family. More than 50 groups meet throughout the week and every member is encouraged to connect to others where they can pray for one another, care for one another, and serve together. As another one of Frazer's core values puts it, "Life is better together; growth happens in groups."

Frazer's size also means it is able to offer all sorts of programs for a wide variety of people—Children's Ministry, Student Ministry, Men's and Women's Ministries, Older Adult Ministry, Sports and Fitness, Music, Media, Prayer and Care, and many more. As a result, the church brings people together from all generations and backgrounds. Frazer is particularly proud of its growing racial diversity in a city that has contributed so much to the long struggle for racial integration in our nation.

Perhaps the most common nickname for Frazer in the community is "the church that serves." Frazer has long practiced a third core value, "Everyone matters, everyone ministers," which means that every Frazer member is encouraged to participate in one of more than 200 volunteer areas each year. The church provides millions of dollars of support to missionaries and community agencies that serve the poor, vulnerable, and marginalized right here in Montgomery and around the world. Ultimately, Frazer members are encouraged to not only give of their money and time through the church, but also to look for everyday opportunities to share the love of God with their neighbors.

Looking to the future, Frazer will continue to look for new ways to serve others, welcome all people, and share the love of God in Montgomery and beyond. Whatever other nicknames the church may garner, Frazer hopes to be known as a church that lifts up the name of Jesus.

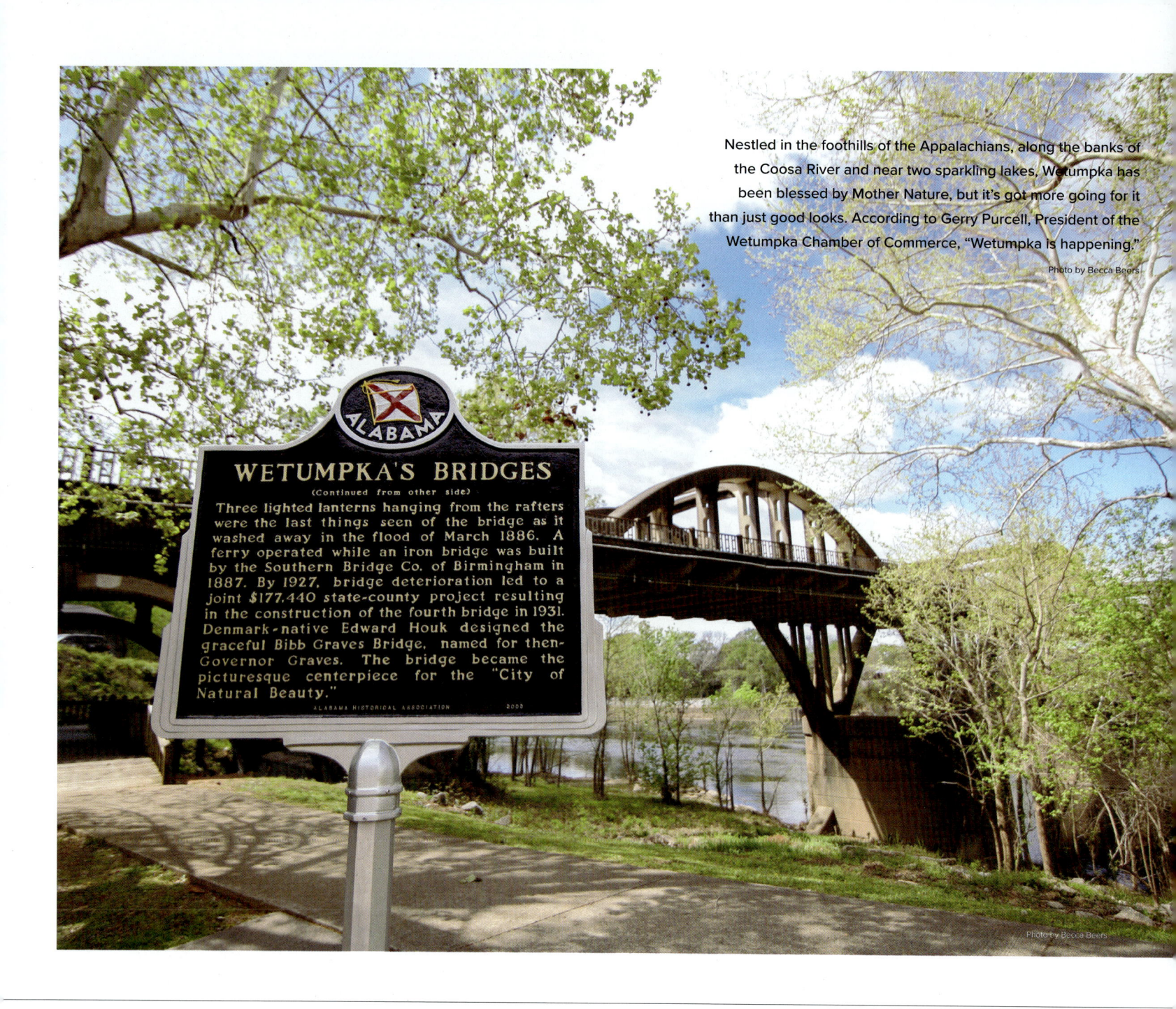

Nestled in the foothills of the Appalachians, along the banks of the Coosa River and near two sparkling lakes, Wetumpka has been blessed by Mother Nature, but it's got more going for it than just good looks. According to Gerry Purcell, President of the Wetumpka Chamber of Commerce, "Wetumpka is happening."

Photo by Becca Beers

WETUMPKA'S BRIDGES
(Continued from other side)

Three lighted lanterns hanging from the rafters were the last things seen of the bridge as it washed away in the flood of March 1886. A ferry operated while an iron bridge was built by the Southern Bridge Co. of Birmingham in 1887. By 1927, bridge deterioration led to a joint $177,440 state-county project resulting in the construction of the fourth bridge in 1931. Denmark-native Edward Houk designed the graceful Bibb Graves Bridge, named for then-Governor Graves. The bridge became the picturesque centerpiece for the "City of Natural Beauty."

ALABAMA HISTORICAL ASSOCIATION 2003

Photo by Becca Beers

Photo by Brooke Glassford / Colorbox

A City to Enjoy

- Gerry Purcell, President of the Wetumpka Chamber of Commerce

"Wetumpka's rich arts culture and history, plus its natural beauty, create an awesome combination for visitors and residents. People are coming to see the 80-million-year-old meteor crater, fish and paddle our waters, tour Jasmine Hill Gardens, have an amazing meal at one of the nicest hotels in the South, Wind Creek, take in hundreds of years of history at Fort Toulouse-Jackson, see a play at the famous and award-winning Wetumpka Depot Players or one of many other activities we offer. Our downtown is revitalizing, aiding increased economic development and preserving our heritage, and the Chamber's impressive Innovation & Incubation Center is attracting new companies. All of these things and more make Wetumpka a special and wonderful place to live."

There is a lot to love about living in Wetumpka, particularly for those interested in the outdoors. The city's abundant natural beauty is always on display and provides a wealth of fresh-air fun.

Photos courtesy of the Montgomery CVB / Carter Photography & Design, LLC

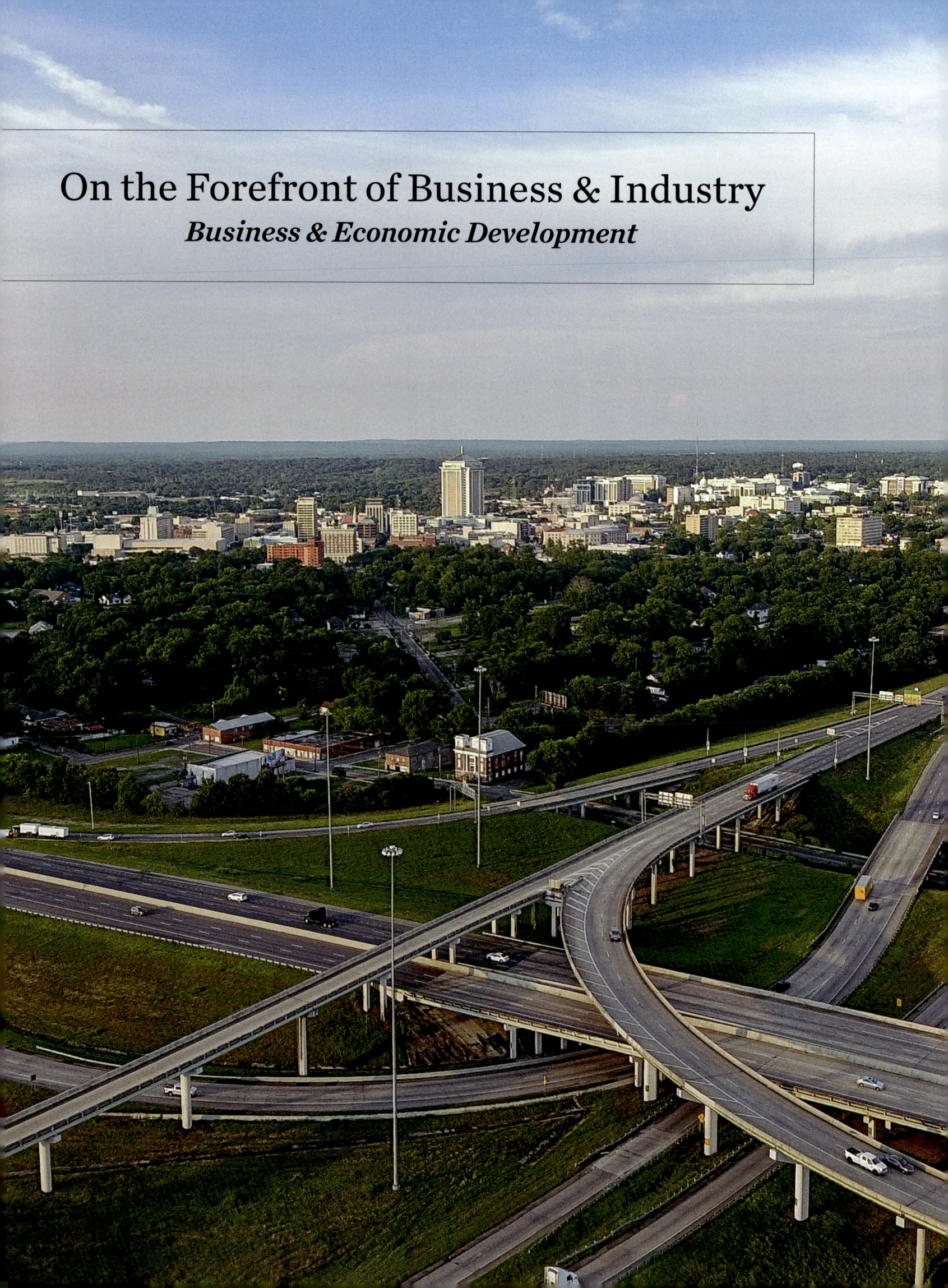

On the Forefront of Business & Industry
Business & Economic Development

When the city of Montgomery and surrounding areas were founded, the Alabama River was an integral asset and a driving force behind the economy. As the region grew, so did its businesses. Fast-forward almost 200 years. Could the area's founders have foreseen what their initial visions would become? While the waterway is no longer the sole source of transportation for trade, Montgomery and the River Region remain important centers of commerce and on the forefront of business and industry. In 2016, the capital city led the state in announced new jobs, an impressive indicator of a robust business climate.

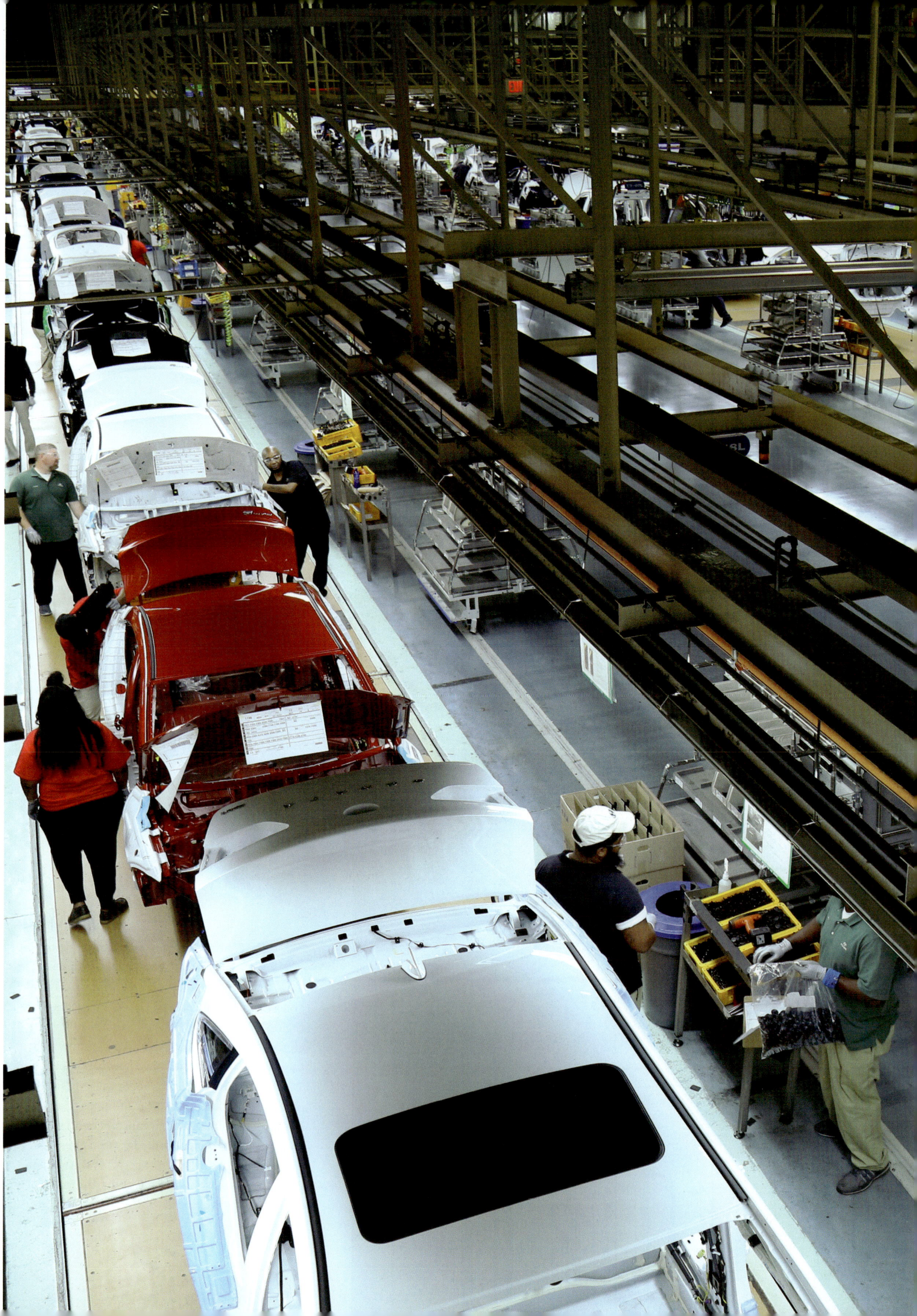

Major economic development achievements in the last 15 years have bolstered Montgomery's continuing success. Companies locating here, giants like Hyundai Motor Manufacturing Alabama, have spurred billions of dollars in economic impact and created jobs for thousands. In 2016, the city was selected as the location of the first North American facility for German automotive supplier Gerhardi Kuntsto£technik. The deal amounts to $37.9 million in initial investment and 235 jobs. In fact, four of the top 10 global automotive suppliers, Denso, Mobis, Faurecia and Lear, have offices and facilities in Montgomery.

continued on page 178

THE MONTGOMERY AREA CHAMBER OF COMMERCE

The mission of The Montgomery Area Chamber of Commerce is simple: as a fully integrated economic development organization, dedicated to both job creation and job preservation, it is focused on growing markets for its members and growing the River Region economy to provide a better quality of life for all. The pursuit of this objective is not so simple. It takes dedication, efficiency, talent and teamwork. Since 1873, the Chamber has proven it possesses all of the above, and credits the unparalleled partnership of local government with business and community leaders as the secret sauce behind Montgomery's success.

In 1910, the fledging member-based organization scored its first economic development win. Orville and Wilbur Wright were searching for the perfect spot to put their civilian flight school, and Chamber leaders wooed them away from other promising locations and brought the school to the capital city. That site today is the home of Maxwell Air Force Base.

A long list of successes followed, including recent triumphs like Hyundai Motor Manufacturing America (HMMA) putting its first U.S. manufacturing plant in Montgomery in 2005 and the resulting network of automotive parts suppliers, providing additional economic investment and employment opportunities for the River Region. In 2015, HMMA celebrated its 10-year anniversary with a $2.4 billion impact in Montgomery County and a statewide economic impact of $4.82 billion. In 2016, Montgomery also was selected as the location of the first North American facility for Gerhardi Kuntsto£technik. The German automotive supplier will invest $37.9M and employ 235 workers. Today, Montgomery is home to four of the Top 10 global automotive suppliers – Denso, Mobis, Faurecia and Lear.

In late 2017, the list lengthened with the historic announcement of Montgomery's selection for a fleet of F-35 jets, the most technologically advanced planes in our Air Force, bringing an estimated annual economic impact of more than $100 million. "The support displayed across all aspects of the community for the F-35 project, from our congressional delegation to local leadership, the business community and the public at-large, was unprecedented and embodied the spirit of partnership that makes Montgomery and the River Region a very special community," said Chamber Chairman Judge Charles Price.

These and many other accomplishments can be credited to the unique spirit of partnership and collaboration that is part of the very fabric of the city. "It is incredible how much progress can be made when everyone works together around shared priorities. The Chamber's economic and community development planning process helps set forth those priorities, with the ultimate vision of creating jobs, economic prosperity, and a better life for Montgomery and the River Region," said Chamber President Randy George.

That spirit of partnership fuels the Chamber's multi-faceted approach to economic development. From tourism to military affairs, small and minority business support, talent retention and recruitment, to more traditional economic development functions, the Montgomery regional chamber works across all spectrums.

In addition to focusing on large companies and manufacturing, the Chamber is also a one-stop resource for the start-up and growth of small and minority-owned businesses. "Small businesses make up 80 percent or more of the local economy, and are a critical part of every community, but particularly here in the River Region," said George. The Chamber offers everything from pre-business counseling, mentorship, incubation support, as well as connections to the resources and training needed at every stage in the developing business life cycle. The addition of the MGMix Internet Exchange has word quickly spreading that Montgomery is an ideal location for entrepreneurs and small businesses to start and thrive. "Our innovation district offers the unique opportunity for direct high-speed connectivity to the state of the art RSA Data Center and MGMix internet exchange, set against a backdrop of world-changing history," said Chamber Chairman Price.

Tourism is another facet of the Chamber's economic development work, and it's become big business in our area: Visitor spending totals almost $1.5 million every day, and annual lodging taxes keep hitting all-time highs, saving every Montgomery household hundreds of tax dollars annually. The Chamber plays the lead role in city and county tourism efforts, with its Destination MGM team focused on bringing leisure travelers, business travelers and meetings of all sizes to Montgomery by promoting and enhancing Montgomery's image and offerings. And the work has paid off; Montgomery has garnered a slew of praise from major media outlets including *The New York Times, Garden & Gun, USA Today*, Thrillist, Zagat and more.

While the Chamber is committed to connecting with people outside the area's borders, it is equally committed to strengthening several already strong relationships here at home. The Chamber's military affairs program is a model for communities around the nation, and the primary reason why Montgomery has been called the "best hometown in the Air Force." Since that first night flight by the Wright Brothers, Montgomery has been building a deep and lasting legacy in support of our military. Maxwell-Gunter Air Force Base has an impressive annual economic impact of $2.6 billion, not to mention the tremendous impact of our military men, women and families in our neighborhoods, churches, synagogues, schools and civic endeavors.

The Chamber knows the foundation of true, lasting prosperity for any city and region is its ability to attract and retain talent. That's why the Chamber's leadership is committed to championing public education, and working to establish a high-performing regional workforce development delivery system. Linkages between K-12, the community colleges, and four-year institutions are vital, along with the partnership of outstanding resources like AIDT and the Montgomery Regional Workforce Training Center. Developing leaders, recruiting talent and spearheading community strategies that lead to solutions in education and talent development are goals the Chamber is striving for like never before.

Balancing the many responsibilities that make up its mission is never easy, but the Chamber continues to excel for one reason: an amazing team. "The Chamber is a reflection of the dedicated leaders in Montgomery and the River Region who care deeply about the future and are committed to creating opportunities and a better life for all who live here. We are honored to have the trust of the city, county, state and congressional delegations, our military partners, and close to 2,000 companies and organizations who, because they believe in Montgomery and the River Region, chose to belong to the Chamber," said George.

In late 2017, the city and River Region attained one of the most exciting and far-reaching goals the area has ever set: landing the F-35 Lightning II jet program here. The end result of a massive, strategic team effort that saw city, county, Chamber of Commerce and other community leaders working hand-in-hand with officials at Maxwell-Gunter Air Force Base and the area's congressional delegation, it will have a staggering annual economic impact of $100 million.

continued on page 182

Photo courtesy of Lockheed Martin

JMR+H ARCHITECTURE, P.C.

Unparalleled Service for Public and Private Sector Clients in the River Region and Far Beyond

JMR+H Architecture, P.C. has its roots firmly planted in Montgomery, and some of its work plays a key part in the city's role as Alabama's capital. The full-service architectural firm designed the Alabama Statehouse, the building that houses the Alabama Legislature and the associated political activity that swirls inside this state government epicenter. While it's certainly a notable project, it's only one example in JMR+H's large portfolio, which showcases a diverse array of work for a broad base of public and private sector clients throughout the Southeast and Gulf States region.

By providing a wide range of architectural services, the firm has evolved over the past 35 years through internal growth, staff development and business mergers to become the current entity managed by Senior Principals Mike Rutland, AIA and Tim Holmes, AIA. Principals Jeff Cahill, AIA and Durand Seay, AIA are also a part of the firm's leadership.

Other highly visible projects in the city include designing the renovations of the former Montgomery Advertiser building. This adaptive reuse project encompassed additions and alterations to the historical 1930s building with 85,000 square feet of repurposed space for Montgomery County business functions and the Montgomery County Commission.

The firm also completed the RSA Dexter Avenue Building in 2009 – one of the most impressive additions to Montgomery's revitalized downtown – where it now has its offices. The former Federal Judicial Building was wrapped within the new 12-story office building as a contradictory complement to the contemporary glass, steel and concrete structure. Among its standout features is a dramatic four-story lobby/atrium with high limestone walls and grand staircase with elevators covered in polished granite and stainless steel. The restored portions of the project include premium executive office space and the historic original Supreme Court Chamber and Lobby, which have been adapted into a state-of-the-art conference and multi-purpose center. An adjacent exterior Honor Court pays homage to the State of Alabama Chief Justices with bronze sculptures dotting the landscape of the State of Alabama and their home districts.

In response to the firm's stellar work on this complex project, RSA has continued its relationship with the firm within many of its downtown buildings. JMR+H has worked in all RSA properties, providing interior architectural services for myriad state government and private sector clients.

Auburn University at Montgomery has also been a long-time client in the educational sector of the firm's portfolio. Work on the East Montgomery campus dates back to the School of Nursing and Health Sciences and, most recently, renovations and repurposing of the existing Taylor Center into a one-stop facility for daily student activities. In addition, the Montgomery Public School System has commissioned the firm with Brewbaker Jr. High Technology Magnet School, George Washington Carver High School and Montgomery Preparatory Academy for Career Technologies in the repurposed Montgomery Mall facility.

Its longstanding relationship with the Alabama National Guard is further proof of the success JMR+H continues to enjoy with its many repeat clients. In the Montgomery area, the firm has been immersed in the Joint Forces Headquarters work and most notably Ft. George C. Wallace Readiness Center. But this relationship has also taken the firm all over the state, with sizable projects including the 20th Special Forces Group Headquarters at the Birmingham Airport and many other Readiness Center projects.

Much of the firm's public sector work also extends statewide, including into more than 40 counties that have relied on JMR+H for the creation of county courthouses, administrative buildings, jails and emergency management facilities. Among local public projects, work includes the new police/fire stations at Montgomery Mall, as well as the Prattville Public Safety Building and Prattville Area Chamber of Commerce facility.

In addition to its public sector focus, JMR+H touches a considerable amount of private work as well. Midtown Shopping Center, Westminster Shopping Center, Chappy's Restaurants and Central Restaurant are among some of the local design work. The firm has completed medical work with River Region Cardiology, Mitylene Medical Facility and, most recently, completed the cutting edge oral surgery facility for the Oral Maxillofacial Surgery Group at Halcyon Pointe.

The firm designed a sizeable expansion to the ALFA Corporate Headquarters on East South Boulevard in the 1990s and followed with the design of a business-processing center in 2002. In the latter case, the $45 million, 135,000-square-foot facility was designed as a Tier III protected facility with poured concrete walls, floors and roof structure, housing complete business protection and continuity functions for ALFA Insurance.

The firm also has a significant footprint far outside the River Region. JMR+H is in the final completion stages of the Anderson Towne Center, a 650,000-square-foot mixed-use, lifestyle development in Cincinnati. In 2009, the firm completed design work for Harbor Walk Village in Destin, Florida, a $161 million mixed-use facility.

No matter where the firm is working or what defines each project's size and scope, every member of the JMR+H team remains committed to the company's foundational philosophy: a passion to provide intelligent, creative responses to client wishes alongside unparalleled service.

These companies come — and they stay and expand — thanks to the efforts of city and county leaders in close partnership with The Montgomery Area Chamber of Commerce and other regional entities. They work as a unified team, one that is committed to providing and promoting a positive climate and strong entrepreneurial ecosystem for businesses of all shapes and sizes. Proof is in the wide diversity of the area's many businesses thriving here today, from family owned industrial companies open for more than 150 years to small boutiques, brand new tech start-ups and everything in between.

*"This is not just where
I do business.
It is my home."*
– Sieu Tang Wood

Hometown Connection

"I've been to so many beautiful places, but I love Montgomery and knew when I first came here that I wanted to build my business here. I like the comfortable, friendly feel, and the people have shown my business so much support. That's why I give back as much as I can. This is not just where I do business. It is my home."

**- Sieu Tang Wood,
owner of Tang's Alterations**

SERVISFIRST BANK MONTGOMERY

"Our name really says it all," said Carl Barker, President and CEO of ServisFirst Bank Montgomery. "Service is our hallmark; it's where we truly excel." In an age where personal attention is being rapidly replaced by one-size-fits-all automation, ServisFirst's focus on the unique needs and goals of each individual client drives every decision and has become a mindset in every single ServisFirst employee. It's a take on banking that's both refreshing and greatly appreciated by the many people who the bank serves. The proof is in ServisFirst's expansive growth.

Founded in 2005 in Birmingham, ServisFirst Bank emphasizes commercial and private banking, and is focused on businesses and professionals. It opened in Huntsville in 2006 and now has locations in Dothan, Mobile, Pensacola, Florida; Nashville, Tennessee; Charleston, South Carolina; Tampa Bay, Florida; and Atlanta, Georgia.

It brought its new brand of better banking to Montgomery in 2007. "Most banks in the city are retail banks, and while we are full service, we consider ourselves a business bank. We are the sixth largest bank in Montgomery out of about 18 banks, which is impressive, seeing that we don't do any advertising and we focus heavily on organic outreach," Barker said.

Instead, ServisFirst Bank has relied on the positive word-of-mouth generated by satisfied clients to increase its market share, some of whom have been with the bank from its beginnings, participating in its innovative client/shareholder model to raise initial capital. "These clients shared their experience with their colleagues, friends and family, and we've benefited greatly from these referrals," Barker said. "That continues today, and it speaks volumes about how responsive we are and how well we treat our clients."

ServisFirst's people are the foundation of this success, and their devotion to the bank's "service-first" mission is what sets it apart from the crowd. "Our people and

> "Service is our hallmark; it's where we truly excel."
>
> - Carl Barker, President and CEO of ServisFirst Bank Montgomery

their attitude stand out," Barker said. "We are fortunate to have a fantastic, talented group working for us. We have experienced, knowledgeable commercial lenders. And our folks are out all day long, meeting with our customers all the time, providing face-to-face, one-on-one service."

That's one reason you won't see a ServisFirst branch on every street corner in the capital city. There are only two, one downtown and one in east Montgomery. "Our two locations are good for people who want to walk into a bank," Barker said, "but our clients know that we will come to them, and for the most part, that is how we bank."

Another is ServisFirst's responsible outlook on overhead. Its founding executives implemented a low-overhead business model from the outset, one that doesn't rely on multiple branch locations, allowing the bank to pass its cost savings along to clients in the form of better rates and lower fees.

Another distinction separating ServisFirst from its competitors is its ability to be highly adaptable and flexible. "Most of us at ServisFirst have been at other banks, and we enjoy the flexibility we have here to really build relationships with clients and partner with them on their success," Barker said. "At some bigger banks, if you don't fit in their box, they don't offer a lot of options. But we have the ability to mold our products, services and solutions around our customers."

Yet ServisFirst still has access to a variety of regional resources, meaning its clients get the best of both worlds: the nimbleness of a local bank where decisions are made at the local level – and made quickly – with the offerings of a larger bank, including highly competitive rates and sophisticated cash management products.

ServisFirst's personal approach to banking doesn't mean it shuns technology. It takes full advantage of the latest advancements to make banking easy and convenient, offering a full suite of internet banking services as well as remote deposit express banking to its clients. "We combine our stellar service with cutting-edge banking technology that lets our clients do just about anything online. It's all right at their fingertips," Barker said. And ServisFirst stays ahead of the curve, giving its customers the added assurance of knowing that when emerging technologies roll out, they'll have access to them.

At ServisFirst Bank, the commitment to clients goes beyond banking; ServisFirst is just as dedicated to the community that it and its clients call home. This dedication is obvious in the many ways it gives back. "We encourage our people to get involved in a number of arts and civic organizations and other groups helping to better our community," Barker said. "Montgomery is a special place, a place that I think continues to surprise new people that come here with its warm welcome. There is some real progress going on all over our city, and ServisFirst Bank is proud to be a part of that."

Since 1943, the Alabama Retail Association, based in Montgomery, has worked to promote and protect the retailers who make our communities a vibrant place to live, work and play by representing them before the Alabama Legislature and the U.S. Congress.

Photo courtesy of Alabama Retail Association

Gerhardi (shown here breaking ground on its plant) is just one of the multiple companies drawn to the River Region. One key element of the area's economic development is the hard work and expertise of The Montgomery Area Chamber of Commerce. In addition to supporting the expansion of existing businesses and bringing new ones here, the Chamber holds a variety of events – Business After Hours, the annual Diversity Summit and military appreciation to name a few – that provide its members with amazing networking and educational opportunities. Photos courtesy of the Montgomery Chamber of Commerce.

"Life is about relationships, and I believe Alfa is about relationships."

- Jimmy Parnell, president and CEO of the Alabama Farmers Federation and Alfa Insurance

ALFA

Shaping the Future

"Life is about relationships, and I believe Alfa is about relationships," said Jimmy Parnell, president and CEO of the Alabama Farmers Federation and Alfa Insurance. "Our people — our employees, members and customers — are our greatest asset, and we strive to be a company that truly cares about the people it serves." It's a sentiment that perfectly sums up the philosophy at Alfa, the Montgomery-based insurance company founded in 1946.

Alfa's roots trace back to 1921, when the Alabama Farm Bureau started on Auburn University's campus. Its original purpose was to bring the state's farmers together to form a more impactful and unified voice on matters of public policy affecting agriculture. Soon, there were arms of the Farm Bureau in every Alabama county. In 1946, leaders of the organization saw another way to help the hard-working farmers it represented — creating a mutual insurance group — and Alfa was born.

Since many farms were in rural areas, places not served by municipal fire departments, farmers had a tough time insuring their homes and barns. The Farm Bureau, now Alabama Farmers Federation, raised $10,000 to provide the needed coverage. There was one catch: Those original policyholders had to promise not to file a claim for at least a year.

As word of the new insurance offering spread, others outside of the farming industry were interested in the concept, too. Alfa began selling insurance to non-farmers as long as they joined its Farmers Federation. This is still how Alfa operates. For residents of Alabama to purchase Alfa property or auto insurance, they must be members of the Federation.

The company has grown far beyond these humble beginnings. In the 1970s, Alfa started selling life insurance and then expanded into Georgia and Mississippi. In the 1980s, the name officially became Alfa Insurance and the Alabama Farmers Federation. Today, Alfa writes policies in 11 states and has about 1 million car, home and business insurance policies and $30 billion of life insurance in force. It has more than 2,300 employees, with approximately 1,000 of them living and working in the River Region. It's been at its main campus in Montgomery since 1959, and its

In 1959, Alfa relocated to the East South Boulevard from offices it had occupied since 1948. Remodeling and expansion projects occurred in 1968, 1972, 1986 and 1993. A second building, the Business Processing Center (BPC), was added in September 2006 to ensure Alfa could continue to serve customers when weather disasters strike. At the same time, Alfa also unveiled two mobile response units, 38-foot-long buses that act as a mobile office with connectivity to Alfa's networks. With an emphasis on service at the very roots of the company, Alfa's agents and customer service representatives continue to build relationships with their customers, while employees serve communities through various initiatives, including Meals on Wheels.

facilities have grown and evolved with the times, undergoing several remodels, renovations and additions. It even has its own daycare for children of employees.

The principle that inspired its founding — recognizing needs and filling them with care — remains the guiding light for every step Alfa takes. "We have been an involved community partner here for a long time," Parnell said. "Our employees live in the communities they serve." They are little league coaches, PTA members and volunteers for countless organizations. Company events, including blood drives, fundraisers, bake sales and food drives, allow employees to give back and better the community.

While it has always put an emphasis on caring, the company formalized the concept in 2015 with its "Alfa Cares" initiative. That October, Alfa raised more than $200,000 for the American Cancer Society and its breast cancer awareness campaign through company foundation gifts and donations from individual employees. As part of a recent Alfa conference, Alfa and its county Federations donated $120,000 to Alabama's Children's Hospital, with $20,000 of the donations coming from employees. "We also match employees' time spent volunteering and reimburse them when they take time off for that," Parnell said. "So 'Alfa Cares' is nothing new; it just highlights what we've been doing all along. We are not some distant company based miles away; we are the company that's right here at home."

Being an engaged, compassionate corporate citizen is a hallmark of Alfa, but so is stellar customer service. By operating through a local agent business model, Alfa has set itself apart. "People choose to do business with us because of our service," Parnell said. "Our agents have a personal touch; they are neighbors with their clients."

In Alabama, Alfa has become synonymous with insurance, but the Alabama Farmers Federation is still a key part of the company. The Federation serves the state's farmers through promotion and education, government advocacy, and sharing the story of how modern-day farming feeds the world.

The company has also stayed on the cutting edge of business practices. Recently, Alfa completed a major upgrade to harness the power of technology and give its customers options they want. "It all goes back to relationships, both in caring for our communities and our caring customer service," Parnell said. "We listen to how our customers want to connect and interact with us, and yet, we'll never lose that personal touch. We know that is our strength. No matter how things progress, at the end of the day, we'll never treat folks like numbers. We are focused on each customer and their needs."

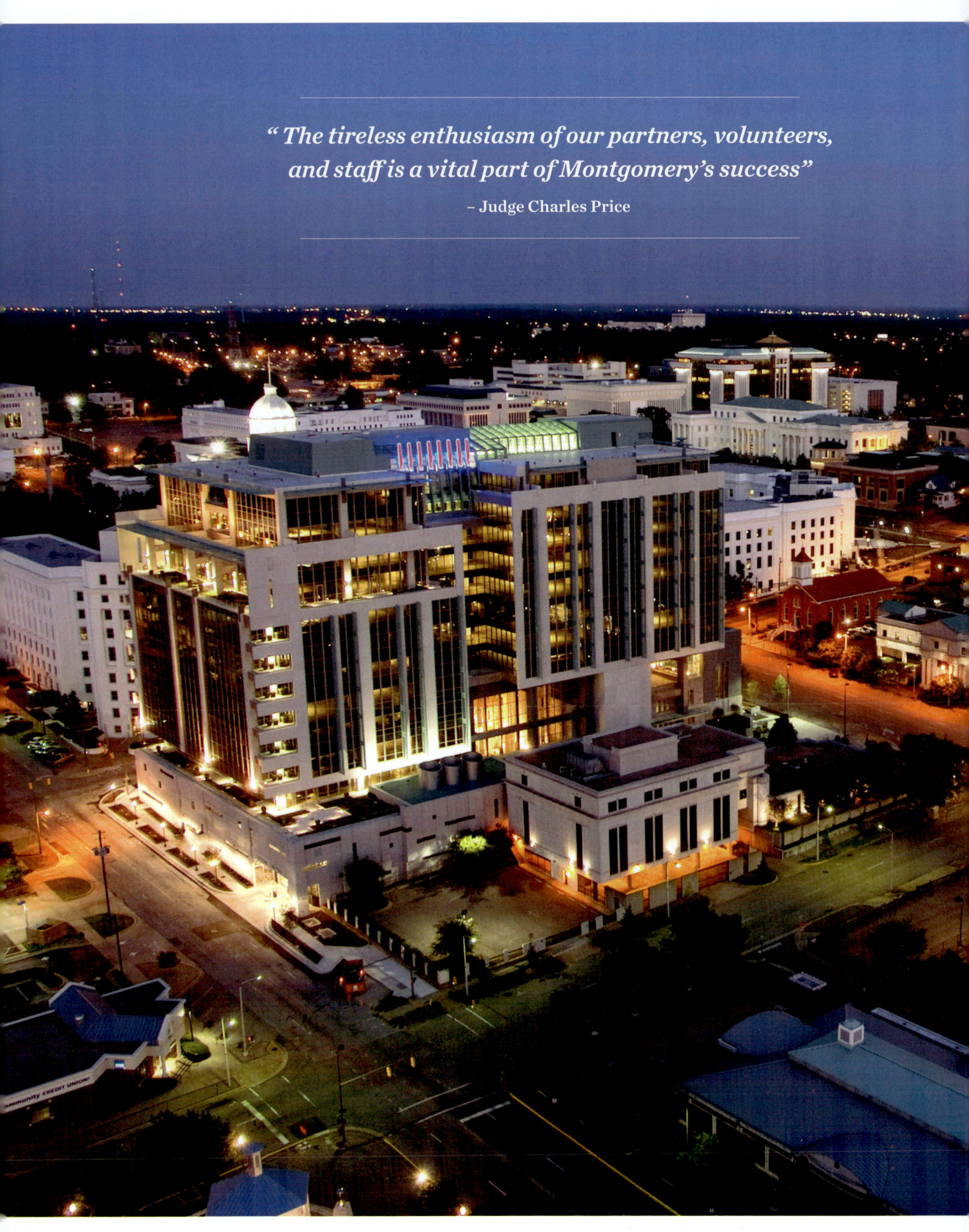

" *The tireless enthusiasm of our partners, volunteers, and staff is a vital part of Montgomery's success*"

– Judge Charles Price

Working Together

"The Montgomery Area Chamber of Commerce has the unique privilege of bringing the business community together around the table to work on the most important issues impacting the economic well-being and quality of life for the area. The tireless enthusiasm of our partners, volunteers, and staff is a vital part of Montgomery's success."

- **Judge Charles Price, Montgomery Chamber of Commerce Chairman**

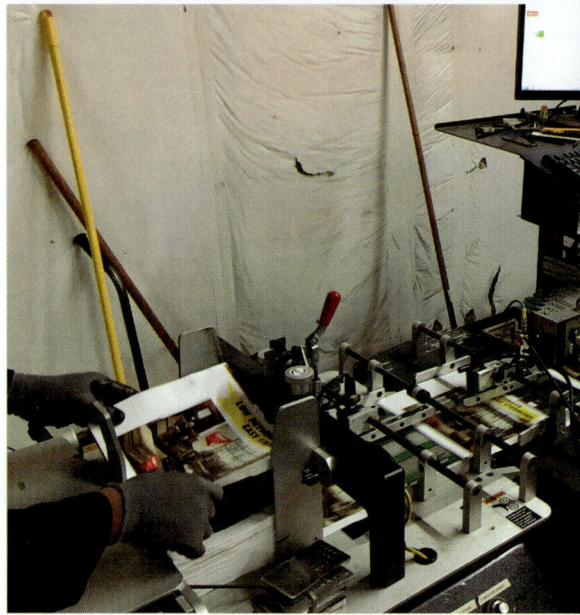

PUBLICATIONS PRESS, INC.

With its emphasis on stellar service, Publications Press, Inc. is striving to show people in the River Region why they should print local. According to the full-service commercial printing company's President Harvey Starling, the list of reasons is pretty long. "For one thing, we've been doing what we do, and doing it here, for two decades, since our founding in 1998," he said. "And we are all from here," he continued. "Everyone at Publications Press is truly a part of this community, so it means a lot for us to do business here. Not just from a dollars and cents perspective; we enjoy serving and giving back by volunteering and donating our services when we can, too."

As a locally based business, Publications Press is able to truly focus on each client and their needs. Additionally, with everyone on the team working together in one spot, the company's operations run smoother and more efficiently, an advantage Starling easily recognizes since he's been in the printing business most of his life. "I grew up around this," he said. "My dad was a pressman. The first job I had was baling scrap paper." He's been with Publications Press since its beginning.

A key thing his experience has taught him is how to take care of clients in a way that shows them they're important. "All of our clients have direct access to all of us. They have my cell phone, and I often get calls at night," he said. "But it is essential that they know they can reach me, and that I'm happy to deal with them directly. I want them to know that their concerns are our concerns. Many of our clients have become my friends."

This high level of personal customer service is based on how much Publications Press values its clients, as Starling explained. "We care about their success and know it is their livelihood," he said. "We also understand that their success equals ours." This client-first philosophy is working; the proof is in the company's roster of loyal clients and their appreciation for Publications Press' work. "We have clients thank us all the time," Starling said. "That's because we treat them the way we want to be treated."

Publications Press' approach also revolves around building relationships that will last for years. "If you treat clients right, they keep coming back. It sounds so simple, but it

Pictured below: Harvey Starling, Robert Starling and Madelaine Gilchrist

can be hard to find," he said. It's a concept that Starling and other company leaders impress on every employee, ensuring that each member of Publications Press' dedicated team of more than 70 people embraces this company culture.

The motto of treating folks right also extends to those employees, as Madelaine Gilchrist, Vice President of Magazine Operations, stressed. "We care about our employees; they're like family, and they know it by how we take care of them," she said. Many have been with the company since it started, and most of the others have been a part of the team for at least a decade.

This longevity provides stability that pays off big for Publications Press' clients in several ways. One is a depth of knowledge that complements the company's broad scope of services. While Publications Press started with just a small web press, by 2006 it moved up to heat-set printing and, since then, has grown and evolved to a 60,000-square-foot facility. It's also committed to staying on the leading edge of advances in printing technology. "That's just part of our promise to always offer the best quality," Starling said. "We have a new, state-of-the-art ink system and the latest and greatest digital press."

Today, Publications Press excels at everything from in-house design to the final finished product in a multitude of printed items including magazines, flyers, signs, point-of-purchase displays, brochures, business cards and more that push it to use almost 400,000 pounds of paper each month. "If it is printed, we can do it," Starling said.

They can do it all, but the company has carved out a niche in the printing world, specializing in glossy publications for newspaper companies. One of its largest customers is the Montgomery-based CNHI, LLC. It also prints many of the lifestyle magazines based in the River Region, just one more way the company is keeping things local.

Going local also means more savings. Publications Press' costs are often lower than an out-of-market printer, especially when they are working with local clients. "We have the largest web press in the state of Alabama for publications work," Starling said. "That makes us faster and means we can do things less expensively."

Publications Press even publishes a few real estate guides itself, adding yet another layer to its expertise. "Since we are on the publishing side of those products, it has given us a better understanding of publishers' needs," Starling said. "But we work hard to understand every client's specific needs, and that's the message we try to put out there: That with us, you can get quality printing, with a great turnaround time combined with some of the best service in the industry, and you can get it all right here at home."

We love our food in Alabama, and the River Region's culinary scene is hotter than ever thanks to good-eating institutions like the more-than-a-century-old Chris' Hot Dogs (bottom right), neighborhood favorite pizza place Tomatino's (top left), and newcomers like Common Bond Brewery. And it's not all about restaurants. Residents find farm-fresh local produce and locally made products at places like downtown Montgomery's Curb Market.

Photo courtesy of Common Bond Brewers / Stephen Poff

Photo by Erika Rowe Tracy

Photo courtesy of the Montgomery CVB / Carter Photography & Design, LLC

Photo courtesy of the Alabama Retail Association

EDWARDS PLUMBING AND HEATING

Serving Customers in Central Alabama for Seven Decades

Edwards Plumbing and Heating was founded in 1948 by Charles W. "Charlie" Edwards and is now in its third generation as a family business.

Early on, Charlie and his brother George ran a combined plumbing business and hardware store on Mt. Meigs Road in Montgomery. "They opened the hardware store in 1953. It didn't stay long," said Chuck Edwards, the founder's son and current company president. When the company expanded into installing mechanical systems in 1959, it dropped the hardware division.

This initial adaptability was probably a sign that a business that has since celebrated its 70th anniversary would stay flexible and keep innovating as it responded to a variety of economic cycles over seven decades.

The company moved to Jean Street in 1963, where it now employs a team of 65 who install plumbing, heating and air conditioning systems for the area's leading homebuilders, as well as completing other residential, multi-housing, commercial and light industrial projects. Currently, Edwards Plumbing and Heating services Montgomery, Autauga and Elmore counties, installing more than 600 systems a year. A service and repair department maintains the number of installations that have been done over the years. The company has more than 35 trucks and three separate divisions – Plumbing, Heating and Air, and a Duct Department.

In 1966, Chuck Edwards was in college at the University of Alabama when his father was diagnosed with cancer, and he was needed back at the business. "I dropped out of school and came home," Edwards said. "I worked with dad for three months until he went in the hospital."

This environment was very familiar, of course. Edwards had grown up in the business, having worked during summers there since the age of 13. Yet now, together with his mother as bookkeeper, he was in charge of a plumbing company that had eight employees. Edwards acknowledged, "It was kind of a struggle to stay in business – 1966, 1967, 1968 were pretty tough economic years."

> "If we weren't doing something right, we wouldn't still be here."
>
> - Chuck Edwards

Above: Founder, Charlie Edwards. Left: In 1953, the Montgomery Advertiser announced the opening of the hardware store on Mt. Meigs Road.
Far Left: Sally Edwards Meacham, Chuck Edwards and Charlie Edwards

Among the company's right steps was an expansion into heating and air conditioning service and installation. "Central air conditioning was just becoming popular in houses to replace window units," Edwards said. His dad had dabbled in heating and air conditioning installation, then by the early 1970s, the company had assembled a team devoted to this growing field. Today it makes up more than half of the company's work.

Chuck's son, Charles "Charlie" Edwards III, joined the company in 1992 and now runs the heating and air department. Daughter Sally Meacham has served as office manager since 1999, and Chuck remains involved after more than a half century at the helm. The company itself is known for well-trained and experienced staff – with very little turnover.

Customers in Central Alabama rely on Edwards Plumbing for a variety of services. The heating and air team is staffed by NATE-certified technicians with experience in residential and commercial air conditioning repair and replacement. NATE, or North American Technician Excellence, is the nation's largest organization for certifying heating, cooling, ventilation and air conditioning technicians.

The company also offers scheduled maintenance plans to help avoid untimely breakdowns and keep air conditioners running in top shape. When it's time to replace a unit, the techs are committed to providing a straightforward and transparent assessment so that customers can make the best-informed decision. They also offer education on equipment, including best practices for safety and energy savings. Importantly, the company provides after-hours emergency service for residential and commercial customers.

The same level of excellence applies to plumbing services, too. Licensed plumbers have installed plumbing in thousands of homes and commercial properties throughout the greater Montgomery area. Whether it's an occupancy inspection, a gas line installed or back-flow prevention, they have a relentless commitment to total customer satisfaction.

Edwards Plumbing and Heating knows that timeliness can save quite a bit of money when faced with a plumbing emergency. Water damage from leaks or breaks can weaken the ceiling, flooring or foundation in a home or business. When a customer calls with an emergency, the priority is to get a technician to the location as quickly as possible. Edwards is always ready to answer a call, 24 hours a day, seven days a week.

In recent years, the company has expanded beyond residential and commercial into light industrial, particularly on automotive supplier buildings in Central Alabama. Chuck Edwards also noted that they have a team in place for "design build" of commercial buildings. "We draw out the heating and air and plumbing to fill out the budget number before the owner makes a determination to bring in the architect," Edwards said. "We've got the capability to do that."

A company that's been around for seven decades still sees growth in the future. As Edwards said, "If we weren't doing something right, we wouldn't still be here. We could never have reached the level of success that we have without our dedicated staff of employees and supervisors. They are our greatest asset."

Alabama State University's impressive stadium is a shining example of the area's stellar architecture industry, but the Historically Black College and University itself is a crucial component of the capital city for more than 100 years. By bringing students and faculty from all over the world, it enriches the community in countless ways, and it's also one of the city's largest employers.

Photo courtesy of the Montgomery CVB

Downtown Prattville

Forward Motion

"The business climate in Prattville and Autauga County have been on a steady growth pattern. Business revenues within the major sectors in the last ten years have risen from 5 percent to 119 percent. Prattville is the fifth fastest growing city in the state. The City of Prattville and Autauga County are averaging 18 to 20 new businesses a year, and Prattville ranks second among the 20 most populous cities in Alabama making it a prime location for even more businesses, entrepreneurs and industries. Add to that the fact that we still have a small-town atmosphere with all the amenities that you can find in larger cities as well as a rich history, and you've got a great spot to do business and to live."

-Patty VanderWal, Prattville Chamber of Commerce President

Photo by Brooke Glassford / Colorbox

PRATTVILLE AREA CHAMBER OF COMMERCE

Welcome to the City of Prattville, a charming New England style village nestled in the heart of the Deep South. A town rich in history, but with a firm focus on the future, Prattville is considered "the Preferred Community" of the region.

In 1835, Daniel Pratt purchased land on Autauga Creek, built his cotton gin factory and became the largest cotton gin manufacturer in the world. Built around industry, much like the classic mill towns in Pratt's native New England, and known as the "birthplace of industry," Prattville's foundation was built on the strength of its people. Visitors today can experience the rich history of Prattville by seeing the dam, millpond and Daniel Pratt's industrial buildings from Heritage Park. The historic downtown retains much of this same feel with unique boutiques, bars and restaurants.

While Prattville honors its rich heritage, the community has become a destination for those who enjoy the outdoors. Listed on the Alabama Scenic River Trails and National Recreational Trails, Autauga Creek Canoe Trail flows for 7 miles through Prattville offering access for canoeing, kayaking and tubing as well as campgrounds. The downtown Creekwalk trails encourage walking, jogging and biking along the banks of the creek. To fully explore the area's natural beauty, Wilderness Park is a must-see. Giant oriental bamboo plants soar 60 feet to form a canopy to the sky. Tee off at Capitol Hill, one of the most popular destinations on the world renown Robert Trent Jones Golf Trail. Capitol Hill's three courses, the Judge, Legislator and Senator, all have earned top honors from *Golf* magazine. Located nearby, Cooters Pond Park provides access to the Alabama River with two boat ramps and floating docks, a river walk, basketball courts, and a dog park. Prattville is also referred to as "The Fountain City," named for the abundance of artesian wells that flow through the town. Some of the city's most historic, free-flowing wells still produce crisp, clean water where visitors can enjoy a drink or fill a container to take home.

Prattville is Open for Business! Significant investments in historic downtown revitalization, retail districts, industrial parks as well as new and significant business and industry projects ensure continued growth and prosperity for the community. A high quality of life, a diverse mix of retail, industry and recreational attractions have transformed this quaint Alabama community into a destination for businesses, newcomers and visitors alike. Prattville's appeal is due to its nationally recognized status as a family-friendly place to relax and play. Designated as a "Community of Character" in 2007, Prattville and Autauga County are striving to strengthen our community by promoting excellence in character for each resident.

Our welcome mat is always out. Come experience our town, rich in history but with a firm focus on the future, and you'll see why we are "The Preferred Community" of the region.

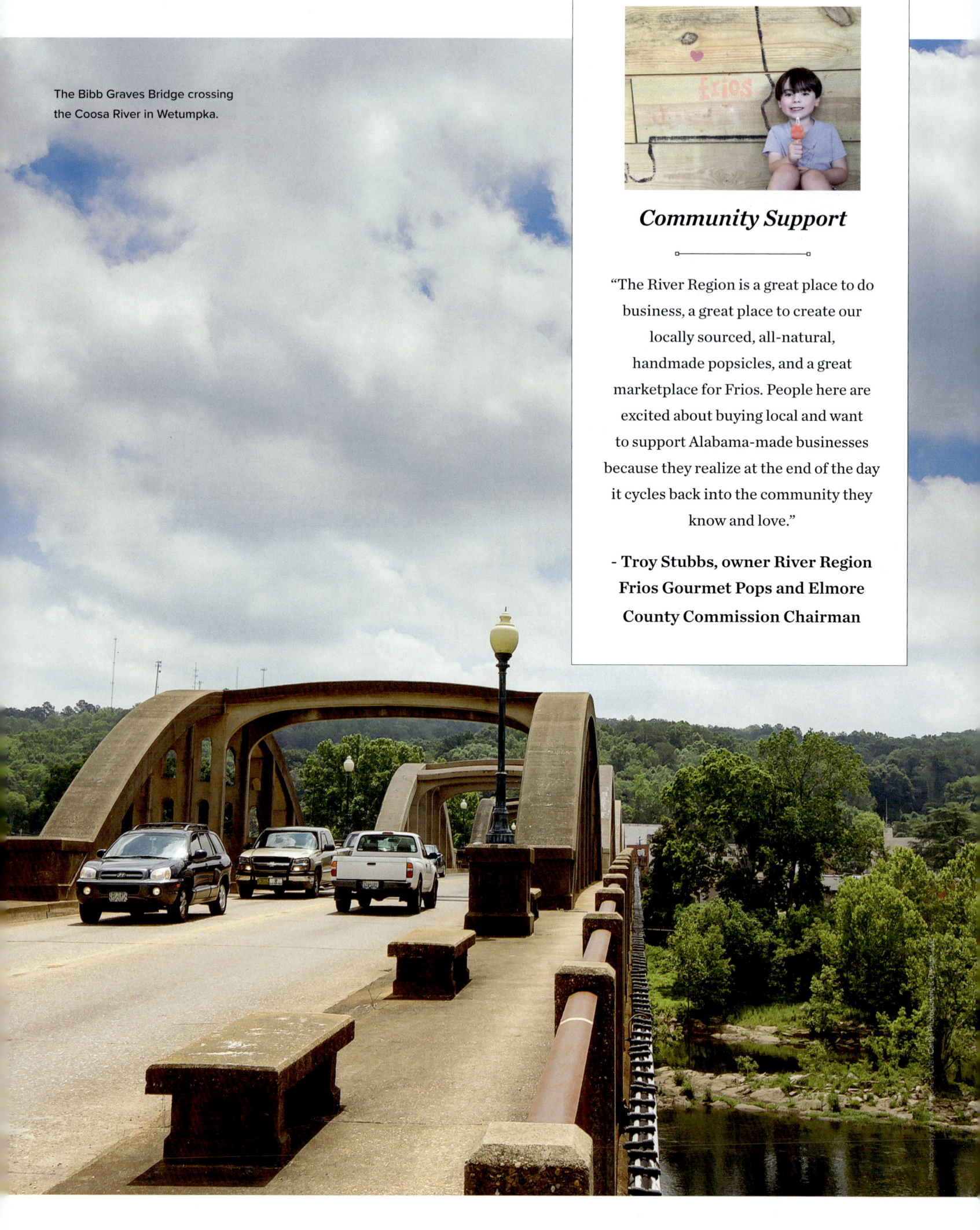

The Bibb Graves Bridge crossing the Coosa River in Wetumpka.

Community Support

"The River Region is a great place to do business, a great place to create our locally sourced, all-natural, handmade popsicles, and a great marketplace for Frios. People here are excited about buying local and want to support Alabama-made businesses because they realize at the end of the day it cycles back into the community they know and love."

- Troy Stubbs, owner River Region Frios Gourmet Pops and Elmore County Commission Chairman

WETUMPKA AREA CHAMBER OF COMMERCE

Preserving a Rich History – Building a Bright Future!

Vital Mission
The Chamber is the voice of business for the Wetumpka area. With nearly 400 members and growing, our voice is strong and growing stronger. The Chamber provides member benefits and services, networking opportunities, operates a visitors and tourism center, organizes events, and provides business development assistance and economic development, all with the mission to enhance the business vitality and quality of life in the Wetumpka area.

Rich History
While the original Chamber of Commerce was organized in 1952, the Chamber as we know it today was established in 1987 with 50 charter members, set in motion at the behest of then-Mayor Jeanette Barrett. Incorporation papers were filed on February 24, 1989, to establish The Wetumpka Area Chamber of Commerce, with William M. Gray serving as the first elected president.

Early in 1995, the Chamber sought a permanent home, gathered commitments from its membership, and made a leap of faith and purchased the historic building at 110 East Bridge Street. This two-story white masonry location originally constructed in 1905 of limestone was the Bank of Wetumpka. After the demise of the bank in the years of the Depression, the historic building served to house a variety of business ventures—barber and beauty shops, a jewelry store, insurance and accounting offices, a gift shop, a restaurant and eatery, a drug prevention and treatment program and finally, June 1, 1995, the official home of The Wetumpka Area Chamber of Commerce. This beautiful building became the anchor building for the Impact Wetumpka redevelopment.

Bright Future
The Chamber made significant progress toward realizing its vision in 2016. Marshaling the hopes and collective resources of a can-do community, a small town with a big vision and heart, the Chamber opened the doors on a $1.4 million renovation of a city block in the heart of historic downtown Wetumpka.

The Impact Wetumpka campaign became the standard and catalyst for downtown transformation. The facility, with its official address at 116 East Bridge Street, features a state-of-the-art expansion with an Innovation Center and Incubator, expanded Chamber offices and meeting space, and a newly renovated Visitor's Center – all made possible through the generosity and goodwill of local citizens and businesses.

In just two short years, the strategic mission of Impact Wetumpka is beginning to be realized as more businesses start in – or relocate to – Wetumpka. The bold project is also gaining notice of other cities and towns across Alabama and the South. Indeed, the future is bright.

It is truly a privilege to serve the businesses in our area as well as the City of Wetumpka and Elmore County at large.

BROWN STUDIO ARCHITECTURE

Brown Studio Architecture has had an important and durable impact on the vibrancy created in downtown Montgomery and the River Region. The firm's 40-year history includes solutions for many clients across the spectrum of project types including city and master planning, historic restoration and adaptive reuse, medical, industrial, educational, commercial, retail, housing, and mixed-use developments.

Downtown Montgomery

In Montgomery, our landmark projects have brought change and excitement. Downtown projects include: the Riverwalk, the Amphitheater, Riverwalk Stadium and the Alley restaurants, rooftop event space, downtown historic lofts and zoning advocacy encouraging urban development.

In the early 2000s, Brown Studio plans fueled the redevelopment of the riverfront and the entertainment areas. These improvements provided a long-term growth plan with walkable neighborhoods, offices, mixed-use development and cultural facilities and the adoption of Montgomery's downtown building code in 2007.

We have preserved and redesigned notable historic structures in the region: The Statehouse and State Capitol, Segall Ice House lofts, Winter Loeb building, Vintage Year restaurant, Old Alabama Town and the award-winning Moton Air Field in Tuskegee.

Leading Edge Solutions

Our portfolio of health care architecture includes new construction and renovation to public and private health care facilities to incorporate leading-edge solutions for the changing world of health care: River Region Health Center, LifeSouth Community Blood Center, Fresenius Medical Care, and Baptist Health. Our work extends across the gulf states region.

Innovative Places of Today and Tomorrow

We are committed to creating innovative places. Several projects at the University of Alabama, Auburn University, Alabama A&M University, and Alabama State University provide built environments for education, housing, wellness services, and athletic stadiums. Alabama State University adopted our master plan to use as a road map, and it includes a 26,000-seat football stadium and dormitories.

Our team provides environments that best represent the client and consumer from the broadest planning to the finest detail: Jack Ingram Motors, Dixie Electric Cooperative, and Neptune Technology Group. Our contributions with the Poarch Creek Indians produced the Wind Creek Casino and Hotel in Atmore, an award-winning facility with unique design highlights including a spa, cooking school and hotel.

Valued Solutions

Brown Studio has been fortunate to become the trusted advisor to many clients on a continuous basis. Established in 1977 by Don Brown, FAIA, the firm has an accomplished staff of architects and project managers who have worked together for many years. The team has leading-edge capability to craft top-tier energy-conscious solutions to create economical, sustainable, durable and elegant design solutions. The firm has completed over 2,000 projects in virtually every market at a value of over a billion dollars. Brown led the team nationally that created the country's new model building code for energy and resources.

Our mission is to make the world a better place, providing valued solutions for every client, one project at a time.

Pictured left: Warren Averett proudly provides A+ service to our A+ clients, like the Civil Air Patrol, which is headquartered in Montgomery, Alabama. (Pictured left to right: John Salvador, Civil Air Patrol COO; Lee Parks, CPA, Warren Averett Member; Paul Gloyd, Civil Air Patrol COA.) Above left: The Warren Averett Young Professionals group volunteering for Habitat for Humanity. Above right: Warren Averett gives back to the community, both financially and through volunteering. (Pictured left to right: Brenda Hellums and Lynn Bius.)

WARREN AVERETT CPAS AND ADVISORS

Solutions to Help You Thrive

Warren Averett is located conveniently on Interstate Court in the center of Montgomery, yet this three-story building is only a hint of the size of this regional accounting, tax and advisory firm.

With offices in Alabama, Georgia and Florida, and affiliate locations in Texas and Grand Cayman, Warren Averett is the largest CPA firm in Alabama, the second largest in the Gulf Coast states and the fourth largest in the Southeast. More than 800 employees work with clients having operations in all 50 states and 36 countries outside the U.S. In addition, seven affiliated companies provide a versatile range of business services, including asset management, benefit consultation, staffing and recruiting, technology solutions, turnaround services and workplace solutions, as well as financial planning for the emerging affluent.

The firm's history traces back to the early 1970s when Wilson, Barfield & Co. was founded by Jim Wilson, Sr. In 1997, the firm became Wilson, Price, Barranco, Blankenship and Billingsley through a Montgomery-based merger and continued to experience growth serving many businesses in the River Region. In 2012, the accounting firms Warren Averett, O'Sullivan-Creel, and Wilson Price merged to form the current Montgomery office of Warren Averett. Along with subsequent mergers with Tampa-based and Atlanta-based firms, Warren Averett has continued to expand its footprint throughout the Southeast.

Locally, 123 employees occupy the Montgomery office, which includes both the Warren Averett firm as well as an affiliated company, Warren Averett Technology Group.

One of Warren Averett's core values is "Sharing Our Success," which encompasses a commitment to giving back to the community both financially and through volunteering. Employees are encouraged and rewarded for their community involvement, and the firm and its staff are involved with a wide range of civic, charitable and economic groups that continue to help the River Region thrive. Warren Averett has been a long-time supporter of several local organizations including the Alabama Shakespeare Festival, Montgomery Museum of Fine Arts, Family Sunshine Center, Tukabatchee Area Council Boy Scouts of America, Child Protect, Brantwood Children's Home, Montgomery Area Food Bank and many others. Members of the firm also take active roles in the Montgomery Area Chamber of Commerce, area nonprofit boards and professional associations.

Warren Averett
CPAs AND ADVISORS

Built on Smart Growth principles, neighborhoods like Hampstead in Montgomery and The Waters in Pike Road include a mix of both commercial spaces and homes, creating a true sense of community. Construction in these spots – and all over the region – also represents an integral segment of the area's economy, providing thousands of jobs.

207

DAVMOOR

Helping owners and their leadership teams get what they want from their business

As a business owner, have you ever wanted to scream because of your frustrations with personnel conflicts, profit woes, inadequate growth or decisions that never seem to get made, or, once made, failed to be properly implemented?

Since the late '70s, Gene Moorhead has faced those issues, not only with his own businesses in Montgomery, but with his clients as well. As an owner/manager of broadcasting stations and then an advertising/marketing/brand development agency, he worked with hundreds of local and regional businesses on ways to help them grow their business. While working with leadership teams he learned firsthand how companies struggle with all the components of growth and learned that real growth happens because of what the owner and leadership team do inside the four walls of the organization and not because of a marketing program.

In 2013 he was introduced to the Entrepreneurial Operating System (EOS) based on the book *Traction* by Gino Wickman. He knew he would be able to help businesses grow more effectively and profitably with EOS. After training, he became a professional EOS Implementer.

He helps business owners and their leadership teams get more of what they want from their businesses by implementing a simple business operating system with practical tools that help them do three things:

Vision – getting the leadership team all 100 percent on the same page.

Traction – getting the leadership team all more disciplined and accountable.

Healthy – getting the leadership team to function like a cohesive team.

The leadership team and eventually everyone in the organization is crystal clear on the vision, is disciplined and accountable, and advances as a healthy, functional, cohesive team.

There are more than 4,000 companies running on EOS worldwide. With over 18,000 full-day working sessions, there is no theory – just timeless field-tested tools that work.

Some client comments:

"My boys have noted that I have more balance in my life even while the business continues to grow and is busier than ever." Publisher

"44% – that's our compounded annual growth rate for the past three years since we started EOS." – Multi-media

"I don't know where we would be without EOS today. We are more organized and able to focus on what absolutely has to be done ahead of time." – Alabama global food processor

Gene is a former board of director member of the Capital City Rotary Club and Hospice of Montgomery, and a longtime supporter of the Montgomery Salvation Army, Montgomery Area Council on Aging and the Montgomery Area Food Bank.

www.davmoor.com

GOODWYN, MILLS AND CAWOOD

Goodwyn, Mills and Cawood (GMC) is one of the largest firms of its kind in the Southeast. Its multi-discipline offerings include architecture, engineering, environmental and more, and while it's based in Montgomery, it has 15 additional offices in key markets around the region. Yet everything the company and its employees do is built on a foundation laid at its beginnings in 1947. Every plan conceived, design rendered, schematic drafted and site surveyed is centered on GMC's commitment to construct more than brick and mortar structures and to build communities. Its mission statement says, "We believe in community, collaboration and using the power of creativity and hard work to make a difference — in our hearts, homes, city, nation and world." Executive Vice President and Board Chairman David Reed stressed that this thought is more than a motto; it's a mantra. "Throughout the history of this company, the importance we place on getting out into our community, supporting it and working to better it has been a big part of our success," he said.

GMC has put this sentiment into action in Montgomery, proving itself an integral community partner by working with city leaders and the Chamber of Commerce on economic development projects, often in a volunteer capacity. "We donate our time to serve as consultants when our community's economic development team is showing sites and facilities to prospective industries," said Galen Thackston, Chief Operating Officer. "From the engineering or architecture side, we highlight the benefits of different sites."

Thackston also pointed to the work environment at GMC, one that encourages every employee to play a part in the big picture, as another crucial piece of the company's story. "We are a team, but we also value and promote individual drive and an entrepreneurial spirit here," he said. "We want our employees to bring us their ideas, seize business opportunities they see, and understand that they are not just a cog in a wheel. Giving them the chance to succeed pays off for the firm overall in the long run."

In addition to a giving and motivational corporate culture, Reed noted a key aspect of the company that underpins its growth, its diversity of services and markets. GMC's scope has evolved to offer many branches of architecture, civil engineering, land surveying, electrical engineering, transportation engineering, environmental engineering, community and master planning, landscape architecture, airport planning, geotechnical engineering and municipal engineering, all serving a wide array of markets, including commercial, manufacturing, education, recreation, health care and more. It's grown in size too, with two subsidiary entities swelling its employee ranks to almost 700 people.

Today, 70 years after its founding, GMC and all of its people still remain focused on that original vision: to make the places we share better for us all.

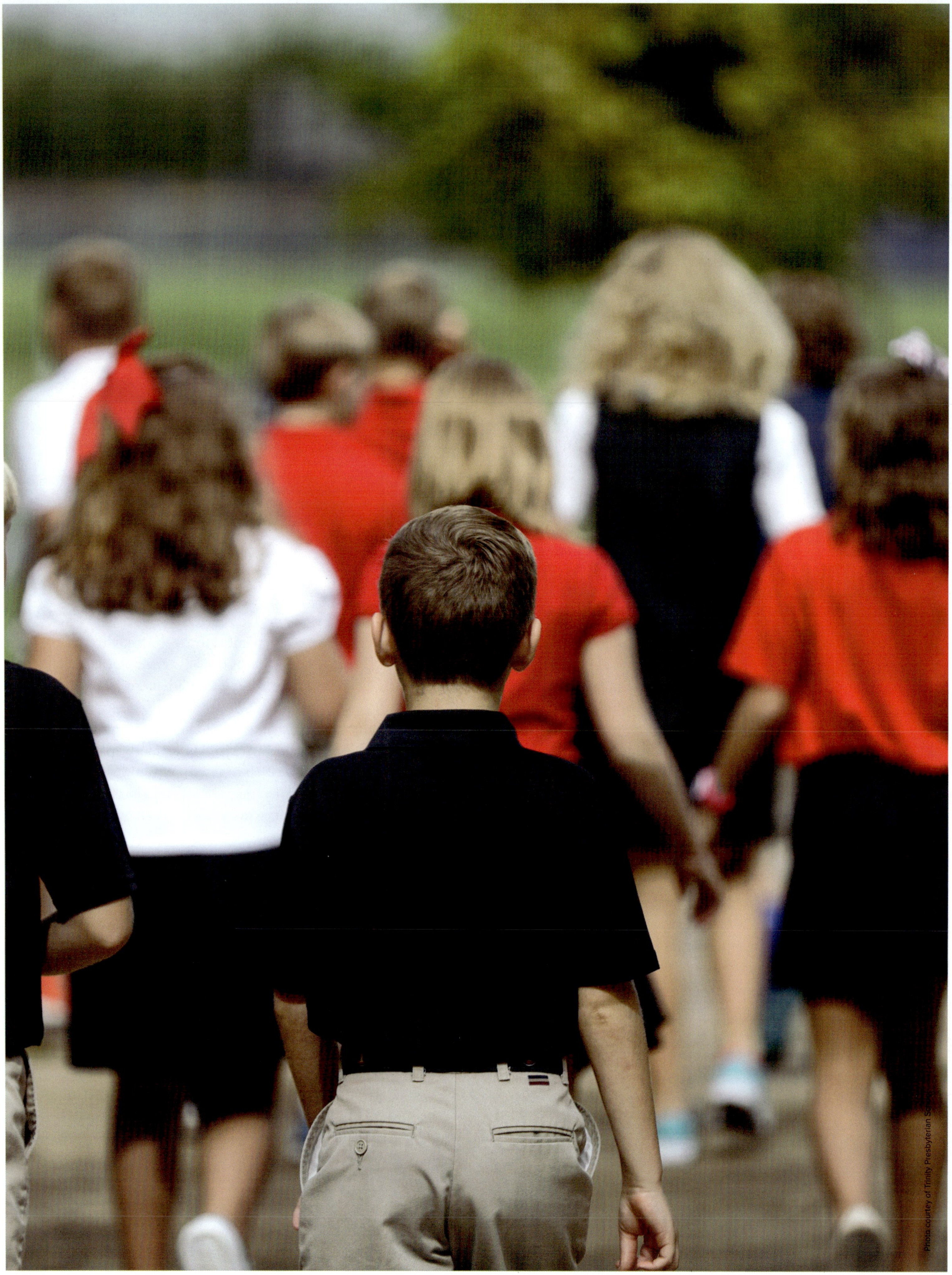
Photo courtesy of Trinity Presbyterian Sc

River Region leaders are keenly aware of the link between quality education and economic development. It's why area schools like Montgomery's Montessori Academy are applying innovative techniques and technology early, and why strategic partnerships have been formed to ensure we're teaching and training the workforce that tomorrow will demand.

LARRY E. SPEAKS & ASSOCIATES, INC.

Consulting Engineers and Land Surveyors

For more than 40 years, Larry E. Speaks & Associates, Inc. has been providing engineering consulting and land surveying in the River Region and other parts of Alabama. Steven Speaks, son of Larry, began working with his dad in the summer of 1980 when he was 16 years old. After he earned a bachelor of science in business administration from Auburn, he added a bachelor of science in civil engineering to his resume. Greg Gillian joined the company in 1986 after completing a bachelor's degree in civil engineering from Auburn University.

Today, these gentlemen own the firm that was founded by its namesake in 1976, and they lead a staff of 22 employees that includes Registered Professional Engineers, Registered Professional Land Surveyors and Environmental Scientists. In this family-oriented company, most of the members of the team have been on board for more than a decade – and many for more than 20 years.

In the civil engineering arena, the firm's full scope of services range from site evaluations and assessments to roadway, subdivision and storm drainage design. They work with sewage and water treatment facilities, collection and distribution systems, as well as municipal works and park and recreation facilities. They also provide construction management, environmental permits, land development planning and design, and land use studies.

The firm provides design for individual on-site sewer systems, decentralized wastewater treatment and disposal, and larger wastewater treatment facilities. They work regularly with the Alabama Department of Public Health and ADEM on permitting these systems. In addition, the fully integrated surveying and drafting staffs perform all types of land surveying services, while the environmental staff provides environmental permitting at the local, state and federal levels. They also work with the U.S. Army Corps of Engineers on wetland delineations and permits.

Many drivers in downtown Montgomery will have experienced one example of the firm's roadway engineering work: in 2006, the Court Square Roundabout at Dexter Avenue and Commerce Street was improved and returned to a square similar to its layout in the 1800s. The company also provided engineering for improvements to Madison Avenue. Among numerous other examples, the company's engineers worked with the logistics firm Vectrus on various projects at Maxwell Air Force Base and Gunter Annex, including water connectivity improvements, relocation of the natural gas infrastructure, erosion repair along the Alabama River, improvements to the base golf course, and resurfacing of the road that surrounds the airfield.

Russell Lands in Alexander City is another long-standing client, and the firm has done a considerable amount of work in the Lake Martin Area. They've been the engineers on several of their significant developments including residential developments, marinas and Russell Crossroads. They also work with municipalities, water authorities and private development as well as private residences. The company is licensed in Alabama, Georgia and Mississippi.

WEALTH MANAGEMENT PARTNERS, LLC, CERTIFIED PUBLIC ACCOUNTANTS

High Quality Services for Government and Commercial Clients

Wealth Management Partners, LLC, Certified Public Accountants (WMP) was formed within the Montgomery Chamber Business Resource Center in 2007. Based upon the challenges and opportunities experienced during the early years (2007 through 2009), the firm has built a solid foundation around its core principles of integrity, responsiveness, professionalism and excellence. Initially, the goal of WMP was to provide comprehensive financial and tax planning for high net worth clients. However, when the economic downturn occurred in 2008, WMP quickly refocused into a more traditional CPA firm offering a full scope of services. In addition, as a result of relationships established by its founder Keary L. Foster, WMP was successfully able to enter the Federal government contracting space. WMP first teamed with IT companies on smaller contracts, and was selected in 2012 to provide Financial Improvement and Audit Readiness (FIAR) support for the Department of Defense.

Today, WMP maintains a government and commercial sector presence, and operates a team of professionals from three primary locations – at Maxwell Air Force Base's Gunter Annex, at Wright-Patterson Air Force Base in Dayton, Ohio, and a headquarter office in downtown Montgomery. The firm specializes in accounting/auditing, financial and IT process controls, auditing/remediation techniques, risk management/cybersecurity compliance consulting and business process re-engineering support and analytics.

Most local clients are developed from referrals, which stem from the firm's growing reputation and community involvement. WMP supports a number of local physicians in the areas of practice management, out-sourced CFO services, bookkeeping, tax preparation, and back office support. Moreover, WMP prepares financial statements for various businesses needing to maintain licensure.

Foster, who serves as CEO/President of WMP, is a native of Eastaboga, Alabama, and received both a Bachelor of Science in accountancy and Master of Science in taxation from the University of Alabama. He is a military veteran, having served for eight years in the U.S. Army Reserve, and was recently invited to participate in and completed the Goldman Sachs 10,000 Small Business Program – a course designed for small businesses held at Babson College in Massachusetts, one of the premier institutions for entrepreneurship.

Active in the River Region community, Foster has served on the board for the Jubilee Community Center, and helped start the local program for Impact Alabama, which provides free tax services for low-income families. Among other activities, Foster has taught accounting and tax classes at Troy University in Montgomery, served as a presenter for several organizations on financial and accounting related topics, and talked to school groups on accounting topics as well as fulfilling life goals.

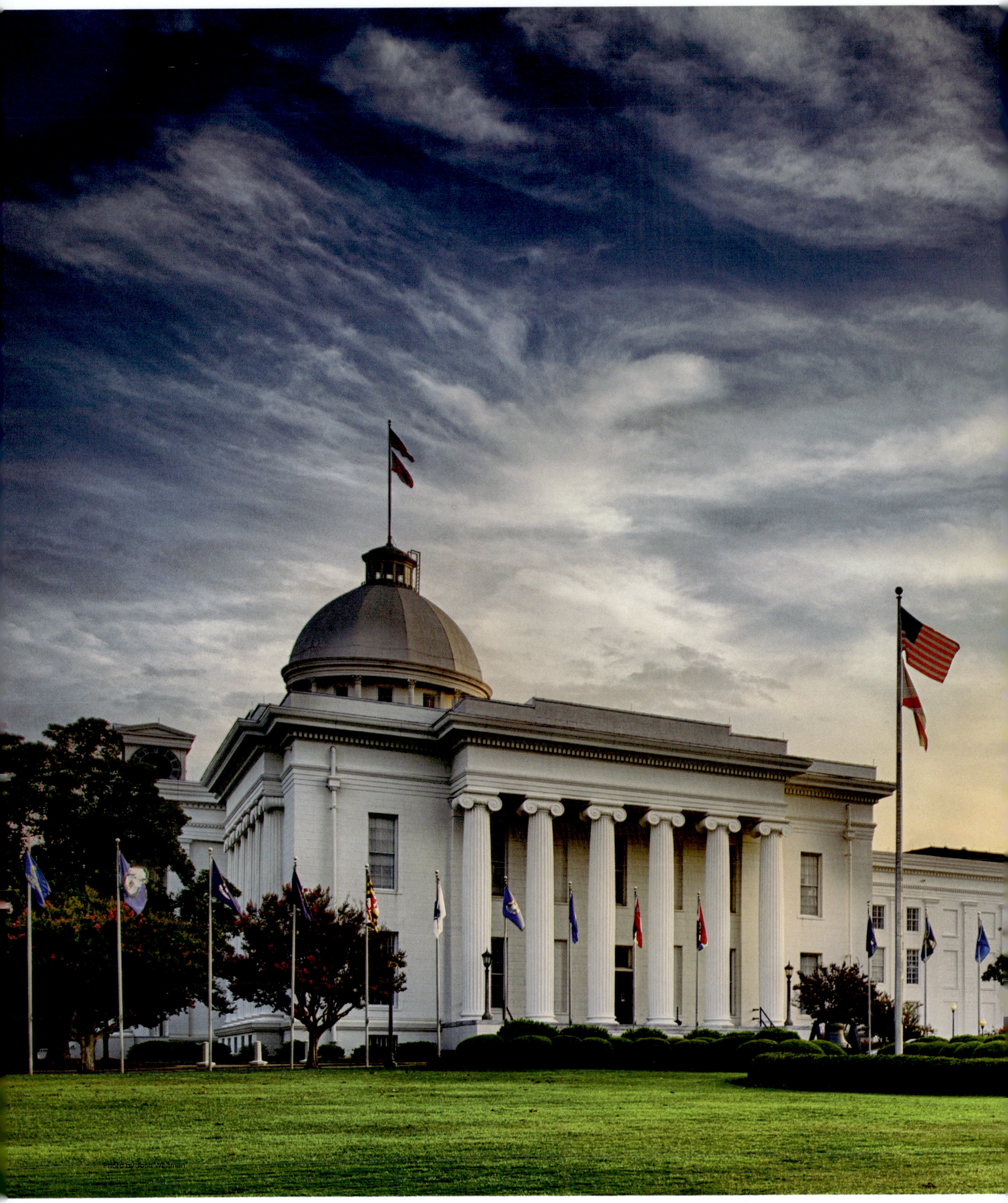

The Alabama Capitol building is a beautiful and imposing piece of architecture, but it's also a bright beaming symbol of the positive impact state capital functions have on the region. The State of Alabama is the city's second largest employer, providing more than 11,600 jobs.

WOOLARD BROTHERS COMMERCIAL CONTRACTING, INC.

Four Generations. 80 Years in Business. Hundreds of Impressive Projects.

Woolard Brothers Commercial Contracting, Inc. traces its beginnings to 1932 when A.F. "Ted" Woolard and O.D. Bonner founded Columbus Plastering Company in Columbus, Georgia. After an interruption during World War II for the founders to serve in the military, the company moved to Montgomery in 1949.

In 1964, the second generation took over as Fred Woolard assumed the reins at the young age of 23 when his father passed away, and soon his younger brother Gary joined him in the business that became known by the name Woolard Brothers. At their retirement, Fred Woolard's son, Paul Woolard, and partner Greg Bozeman took ownership.

"My grandfather started this company as a plastering contractor," said Paul Woolard, company president. "My dad and his brother continued plastering and moved into drywall." Today the company is still doing plastering projects like the Downtown Kress building renovation and bids commercial contracting projects for metal stud framing, drywall, stucco, EIFS, acoustical ceilings, acoustical wall panels, GFRG and GRC.

In recent years, Woolard Brothers has worked on a variety of projects for state government, higher education, utilities and the military.

For example, Ross Bridge Golf Resort and Spa, the RSA Activity Center, the RSA Judicial Building, and the Renaissance Montgomery Hotel and Convention Center are notable projects, as well as the recent Gulf State Park Hotel and Convention Center. The company's portfolio also includes state office buildings such as the Alabama Department of Transportation, State Health Department Building and Alabama Department of Public Safety, and the company assisted in a renovation of the State Capitol Building in the 1990s.

Projects in the higher education sector include the Levi Watkins Library at Alabama State University, the Wellness Center at Auburn University Montgomery, the library at Central Alabama Community College, and Hawkins Hall at Troy University. The company is also slated to work on a North End Zone addition for the Troy football stadium. In addition, the company has worked on several buildings at Maxwell Air Force Base and assisted with renovations for Pea River Electric Cooperative, Central Alabama Electric Cooperative and Covington Electric Cooperative, among others. Though the company has completed work around Alabama and as far away as St. Louis, Woolard said, "Most of our work is in the River Region. We prefer to stay here and work for this community."

Along with a third generation of the family business now at the helm, the fourth generation is also in place. Paul's son Wesley Woolard and nephew Campbell McNab are part of the business, as is his partner's son Ryan Bozeman.

eSOLUTION ARCHITECTS, INC.

Montgomery Small Business Provides Global IT Services

In 2005, Air Force veterans Bill Woodhouse and Stacy Waldrep continued their service to the country when they began applying their military-based information technology experience in a new company they formed with partner Tim Castro, an IT professional well-versed in government contracts.

Today, the gentlemen lead eSolution Architects (eSA), a firm headquartered in Montgomery that largely provides programming services for the U.S. Department of Defense. "We're very good at what we do," Woodhouse said. Regarding their responsibilities, he said, "We maintain the Air Force network worldwide, and we develop and sustain Air Force enterprise level software."

eSA relies on a talented team of 70 employees, many of whom are highly certified. "They can't work on DoD systems unless they have those certifications," Woodhouse said. Team members also include those with a top secret security clearance. "We go from 'no clearance' all the way to 'top secret,'" Woodhouse said.

The eSA staff even includes a cybersecurity certified ethical hacker. "Some people call them the white hats," Woodhouse said. "They're looking for holes, trying to identify the gaps in security and work with organizations to fix their security systems."

In addition to office locations in East Montgomery, the firm also has locations at the Gunter annex of Maxwell Air Force Base, as well as locations in San Antonio, Texas, and Washington, D.C. They appreciate being headquartered in the River Region, providing jobs and contributing as a local company.

"We're dedicated to seeing the local economy thrive and do well and to assist in making that expansion as much as possible," Waldrep said.

The company also works to train the next generation of IT professionals. Through the Air Force Communications and Electronics Association (AFCEA) internship and scholarship program, they've introduced high school graduating students to the IT field. They've also hired students pursuing computer science studies at local universities. "We expose our interns to leading edge technologies and help them get familiar with how IT companies work," Waldrep said.

Waldrep said, "We're looking at new cloud technologies, growing into cloud services, and mobile device apps for increasing service to the military." In addition, eSA plans to expand its work with the commercial sector.

"We have a lot of experience in enterprise systems," Waldrep said. "The DoD is really high on servicing the network. Commercial companies need that."

eSolution Architects, Inc., a privately held, minority- and veteran-owned company, is a U.S. Small Business Administration 8(a) Business Development Program company and Small Disadvantaged Business certified since January 2009.

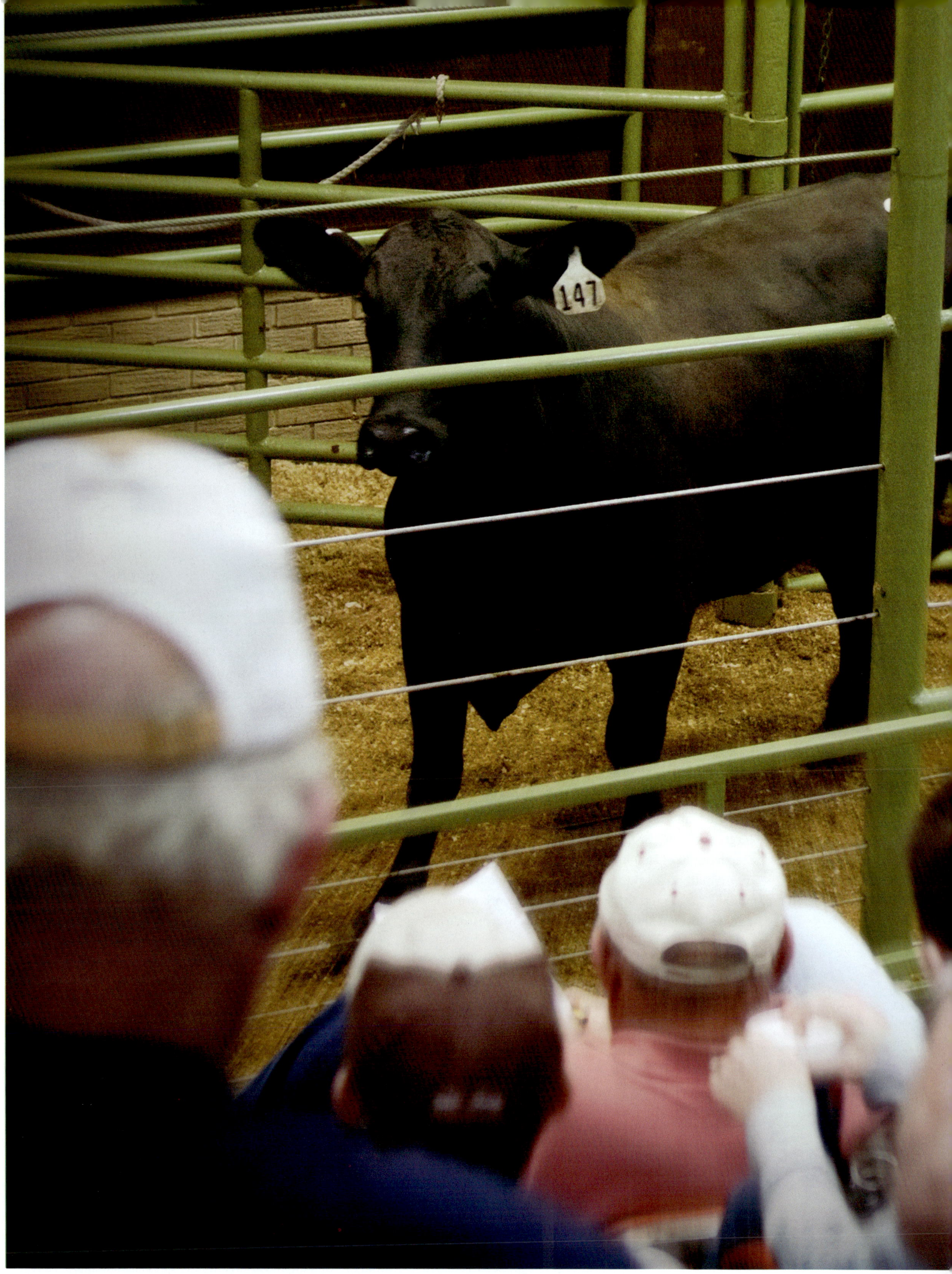
147

In the Field

The cattle industry in our area is big business. According to the Alabama Cattlemen's Association, which is based in Montgomery, Montgomery County is the largest cow county in the state with 73,000 head of cattle being raised. The prevalence of agriculture in our area is one aspect that makes it special to Erin Beasley, the ACA's executive vice president. "It doesn't take very long to drive out of the city limits and hit pasture and cropland. Agriculture certainly has its footprint in the River Region, especially in terms of cattle numbers and the rich history our industry has in this area," she said. "So many of the ACA's great leaders have been from this area and have influenced the association in a positive way. An interesting tidbit: Alabama has only had one president ever serve for the national cattlemen's organization, Mr. John 'Bubba' Trotman from Montgomery County, until his death in 2018."

CEDRIC BRADFORD

Well-Known Insurance Agent Serves River Region Clients

Cedric Bradford is a successful State Farm insurance agent who's been serving River Region clients for 30 years. His route to this profession came through unexpected turns.

A native of Montgomery, Bradford attended elementary and high school at St. Jude. After earning a degree in communication from the University of Alabama in 1976, he returned to Montgomery to work with WKAB TV. Then he began a career change.

"I had a cousin starting up a food service business, and I planned to work for him," Bradford said. Unfortunately, his cousin died unexpectedly right as he was taking the new position, so a new career path was headed his way.

In 1977, Eastdale Mall was opening on Atlanta Highway, and Bradford took what he thought would be a temporary position with Musicland. "Eleven years later, I was still there," he said, smiling. The timing was just right, however, for his next turn.

"One Christmas, the State Farm manager was at Musicland getting Christmas gifts for agents," Bradford said. "Because he had a lot of purchases, I helped him take them to his car." That initial meeting eventually led to an interview, and in 1988 Bradford was recruited to become the first African-American State Farm agent in this area.

"I knew a lot of people that owned houses and cars. I took a shot at it," Bradford said. He had help right away from family and friends. "My mom and dad were probably my biggest recruiters. The business was kind of instantly built." It's stayed strong ever since.

"State Farm is the number one insurer in the U.S. for auto and homeowners," Bradford said. The insurance company also offers much more, including property insurance, life insurance, business insurance and annuities. "We offer over 70 different products."

Each State Farm office operates as a privately owned business. Bradford's office includes a staff of three that are also licensed agents. Office manager Connie King has been with his office for 29 years. Assistant manager Octavia Sullen joined the team about 10 years ago, and Gwyneth Bias serves as receptionist and property and casualty specialist

Bradford's office is a platform to showcase his passion for hard work and serving others. His greatest reward comes from helping a client in need, and his caring desire to help others has led him to become one of the top agents in the city of Montgomery.

Bradford and his wife Audrie have three daughters and five grandchildren. One of their daughters, Dr. Porcia Bradford Love, is the owner of River Region Dermatology & Laser. Amber Bradford Buchanan is Corporate Account Manager for Halyard Health in Alpharetta, Georgia, and Caryn Bradford is IT Procurement Specialist for Randstad USA in Atlanta, Georgia.

ROBINSON AND ASSOCIATES ARCHITECTURE, INC.

Small Architectural Firm Helps Provide Big Welcome for Travelers

Robinson and Associates Architecture, Inc. was established by Wm. Barry Robinson in 1998. Located on South Perry Street in Montgomery, the firm also includes intern architect Damian Barnes and project manager Glazer Robinson, the founder's son.

Over the years, the small firm has provided architectural design services for educational institutions, municipalities, residential and multi-family, churches, historic preservation and many other projects. As a matter of fact, thousands of drivers entering Alabama are welcomed by their work every day.

The Alabama Department of Transportation (ALDOT) selected Robinson and Associates to design and produce construction documents for a replacement of the Welcome Center at the Alabama/Mississippi state line on I-10 East as well as the Welcome Centers at the Alabama/Georgia state line on I-59 South & I-85 South. Robinson and Associates were also selected to design and produce construction documents for a replacement of the Welcome Center at the Alabama/Tennessee state line on I-65 South. A longstanding client, ALDOT selected Robinson and Associates to provide architectural services for interior renovations for the Central Office Complex in Montgomery, and the firm has worked on divisional and regional office buildings in other parts of the state.

River Region residents and visitors also see examples of the firm's quality work in the main buildings at Gateway Park. The firm provided design and architectural services for the clubhouse, a two-story, 12,000-square-foot building incorporating timber framing and large glass windows that offer beautiful views of the golf course and driving range. In addition, the lodge is a one-story, 11,700-square-foot building designed for community meetings, family gatherings, and large-scale parties. The building exteriors are composed of brick, cultured stone, synthetic slate roof and engineered wood deck.

Also in Montgomery, the firm worked on the renovation of the historic Greyhound Bus Station in downtown. Exterior restoration included a new sign circa the early-to-mid 1960s and an exhibit telling the story of the attack on the Freedom Riders in 1961 during the Civil Rights movement.

Projects at Alabama State University, which were conducted as a joint venture with Barganier Davis Sims Architects, have been part of the firm's work in the educational sector. These included major renovations and addition to a sports arena that was converted into a 39,000-square-foot dining hall. The firm also worked on the programming and design of a 78,000-square-foot Student Services Center.

In addition, the firm provided architectural services for Tuskegee University, the alma mater for the three gentlemen. Milbank Agriculture Building, which was built in 1909 and is still in use, was experiencing a problem with water seeping through basement walls. Robinson and Associates was hired to correct this ongoing problem and renovate the damaged areas.

Business in the River Region knows no boundaries. In traditional office parks and centuries-old historic houses in the Old Alabama Town Business district, work is getting done.

In addition to the multiple RSA buildings adding their shapes to the capital city skyline, the Retirement Systems of Alabama has an extensive positive effect on the region, most visibly in the lush green fairways of the Robert Trent Jones Golf Trail courses that are scattered throughout the state and provide a big tourism boost.
Photo by Robert Fouts

MERRILL LYNCH

Merrill Lynch has had a strong presence in Montgomery since 1935, when it first opened its office downtown. It's one of the oldest wealth management firms in the city, and one of the largest, with more than $2 billion in assets and liabilities under management. Its longevity, stability, size and scope are impressive, but according to Cindy Clark, Resident Director, the firm's real strength is its unwavering commitment to its clients and its community.

Merrill Lynch provides more than 200 financial and investment products and services like estate planning, insurance, mortgages and more to a diverse array of clients helping them reach their unique financial goals. "We strive to meet and exceed client expectations every day," Clark said. The firm's investment professionals create a wealth outlook for clients that focuses on seven key areas. It's a custom approach that's at the foundation of the firm's client-centered philosophy.

The firm's technological advances is another key role in the firm's approach to meeting their clients' needs. Merrill Lynch strives to stay on top of the digital advances and the leading edge of technology.

This also includes the firm's philanthropic mindset. Merrill Lynch has a charitable budget that ensures emphasis is placed on boosting the efforts of local non-profits. "We have a huge level of community involvement, and I've always been proud of that," Bob Runkle, a longtime financial advisor, said. "We're big believers in giving back." "We live here and are invested in Montgomery's future," they both added. "Many of our employees serve on boards and volunteer with civic and charitable organizations of all kinds."

When the firm's employees are doing well, they're in a good place too. Merrill Lynch provides a working environment that helps employees thrive, proven by their long tenure. Many of their employees start and end their careers there, which is another benefit to their clients. Altogether, their employees represent hundreds of years of combined expertise and experience.

Merrill Lynch employees enjoy a supportive corporate culture that's inclusive, with a focus on diversity, from the corporate level down to Montgomery's firm. It's just one more way they're dedicated to their clients. In their words, "A more diverse office lets us better serve a diverse clientele."

All the firm's clients benefit from the depth of resources a global investment company like Merrill Lynch can provide combined with the personalized service that comes from a true relationship with their local investment advisor. They say their clients become like family, and they treat them as such.

Dollars and cents aside, Merrill Lynch clients can rest on the firm's proven responsibility, and its ability to provide something more valuable than money: peace of mind. "Merrill Lynch has always been on the forefront of this industry," Runkle said. "When markets find themselves in turmoil, we provide solid leadership and always lead with a sense of confident direction and integrity."

Far left: Jackson Thornton Young Professionals (otherwise known as JTYP) are out in full force to support the Lions Club of Montgomery and our community. Far right: Renee Hubbard, Carlee Sims, Kali Belyeu and Kendall Causby visiting with accounting students at Huntingdon College's "Meet the Firms" event.

JACKSON THORNTON

A Century of Service to the River Region and Beyond

Jackson Thornton was founded in 1919 when Harold Crane opened an accounting office in the Bell Building in downtown Montgomery. The company's long history reflects the growth of Montgomery, the River Region economy and, in many cases, the privately owned businesses that it has served since the beginning.

"Through our century of service, we have worked with many closely held and family-owned businesses. What began with the grandparents has now been passed down to children and grandchildren. It's a privilege for us to be a small part of the growth and success of these companies, which have become so important to the communities they serve," said Ned F. Sheffield, President & Managing Principal.

In the 1960s, the firm began to bear the name of earlier principals Douglass Jackson and James Thornton, and its clients drew largely from the agriculture, lumber, manufacturing, banking, automotive and merchant sectors. Today, Jackson Thornton serves an even wider array of industries and has created specific groups within the firm to specialize in areas like utilities, health care, construction, business valuation, not-for-profit and governmental, to name a few.

Jackson Thornton has also launched a full family of companies, including Jackson Thornton Asset Management, founded in 1999, and Jackson Thornton Technologies, founded in 2001. "Both of these companies began because our clients needed these kinds of services, and it was gratifying to us to continue to serve as a trusted adviser in new directions," Sheffield said.

More than 150 people work in the corporate office on lower Commerce Street and the two other River Region offices in Prattville and Wetumpka. There are also three additional offices in Dothan, Opelika and Nashville, bringing the total number of employees to around 200.

Harold Crane's decision to locate the first office in downtown Montgomery has remained a commitment even during five additional moves. As a matter of fact, Jackson Thornton was part of the initial resurgence of the downtown area when the firm moved to lower Commerce Street in 1980 at the suggestion of James Loeb and the Landmarks Foundation. In 1997, the building was expanded to include a portion of the adjoining property at 210 Commerce Street.

The founder's grandson, Lanny Crane, is a former managing principal of Jackson Thornton and a current principal with Jackson Thornton Asset Management. With his tie to the firm's founding and his contributions as a longtime philanthropist, Crane parallels the company's larger impact on the community in the arts, historic preservation, and philanthropy.

"Community involvement and philanthropy have been and always will be very important to the firm. We invest our time, talents, and resources in our home communities," said Sheffield.

The River Region has proven its appeal to visitors, racking up record tourism numbers (like the most hotel nights) in recent years. The crowds traveling here equal a boom to local businesses that serve both their bottom lines and bring a higher quality of life for all, thanks to more attractions and restaurants and more money going into cities' tax coffers. Photo courtesy of the Montgomery CVB / Carter Photography & Design, LLC

Businesses of all shapes and sizes offer a myriad products and services. From furry-friend daycare and shopping options galore (that draw folks from all over) to banks ready to help with a loan for the next great start-up, the River Region has it all.

GARNER ELECTRIC

Reliable Electrical Services at Competitive Prices

Master electrician and Millbrook businessman Harris Garner founded Garner Electric in 1995. His wife Cathy joined him in the business a short time later, and, since then, Garner Electric's highly skilled staff has worked on nearly 600 commercial projects in Central Alabama.

The company typically works for general contractors, property owners, municipalities and corporations in commercial, light industrial and residential sectors on a diverse array of projects. However, Garner Electric also has a residential service department and works with area homeowners on tailor-made electrical plans, lighting services, wiring upgrades or other electrical services. In addition, many real estate agents call on the company to provide electrical services for rental properties.

"We work on jobs of all sizes," Harris Garner said. "We can wire a $5 million project or change out light bulbs."

Some of the more recognizable projects in the area include LED lighting for Long-Lewis Ford automobile dealership in Prattville, electrical services for elementary and middle schools at Maxwell Air Force Base, and lighting for the sculpture garden at the Montgomery Museum of Fine Arts. Garner Electric has also worked on expansions for the Montgomery County Courthouse and Montgomery City Hall and has worked on churches, banks, schools and medical offices across the River Region.

Most of the company's commercial work involves sharpening the pencil to get a bid just right for a general contractor. And that involves the nuances of knowing what it takes to get the job done right. "They can trust us knowing we'll do a good job," Cathy Garner said.

"If we can't do it right, we're not going to do it," Harris echoed. "We're never going to jeopardize safety."

For a successful electrical contractor, it's vital to stay current with electrical codes and licensure as well as lighting and technology trends. "That National Electric Code changes every three years," Harris said. "With technology changing, we stay up to date with energy and lighting controls and life-safety systems so that we can bring them to our customers," Harris added. "We're knowledgeable about improvements that help them save energy and money."

Garner Electric is also known for its reliability to its own team. "We take care of our employees," Cathy said. "A couple of electricians have been with us over 20 years. We would rather have our people work overtime than overstaff. We've never had a layoff, ever."

UNITED HEATING & AIR

United for Your Comfort

Pictured left to right: Bill Maxey, Jeremy Garner, Doyle Storms, Shane Morrison, Terry Brooks, Wayne Durham, Anthony Snead and Rhett Whynott

Thousands of customers in the River Region trust United for service, repair and installation of the systems that run their homes and businesses. United's founding dates back to 1985 when owner Billy Henderson formed a company handling residential and new construction of heating and air conditioning systems. In 1992, a merger with another company added to the size, and the name was changed to United.

United began light construction HVAC in the mid '90s and by the 2000s had grown to become one of the top three residential air conditioning companies in the area. During that time, the company began replacing systems in existing homes and expanded its service department. The growth continued from there. In 2007, the company added a plumbing division that included service, repair and new construction. In 2014, United added an electrical department for new construction, and small commercial and residential service.

Importantly, United remains locally owned and operated with a fully staffed team of 80 employees that are ready to serve. Longevity is a strength of this team. Several employees have been with the company 25 years or more, and many have served 10 to 20 years. Each contracting trade features its own licensed specialists.

United is also known for its responsiveness and personal touch. The company offers 24/7 service, and if you've got a problem, you get a call back.

In the large warehouse at the Mobile Highway location, United is fully stocked with supplies that are easily accessible for service to customers. This location also features a shop area where it can build its own ductwork, and there are two other locations in Millbrook. The company's sizable coverage area extends as far north as the north side of Lake Martin, as far south as Troy, east to Auburn/Opelika, and as far west as Selma.

United is also heavily involved in the River Region community. For example, the company sponsors local sports teams and also supports charities. At various times, the company has donated $100 for every installation toward a charity such as the American Cancer Society or American Heart Association. United also hosts a golf tournament for the local Boy Scouts of America organization and has raised tens of thousands of dollars over 20 years.

Ultimately, United takes pride in being a "no shortcut" company with a reputation for quality work and treating its customers right.

Ken Hendrick and his wife, Sandy.

Bobby Knepper, Ken Hendrick and Sunny Knepper

> "Our employees and the level of service we provide are what has separated us as a company,"
>
> - Ken Hendrick, owner of Stanley Steemer in Montgomery

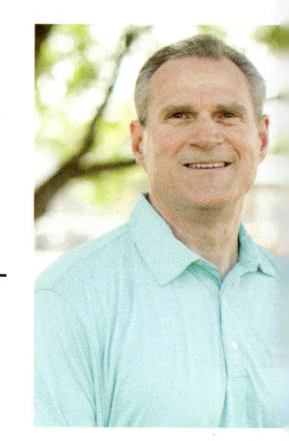

STANLEY STEEMER

With its recognizable yellow trucks, clean-cut uniformed crews and catchy jingles, Stanley Steemer is the company most people associate with quality carpet, hardwood, tile and grout cleaning. The company got its start with founder Jack Bates in 1947 in Dublin, Ohio as a single-truck operation and found early success. In the 1970s, Jack's son Wes joined the company. At that point they began franchising and never looked back. Today, Stanley Steemer has grown into 300+ operations in 49 states and is led by Justin Bates, Wes' son. The Montgomery location opened in 1980, with Richard and Nancy Crunkleton at the helm and built a firm foundation for continued success. Today, the Montgomery location is owned by Ken Hendrick and still making an imprint on households across the tri-county area. It even services customers as far north as Clanton, as far south as Troy, as far west as Selma and as far east as Auburn/Opelika.

When Hendrick went to work at Stanley Steemer in Montgomery in 1985, he never intended to become the owner of a franchise. "It was my first job out of college," said Hendrick. "The only reason I came to work here was because I had a few friends who worked here." For Hendrick, it was intended to just be a part-time job while he waited for the NFL draft. But there were other plans in store.

When his hopes of joining an NFL team didn't go as planned, Hendrick joined Stanley Steemer full-time. A few years later, corporate took notice and hired him to work at the Stanley Steemer headquarters in Ohio. After his stint at corporate, he even launched out on his own, starting a local carpet-cleaning company in Montgomery while still maintaining a good relationship with the Bates family. This eventually led to Hendrick purchasing his first of several franchises in 2000 in North Alabama in Huntsville, Florence and Muscle Shoals. Within one year, he bought the Montgomery location, as well as several others in the state. Today, Hendrick operates the Columbus, Georgia and Montgomery locations. He's proud of the reputation Stanley Steemer has maintained over the years and, most importantly, the team it hires to serve its customers.

"When we hire people I tell them that I'm an example of the opportunities that Stanley Steemer provides," said Hendrick. "The opportunities are unlimited. I had no idea when I started I would own a franchise. I had no experience in business. It was service, which is where my heart is." Today, Hendrick checks on his crews, does estimates and ensures unparalleled service, and that the impression his employees leave in every home sets the tone for a great customer experience. "Our employees and the level of service we provide are what has separated us as a company," said Hendrick.

River-Region-based companies like Goodwyn Mills and Cawood play an essential role in building the area's future, often by doing work far beyond the region's borders.

BORDEN MORRIS GARNER CONSULTING ENGINEERS

Quality Design in Every Project

Borden Morris Garner Consulting Engineers is well known by clients across the Southeast and especially in downtown Montgomery, where the hometown firm has been actively involved in numerous projects revitalizing the city's historic buildings and surroundings. One of the few firms in the River Region that generates MEP designs (which includes mechanical, electrical, plumbing and fire protection), Borden Morris Garner has experience in project planning, project analysis, energy studies, system design, construction supervision and project management. Since its founding in 1985, the firm has completed more than 400 school designs, over 150 church designs, over 200 apartment complexes, as well as projects for local and state governments and commercial and industrial clients. Also of note, they designed the street lighting and power distribution for the streetscape in downtown Montgomery, starting at the Court Square Fountain all the way to the State Capitol. The firm uses the latest design technology to create accurate and easy-to-follow construction documents and stays involved during the construction phase to ensure quality work and to assist the contractor in successful project completion. Located in downtown Montgomery, Borden Morris Garner is licensed in 10 states.

ROSS–CLAYTON FUNERAL HOME, INC.

Serving Four Generations for 100 Years as Montgomery's Oldest Minority Owned Business

In a small space on Monroe Street in the heart of downtown Montgomery in 1918, Robert Ambers Ross, an insurance agent for Mississippi Life, decided to open his undertaking business. Ross soon formed a partnership with a married couple named William and Frazzie Clayton, the former of whom served as embalmer. In 1929, the company became a corporation and continued operating on Monroe Street until 1939 when it relocated to 524 South Union Street. Today, the funeral home conducts business from its new building constructed in 2011 at 1412 Adams Avenue.

The company has stayed in the careful hands of four generations to date as they continue to serve families in the River Region. In 2018, the company celebrated 100 years, making it the oldest surviving minority owned business in the capital city. A proud moment for Ross-Clayton.

Today, the corporation operates under the leadership of David C. Ross, Jr. David has served as president since he was appointed by his father, D. Calloway Ross, in 1978. Ross-Clayton employs 13 Licensed Funeral Directors and Embalmers and more than 30 part-time personnel who continue to carry on the important work and legacy of this honorable and long-standing Montgomery corporation.

Manufacturing in the River Region is moving full steam ahead with companies like Hyundai Motor Manufacturing Alabama and its state-of-the-art facility. But the reach of manufacturing extends beyond the automotive sector. Everything from syrup to steel is produced in plants large and small throughout the area.

Photo courtesy of HMMA

RALPH SMITH MOTORS

Celebrating 75 years in Business

Ralph Smith Motors celebrated 75 years in 2017, making it the oldest active independent automobile dealer in the state. Its story of success begins with a sewing machine salesman with a ninth-grade education named Ralph O. Smith from Balm, Alabama, who came to town to try his hand at sales.

In 1941, Ralph's sales expertise found him selling cars at McGough Chevrolet. It seemed like he might stay forever, but then, in the words of then-President Roosevelt, "a sleeping giant" awoke. WWII changed everything, including automobile manufacturing. Early in 1942, all manufacturing of automobiles stopped. But Ralph did not. Instead, he started his own business. On March 5, 1942, on the corner of Church and Molton Street, Ralph Smith Motors opened for business.

The world wasn't the only place that was divided in 1942. Mr. Smith resolved not to hang the "Whites Only" sign that dominated so much of the commercial landscape in those days. Instead, he treated all as a valued customer, honoring each person and earning their honor in return.

Today, the dealership specializes in used auto sales and in-house financing. As for the secret to the company's longevity? The legacy of Ralph Smith is still seen today in the way they take care of their customers.

STANDOUT: *Montgomery's Oldest Business*

"We have been in business here for 161 years and are still family owned and operated. We've made it this long because we do business by the Golden Rule: We respect our employees, vendors and customers and our word is our bond. There's been a measure of luck too. Plus, Montgomery is a business friendly city and is getting more so all the time. Our citizens are open and welcoming. We've made such progress in the last 100 years, specifically in terms of race relations. The renewal going on downtown is changing the attitude and atmosphere of the entire city. And, we're centrally located. All these things are good for business."

–Keith Sabel, President and CEO, Sabel Steel

JENKINS TIRE & AUTOMOTIVE

Mike Jenkins comes from a long line of entrepreneurs and residents of Montgomery might know his last name as synonymous with the brick industry. However, for the last six years, Mike has been making sure drivers in the River Region have all of their automotive needs met to get where they are going safely and without unexpected problems. And if there is a problem, Mike and his team know how to get you back on the road in no time.

With one location in downtown Montgomery at 38 East Jefferson Street, Jenkins Tire and Automotive is a comprehensive Tire Store and Automotive Service Center. According to Jenkins, the Jenkins Tire and Automotive philosophy is simple. "We always deliver and we always exceed customer expectations. That's why when they need high quality auto repair, Montgomery residents come to us." His team of experienced repair professionals pride themselves on customer service that is unmatched while giving customers the satisfaction of knowing their vehicle is in good hands.

Foundation for Progress
Politics & Government

Anchoring one end of Dexter Avenue atop Goat Hill in downtown Montgomery, The Alabama State Capitol building is the center of the state's political history and current political life, housing the governor's office as well as other executive branch offices. It's also a museum. A designated National Historic Landmark, the Greek Revival building with its stately columns and gleaming white dome was completed in 1851. Several additions have been made throughout the years. Photo by Jonathon Kohn

In its function as the capital city of Alabama (a role it's played since 1846), Montgomery is the center of the state's political life. The governor lives here and the gleaming white dome of the Capitol building casts a strong shadow on our downtown streets. The Alabama Legislature struggles each session to meet the needs of Alabama citizens and find solutions to challenges, resulting in sometimes intense fights for funds, debates over policy and battles waged over bills as they search for the balance that will keep Alabama moving forward.

While this means Montgomery is often ground zero for a large portion of Alabama's political news – the good, the bad and the just plain interesting – the significance of being the state capital goes well beyond the results of the work done here and the attention – and visitors – this draws to the region. From a purely practical standpoint, it's vital to our area's future. State government operations alone employ nearly 12,000 people in the River Region, and federal government jobs come here too, thanks to Montgomery's capital status. With the addition of cities and counties, government jobs form a crucial pillar in the foundation of the area's economic prosperity.

The men and women of the River Region's fire and police departments and other first responders take their call to protect and serve seriously.

Photo by Robert Fouts

Photo courtesy of the Montgomery CVB

Politics (and politicians) often hog the spotlight, but our area's public services, also functions of the government, are essential to our daily lives. Our law enforcement officers all over the River Region ensure safety and order is maintained, and our fire fighters are always ready to answer when called. Public transportation options help keep all of our residents moving, and our public library systems are institutions of information and learning that wield an influence, especially on young lives, that should never be underestimated.

Photo by Jonathon Kohn

"MPD works every day to strengthen our relationship with the community. Working together with the community allows MPD to better serve the citizens of this great city. Our commitment to a safe Montgomery provides security for the city's current and future generations."

-Chief Finley, Montgomery Police Department

Photo courtesy of Montgomery MPD

Serving the City

Patrol Officer Stacy B. McKenzie Jr. has been employed with the Montgomery Police Department since 2015 and became a police officer because he wanted his career to make a difference. "I love seeing the positive change and impact I bring to the individuals in my family, as well as in my community doing this work," he said. "I also enjoy showing children they can accomplish any goal by working hard and staying positive in all situations. Because I was born and raised in Montgomery, I will always have a strong sense of respect for my fellow citizens. I see my job as a way to serve our city." McKenzie is also working to bridge divides in our city, especially among young people. "I live and work by this motto: Peace be still." It's based on the Bible verse Mark 4:39: "Then he arose and rebuked the wind, and said to the sea, 'Peace, Be still!' And the wind ceased and there was a great calm." "Police officers are also known as peace officers, so I strive to cease crime and increase peace," McKenzie said.

The interior of the Capitol dome is a stunning work of art. The eight murals flanking the stained-glass pinnacle of the rotunda depict important moments in Alabama history and were painted by London-born but Alabama-raised artist Roderick MacKenzie in the 1920s.
Photo by Eric Salas

CHIP NIX, ATTORNEY AT LAW

A Montgomery Personal Injury Lawyer Helping His Clients Move Forward

For more than 40 years, Montgomery attorney Chip Nix has been dealing with personal injury claims involving the most serious and catastrophic injuries. As founder of the office of Chip Nix, Attorney at Law, he is devoted to helping injured workers and others recover the compensation they need to deal with their medical expenses and lost income, and recuperate to the maximum extent possible.

From industrial accidents to any type of injury or death at home or on the road, Nix works hard to get his clients the benefits and compensation they need and deserve. He also represents victims of fraud or legal malpractice statewide.

Chip Nix is an attorney who truly cares about the people he represents, and he pursues the best result in each individual case. With his extensive experience, he understands that the first offer is rarely the best offer, and he takes time to fully understand the extent of his client's medical needs and the full amount of the client's legal damages.

During the course of his career, Nix has built a reputation for excellence. He is Board Certified in Civil Trial Practice by the National Board of Trial Advocacy and has served as an Administrative Law Judge in various disputes. He has experience as both a mediator and arbitrator. Nix is also the former president of the Alabama Defense Lawyers Association, a statewide organization that boasts more than 1,200 members.

Chip Nix serves the greater Montgomery area and beyond – from Selma to Phenix City, from Huntsville to Mobile, and all across the state of Alabama. Practice areas include products liability, wrongful death, car accidents, industrial accidents, traumatic brain injuries and truck accidents.

A Montgomery native, Nix attended Montgomery Public Schools and has known since seventh grade that he wanted to be a trial lawyer. He graduated from Auburn University and was awarded Phi Eta Sigma, a scholastic honorary. He then attended the University of Alabama School of Law, where he was on the National Moot Court Team. He began his legal career upon admission to the Alabama State Bar in 1973. Since then, he has spent more than four decades serving clients in numerous cases throughout the state.

Chip Nix provides free case consultation and also offers flexible hours for scheduling meetings, including arranging for hospital or home visits.

A Partnership for Progress

"Beginning in the late 1960s, the downtown area would begin to experience decades of decline and disinvestment. But now, in 2018, downtown Montgomery is renewing itself and moving forward.

The city challenged itself to take on major catalytic investments in the early 2000s, from the Montgomery Performing Arts Center, Convention Center, Riverfront Park and Amphitheatre, Riverwalk Stadium, and Cramton Bowl Multiplex sports area, to more recent projects, like the Alley Entertainment District and Lower Dexter Avenue property and streetscape improvements.

After 2011 and through today, the City of Montgomery has been actively selling buildings and properties for redevelopment on which more than 200 new apartments, a new hotel, and a new national memorial would be built; on which more than $23 million of major renovations would occur. There is more still to come. At long last, the seeds of these revitalization efforts have grown and spread confidently to the private sector. New efforts and new businesses are being initiated completely without city support. Downtown revitalization is now decidedly underway and Montgomery has positioned itself well for future growth."

-Lois Cortell, Senior Development Manager, Department of Development

From left in front Kenneth Shinbaum, Julian McPhillips and Joe Guillot. From left in rear Jim Bodin, Tanitha Finney, Chase Estes and Aaron Luck.

Julian McPhillips and his wife, Leslie.

The entire law firm in December 2017.

MCPHILLIPS SHINBAUM, LLP

And Julian McPhillips, The People's Lawyer

McPhillips Shinbaum, LLP, "The People's Law Firm," reached its 40th anniversary in September 2018. Over the years, it has successfully pursued landmark cases involving civil rights, race, age, sex, and disability discrimination, personal injury, criminal defense and police brutality. Today, the seven-attorney litigation firm represents clients throughout Alabama in state and federal court, routinely fighting against insurance companies, government agencies, and businesses, protecting its clients' rights and providing them with the justice they deserve.

The firm's founder, Julian McPhillips, has long been called "The People's Lawyer." That is also the title of a book written by Carroll Dale Short about Julian in 2000, and co-authored by Julian in a 2005 re-publication. Julian is a "Renaissance man," with many interests; he is senior minister at Christ the Redeemer Episcopal Church and board chair of the Scott and Zelda Fitzgerald Museum. He is also the Johnny Appleseed of high school wrestling (having founded and coached several Montgomery teams), and author of "Civil Rights in My Bones," and "From Vacillation to Resolve: the French Communist Party in the Resistance against the Nazis."

McPhillips puts family first as a father of two grown daughters, one grown son, and five grandchildren. He is also devoted to his wife of 45 years, Leslie, with whom he has enjoyed extensive international travel.

Born in 1946, McPhillips grew up in Cullman, Alabama, where his father headed a successful vegetable canning business before becoming a priest in 1962 and moving the family to Montgomery. In 1964, McPhillips graduated from Sewanee Military Academy in Tennessee; in 1968 with honors from Princeton University (where he was undefeated in four years of Ivy League wrestling and where he and his family celebrated his 50th anniversary in June 2018); and from Columbia University Law School in 1971. He then worked four years on Wall Street before returning to Alabama in 1975. His strong interest in politics fueled a close run for Alabama Attorney General in 1978. He has been a four-time delegate to the Democratic National Convention and a U.S. Senate candidate in 2002.

McPhillips has enjoyed establishing the firm that for 40 years has carried his name, while building a reputation as a tireless advocate for the underdog. The next partner, Kenneth Shinbaum, has been with the firm 33 years and provides strategic leadership, while Joe Guillot, a retired Air Force Lt. Colonel, Aaron Luck and Jim Bodin have been with the firm more than 20 years - all adding muscle and experience in the personal injury, criminal and employment sectors. The two associate attorneys, Chase Estes and Tanitha Finney, provide youthful energy.

The Business Council of Alabama, based in Montgomery, represents the interests of the state's diverse businesses community, from small mom-and-pop shops to Fortune 500 companies.

Linking Past & Present

"Montgomery once served briefly as the capital of a foreign country, until Union victory in the Civil War returned it as the seat of government for the state that will celebrate its bicentennial in 2019. Montgomery is a unique town that has deep links with past traditions and that looks toward the future as Alabama continues to evolve from a largely rural, agriculture state to one in which urban areas strive to dominate the cultural, political and business landscape. Being the seat of government draws the attention of political junkies, tourists and history buffs here. Plus, the Montgomery metro area's thousands of state employees and their earnings, along with significant federal and local government employment, underpin the four-county region's economic well-being."

- Jeremy Arthur, President and CEO of the Chamber of Commerce Association of Alabama

The River Region's municipal governments remain committed to bringing employment opportunities through continued economic development throughout the area and often work in close partnerships for the benefit of the region.

Photos by Becca Beers

"At its core, Montgomery is a pretty small town with small town values that have been lost in a lot of places. While it is culturally a lot different from where I grew up in Michigan, it has been a great place to raise a family. It is a place with a sense of community, good people and a thriving place to raise kids. The biggest change in my 25 years here in terms of politics has been a change from one-party Democratic rule to one-party Republican rule. I don't think either is very good for citizens. I think more than anything, Montgomery's and Alabama's political history are its most interesting political aspects. The George Wallace-Frank Johnson civil rights battles are important historical events for the state and country."

**- John Anzalone, Anzalone Liszt Grove Research,
a public opinion research firm
headquartered in Montgomery**

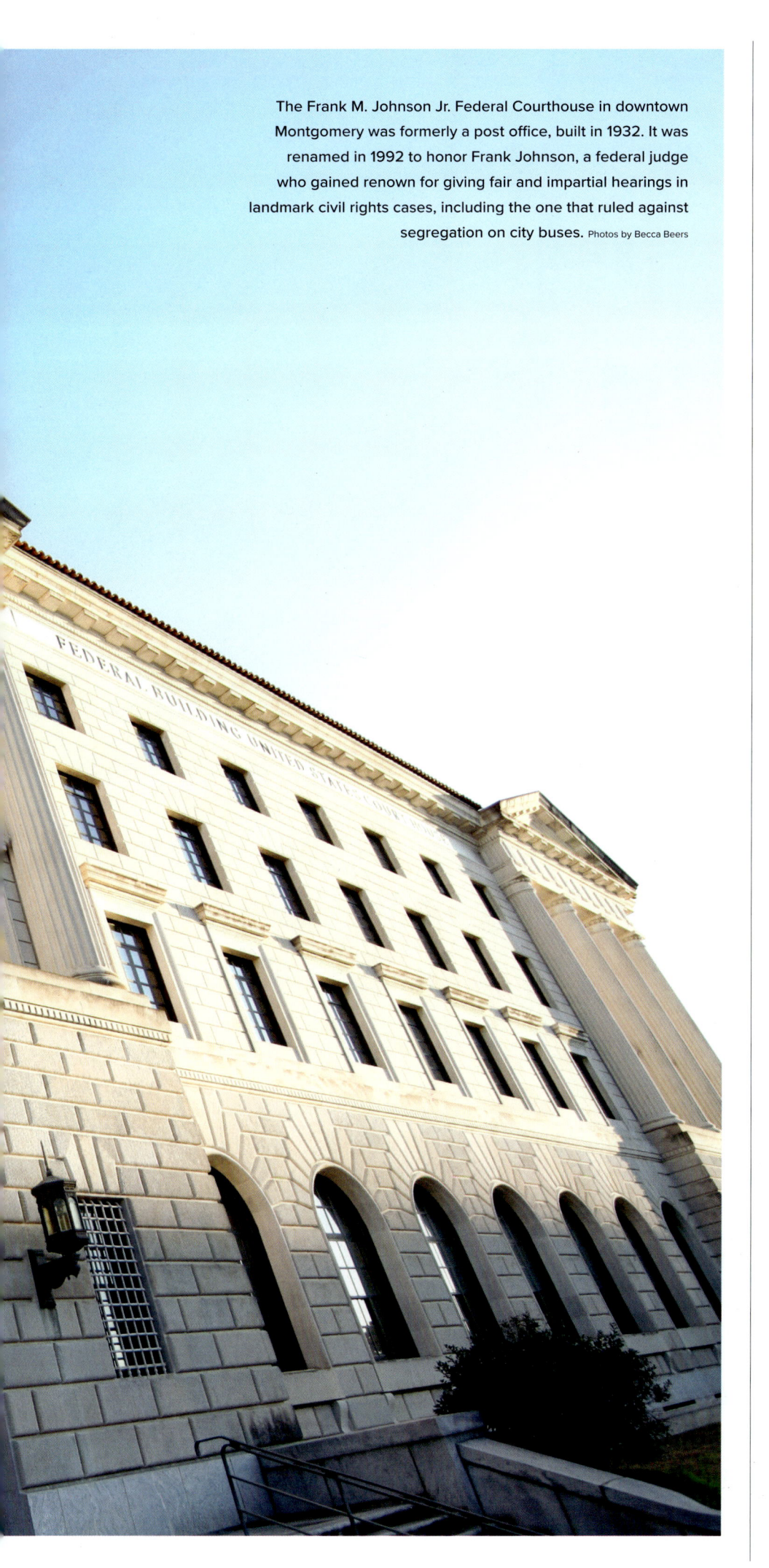

The Frank M. Johnson Jr. Federal Courthouse in downtown Montgomery was formerly a post office, built in 1932. It was renamed in 1992 to honor Frank Johnson, a federal judge who gained renown for giving fair and impartial hearings in landmark civil rights cases, including the one that ruled against segregation on city buses. Photos by Becca Beers

THE JOE HUBBARD LAW FIRM

After serving in the Alabama Legislature and receiving the Democratic party nomination for Alabama Attorney General, Joe Hubbard set out to build an innovative model for legal service in Alabama. Since 2010, Joe has successfully leveraged his political experience and relationships to deliver results for his clients in courtrooms across Alabama and the Southeast.

The Joe Hubbard Law Firm devotes much of its practice to representing individuals and businesses in a variety of litigation matters with the belief that for every wrong there is a remedy. Joe is a leader in delivering out-of-the-box solutions to complicated matters and was even named one of the top trial lawyers under 40 by the National Trial Lawyers Association. The Joe Hubbard Law Firm sets itself apart by providing personal service at a lower cost without sacrificing results. The firm prides itself in offering a passionate, proven approach and top-rate customer service all while delivering the flexibility and responsiveness their clients deserve.

The RSA Dexter Avenue building is an amazing architectural feat. The modern structure encapsulates the historic State of Alabama Judicial Building, former home of the Alabama Supreme Court. In recognition, the building features an Honor Court on its grounds with five life-size bronze statues of past Chief Justices. Photos by Becca Beers

Montgomery's City Hall
Photo by Brooke Glassford / Colorbox

The Force is With Us
Maxwell Gunter AFB

Montgomery has been named the "Best Hometown of the Air Force."

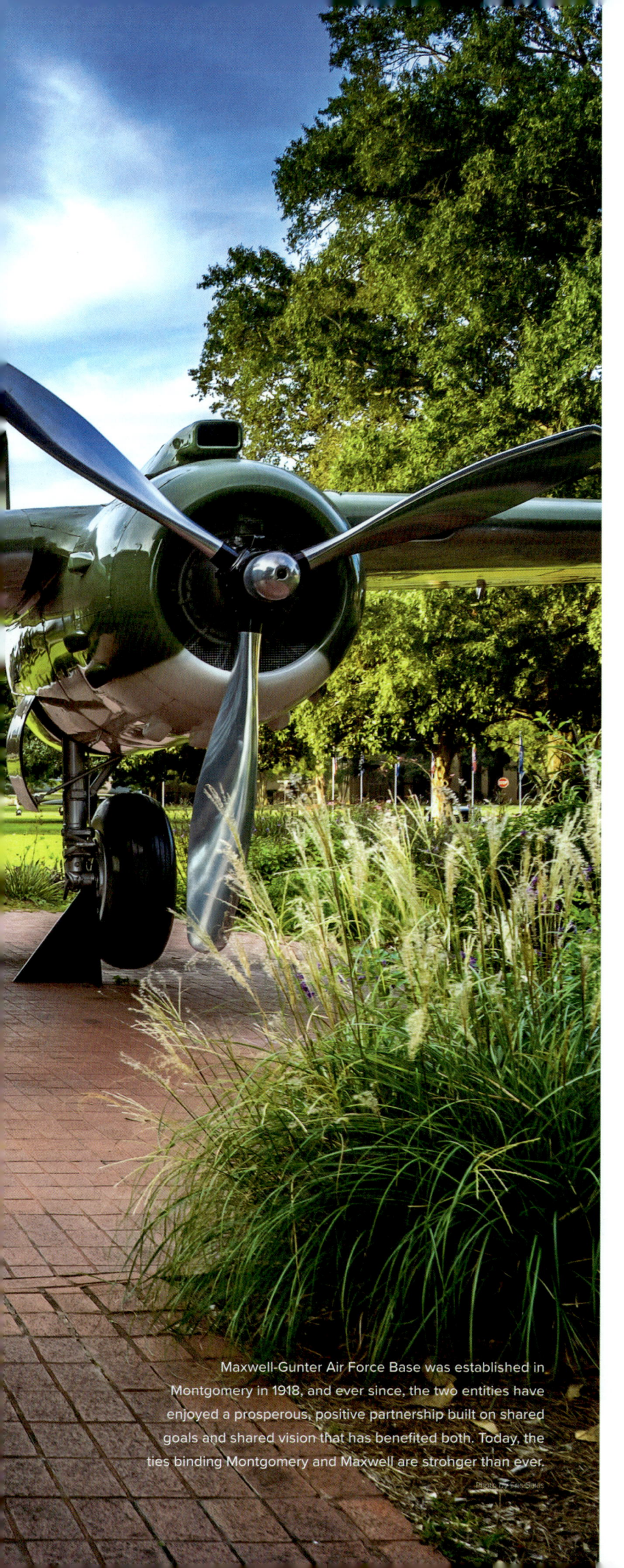

Maxwell-Gunter Air Force Base and the capital city have been proud partners for decades. But it all began more than 100 years ago, when powered flight first took off in Alabama. In 1903, Orville and Wilbur Wright conquered the laws of gravity. Their biplane soared above the sands in Kittyhawk, North Carolina for 12 seconds and ushered in a new age of transport and travel. Seven years later, on March 26, 1910, the brothers established the nation's first civilian flying school in Montgomery at Wright Field. Though the school lasted only a short time, it set the stage for the establishment of Maxwell-Gunter Air Force Base at the very same spot.

The base's presence here contributes much to Montgomery and the surrounding River Region and, in return, area residents and businesses welcome members of the military and their families to the community. It's a mutually beneficial relationship that is key to the area's prosperity and one that continues to flourish.

Base personnel contribute to the local economy simply by being here — Maxwell-Gunter AFB has an estimated annual economic impact of $2.6 billion on the River Region, and airmen stationed at the base and their families continually donate their time and talents to the community, helping at local events and supporting area charities.

By staying on the cutting edge of aviation and information technology, Maxwell has also bolstered Montgomery's efforts to become a "cyber city." In the early 1930s, the precursor to Maxwell-Gunter AFB — the Army Air Corps Tactical School — made the city the country's intellectual center for airpower education. Today, Air University at Maxwell continues that tradition, educating tomorrow's leaders in air, space and cyberspace power for the Air Force, as well as for other branches of the U.S. armed forces, civilians and even international organizations. Its Cyber College, founded in 2017, is ensuring both current and future airmen have the operational knowledge and strategic insights to fight potential cyber attacks. This has helped make Montgomery a hub of military aviation and cyber advancements and has led to multiple information technology companies headquartering here to support the services of the base. Almost 2,000 area jobs are in direct support of the cyber and IT missions at Gunter Annex.

Montgomery has long been proud to have a military institution of such stature as part of its community. In 2015, this pride earned the city a prestigious national award, the Altus Trophy, a recognition presented annually to the city that shows the most "outstanding support to an Air Education and Training Command base." As further proof of Montgomery's dedication to local military, the city has also been named the "Best Hometown of the Air Force."

Maxwell-Gunter Air Force Base was established in Montgomery in 1918, and ever since, the two entities have enjoyed a prosperous, positive partnership built on shared goals and shared vision that has benefited both. Today, the ties binding Montgomery and Maxwell are stronger than ever.

U.S. Air Force photo by Senior Airman Tammie Ramsouer

Photo by Eric Salas

252

As the preeminent source of higher education for the Air Force, Maxwell-Gunter Air Force Base's Air University plays a critical role in our nation's defense.
Photo courtesy of the Montgomery Chamber of Commerce

"It was an amazing team effort that brought this about."
- Leslie Sanders

An array of technical innovations giving it extreme stealth and heightened maneuverability make the F-35 the most advanced fighter jet in the Air Force. It's also more survivable and less expensive to maintain than previous fighter jets.

The Sky's the Limit

The success of the effort to bring the Air Force's fleet of Lockheed Martin's F-35 Lightning II jets to Montgomery marks one of the area's most important economic development accomplishments in decades. These jets — the most sophisticated and advanced aircraft in the Air Force — will be home-based in the capital city with the historic 187th Fighter Wing.

The impact numbers are impressive. The bed down of the F-35s directly protects a collective 4,000 jobs in Alabama. The direct economic impact (salary and operations management) is estimated to be more than $100 million annually.

While they won't arrive until 2023, the boost to employment, image and more started as soon as the announcement came in late 2017. Capital investments are being made, existing jobs are being preserved and new ones created, and that's just the beginning, as Leslie Sanders, Vice President, Southern Division for Alabama Power and chair of the F-35 taskforce, explained. "While the direct economic impact is impressive, the cutting-edge military technology and ongoing missions at Maxwell and Gunter will attract more innovators and technology professionals here," she said. "It was an amazing team effort that brought this about. Every aspect of our community rallied in support — our military partners, business community, civic leadership and our elected leaders."

Photo courtesy of Lockheed Martin

Photos courtesy of U.S.A.F. Thunderbirds

The presence of Maxwell AFB in Montgomery routinely brings the River Region some serious excitement in the form of the Thunderbirds, the Air Force's fighter demonstration team. Their air shows feature F-16 Fighting Falcon jets emblazoned with patriotic red, white and blue performing thrilling aerial acrobatics and other flying feats, all at stellar speeds.

In its more than 100 years of existence, Maxwell-Gunter AFB has built a rich and proud history. It tells the tales of this heritage with monuments and displays around the base. This statue of Lt. Karl Richter honors a decorated fighter pilot who served in the Vietnam conflict and became the youngest pilot to shoot down a MiG jet in combat. He died after being shot down during a mission.

Photo by Eric Salas

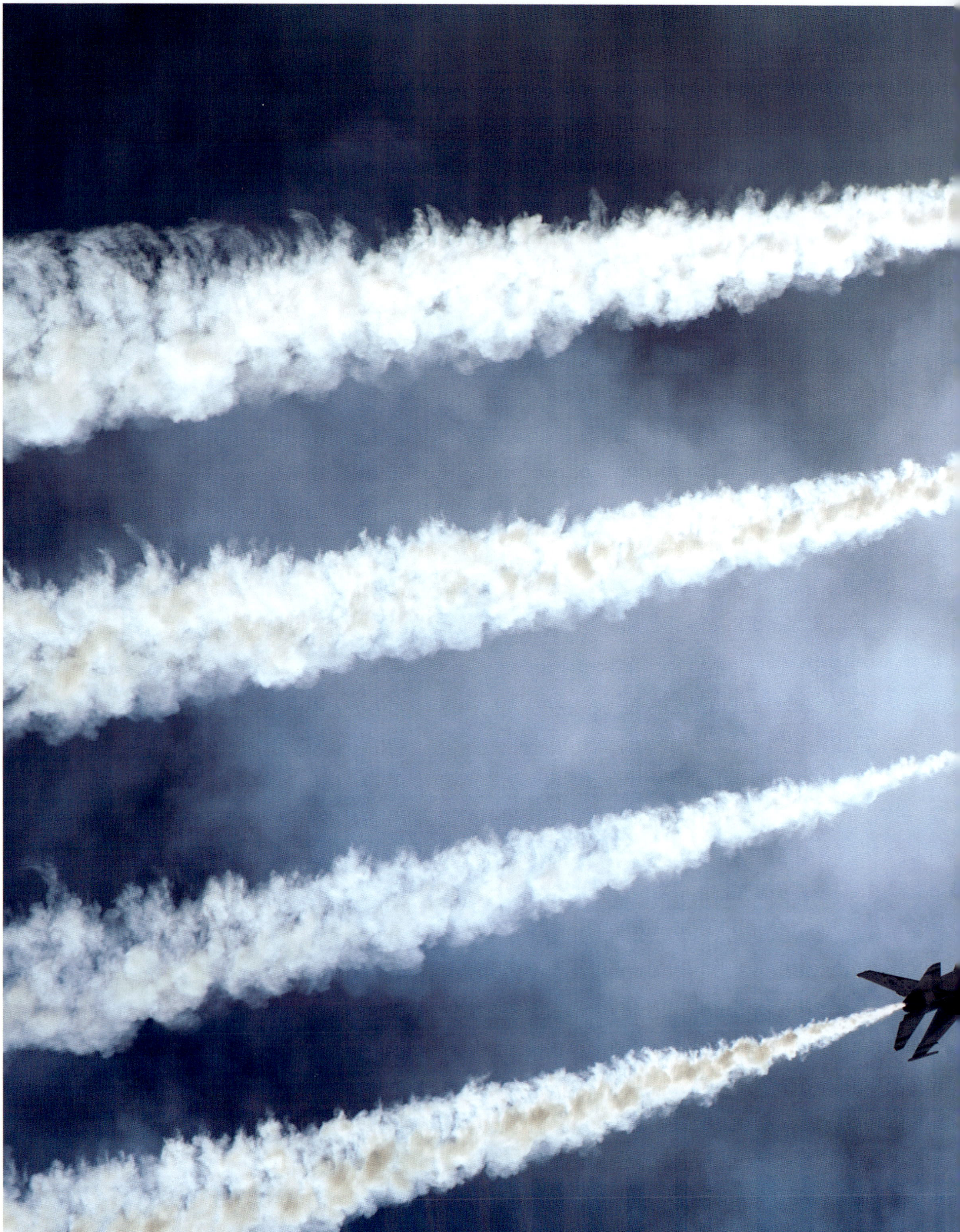

Air University: At the Forefront of Excellence

"I believe Air University is the professional military education standard-bearer, not only for the United States Air Force and its sister military and civilian services, but for this nation. While I am certain that Air University is indeed on the cutting edge — and that our great men and women are doing an awesome job in their mission of educating and developing our future leaders — we simply cannot rest on our laurels. We must constantly lean forward, think outside the box, and even look over the horizon for future threats to this nation. I also believe Montgomery and the greater River Region communities that we partner with are essential to our continuing success as a preeminent academic institution for the military. This synergistic partnership with the River Region keeps Air University at the forefront of academic excellence while, at the same time, supporting the defense of our nation in a very dangerous world of peer, near-peer, cyber, and terrorist threats."

– Lt. General Anthony Cotton, Commander of Air University

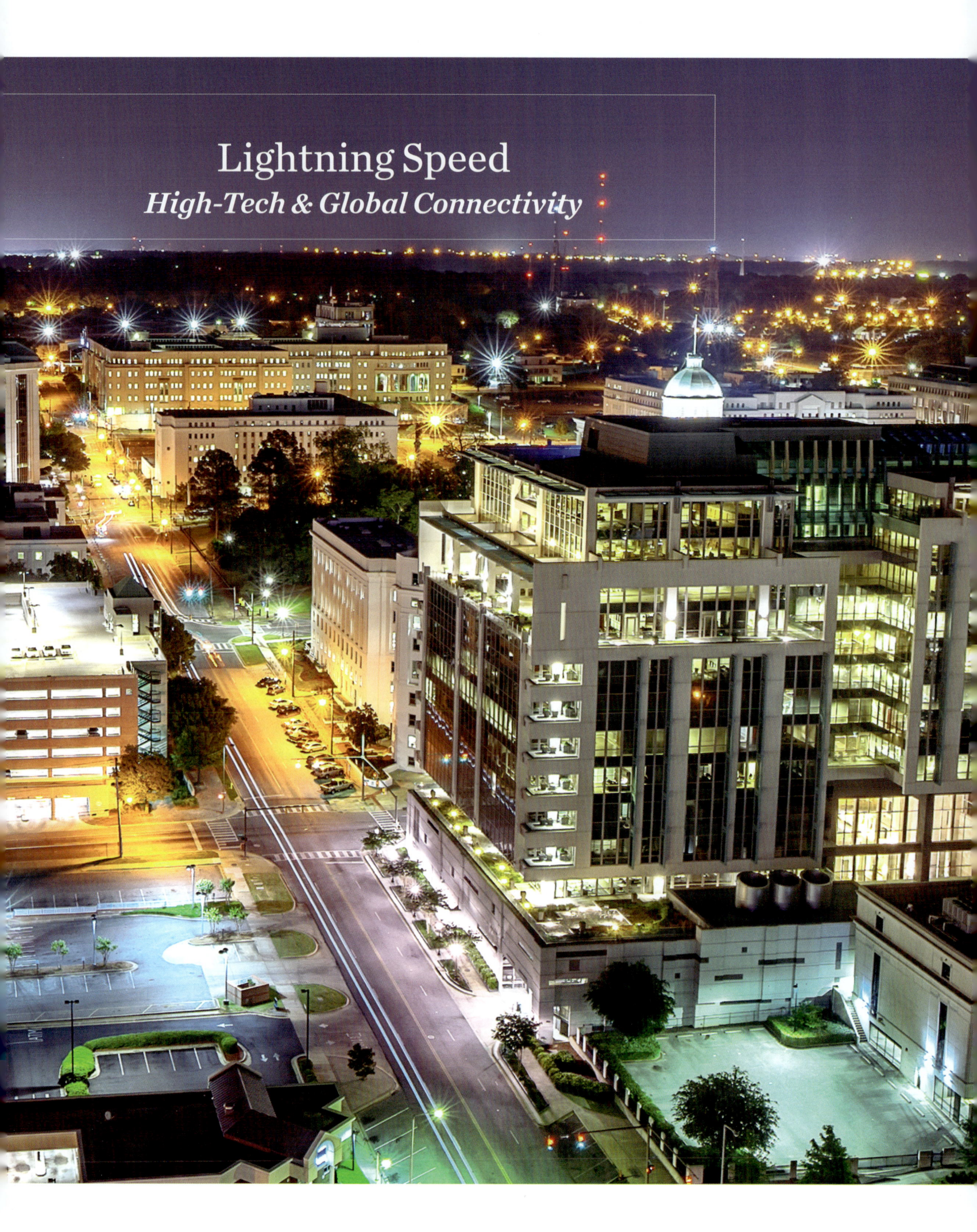

Lightning Speed
High-Tech & Global Connectivity

For Montgomery and the River Region's future growth, connectivity is key. It's a fact leaders in both the public and private sphere have acknowledged, and they are working together to fulfill the region's potential in the global marketplace.

By connecting its unique supply of cyber talent and resources, Montgomery is becoming one of the region's most vibrant and strategic "cyber cities." The continual cutting-edge advancements made at Maxwell-Gunter Air Force Base, the MGMix Internet Exchange (the only one in Alabama and one of only four in the Southeast) and the associated datacenter (one of the largest in the region), along with the city's commitment to supporting and spearheading tech-focused initiatives, have created an atmosphere of innovation benefiting both businesses and residents with lower costs for services and increased job opportunities. The area's five universities and strong partnerships between the region's local governments also play a crucial part, creating a perfect environment for exciting progress.

Montgomery's close proximity to some of the biggest metropolitan areas in the Southeast, combined with the convergence of two major interstates to connect them, makes the city a prime location with the transportation necessary for distribution and the access needed to support continued economic development.

The city's regional airport is a critical piece of the connection puzzle as well, making Montgomery and the River Region easily reachable for businesses, state government and more and linking the region with the world. And thanks to its low prices, reliability and stalwart support of community initiatives and area businesses, Alabama Power, which provides electricity for the majority of the River Region, is both literally and figuratively the power that drives much of the area's past, present and future advances in digital infrastructure and the benefits that follow.

Photo by Eric Salas

The RSA Dexter Datacenter

"The RSA Dexter Datacenter is a world-class colocation datacenter and home to the 100 gigabyte-per-second Montgomery Internet Exchange (MGMix.net) and some of the most prominent names in Alabama and the surrounding states' business community, including health care, education, real estate, accounting, government, recreation, communications, utilities, 911 services, banking, insurance, pharmaceuticals, law enforcement, legal, hotels, IT managed services, trucking, transportation, television, newspapers, plus bandwidth and networks from some of the largest providers in the world."

-Michael Blevins, Director of RSA Dexter Datacenter

The state-of-the-art, super-secure, 42,000-square-foot RSA Datacenter in downtown Montgomery is one of the most sophisticated in the country. It facilitates the MGMix Internet exchange, and both are crucial elements in building an innovation district that's drawing high-tech talent and high paying IT and cyber jobs to the region.

Photos courtesy of the RSA Dexter Datacenter

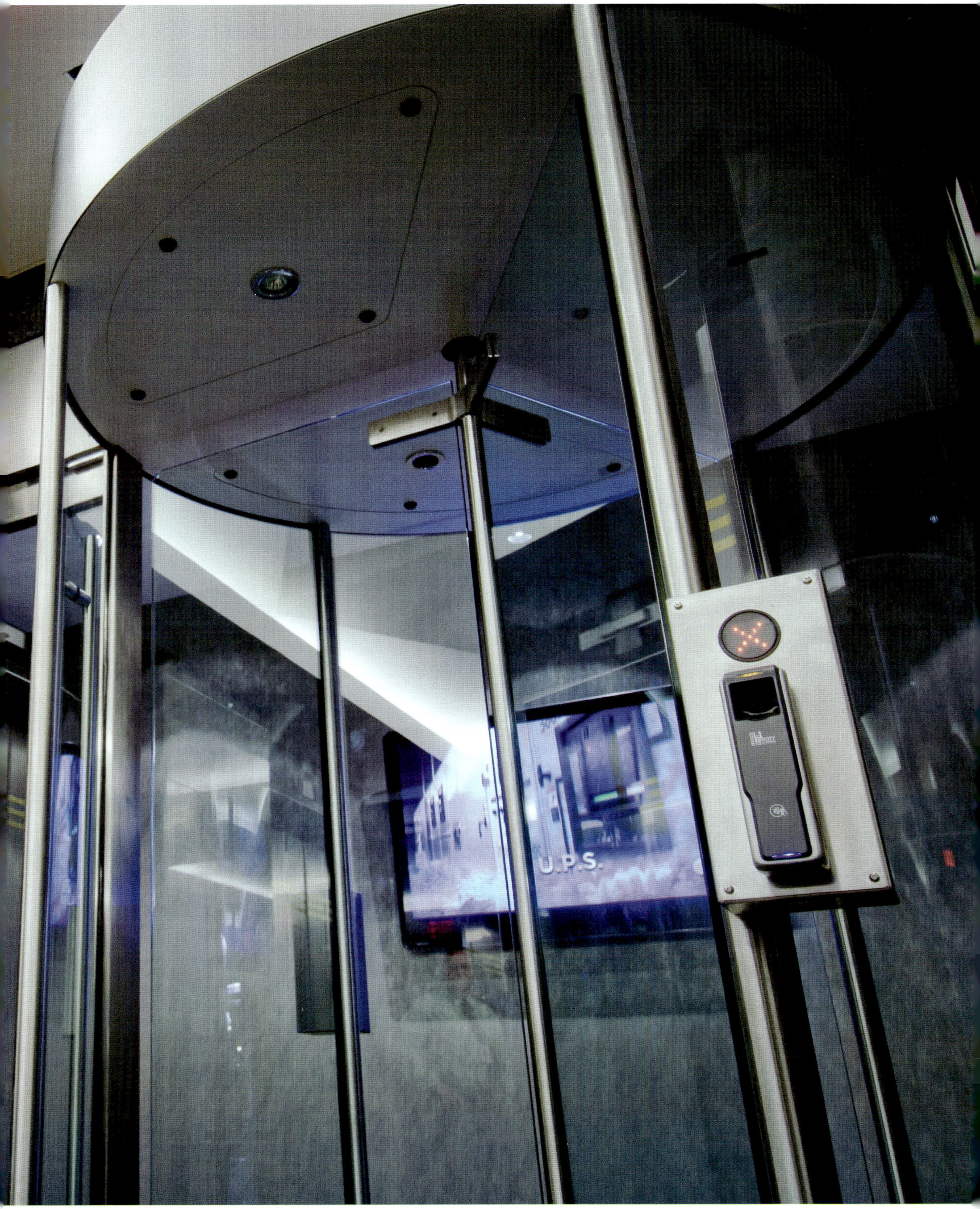
U.P.S.

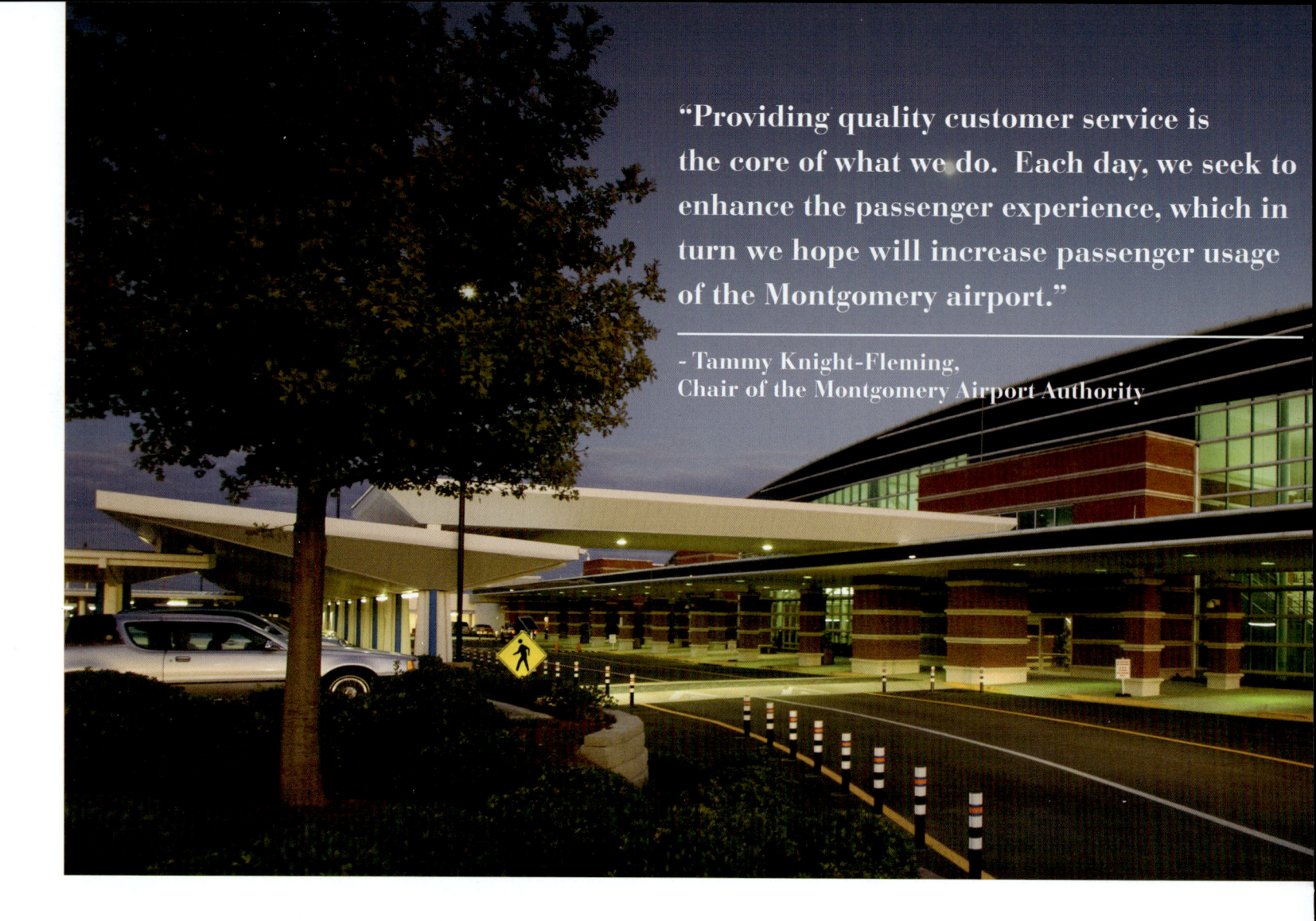

"Providing quality customer service is the core of what we do. Each day, we seek to enhance the passenger experience, which in turn we hope will increase passenger usage of the Montgomery airport."

- Tammy Knight-Fleming, Chair of the Montgomery Airport Authority

MONTGOMERY REGIONAL AIRPORT

The Montgomery Regional Airport has an impressive history that can literally trace its roots to the birth of aviation. Montgomery secured its place in the history of aviation when the Wright brothers established a civilian flight school there in 1910. Building on that legacy, military aircraft were stationed and flew from Wright's Field when the United States entered World War I in 1917. After the war, commercial airline operations as we know them today actually began at Wright's Field, later renamed Maxwell Field, in the 1920s. Maxwell Field, now Maxwell Air Force Base, is home to the 42nd Air Base Wing. It is a major training, educational and technical center for the United States Air Force and international officers from around the globe.

In 1929, Montgomery's mayor, William A. Gunter, spearheaded the effort to establish a municipal airport in Alabama's capital city. The new airport was later named Dannelly Field in honor of Ensign Clarence M. Dannelly, Jr., a Navy pilot generally considered to be the first Montgomery native to lose his life in defense preparations for World War II when he crashed in a training accident at Pensacola Naval Air Station in December 1940. In 1946, Montgomery Regional Airport (Dannelly Field) became home to an Alabama Air National Guard Fighter Wing that is still based there today, continuing Montgomery's rich partnership with the military community.

"There is no question Montgomery Regional Airport has an amazing history, but as exciting as where we've been, we're even more excited about where we're going," said Mark Wnuk, Executive Assistant. "Our legacy gives us momentum to move forward, improve what we have and make plans for the future."

In the past 15 years, for example, the airport has experienced tremendous growth, completing a three-phase, $40 million expansion that included upgrades in every area from baggage claim to parking, ticketing and passenger gates. The airport expanded its focus on customer service, adding amenities like a coffee shop and other food services, as well as the Sky Cap Ambassadors concierge service, which provides curbside baggage assistance and specialized assistance for elderly passengers and passengers with disabilities.

"Each day, we seek to enhance the passenger experience, which in turn we hope will increase passenger usage of the Montgomery airport," said Tammy Knight-Fleming, Chair of the Montgomery Airport Authority. "I believe that service standards will be critical to helping develop the use of MGM and to bringing more airlines here, which is our number one strategic goal."

Montgomery has seen three straight years of passenger growth. Three commercial airlines currently serve Montgomery. American Airlines offers three flights daily to Charlotte and two flights daily to Dallas. In 2018, American began non-stop service to Washington, DC, direct to Reagan National Airport. Delta Air Lines has seven flights daily to Atlanta. In 2017, Montgomery gained its third airline, Via, which provides service to Orlando-Sanford airport. As home of Hyundai Motor Manufacturing North America and its many suppliers, Montgomery also is an important connection for air travel to and from Korea. As of June 2017, four daily flights, two American and two Delta, to and from MGM carry Korean Air flight numbers.

The Montgomery Regional Airport is increasing the number of people who choose MGM for travel through the use of cutting-edge digital marketing efforts. This not only positions the airport to target its audience of potential customers based on location – saving time and advertising dollars – it dovetails with the City's initiative to grow technology. "Promoting Montgomery as both a departure and destination city is central to what we do. The Board views the City as a partner in that effort. We want to stay connected with the City's initiatives, which include moving technology forward with the development of the Internet Exchange," Knight-Fleming says.

An important initiative in 2017 with an eye to the future was the Montgomery Regional Airport's effort to bring the state-of-the-art F-35 fighter aircraft to Montgomery. The Montgomery Airport Authority worked tirelessly in conjunction with the City of Montgomery, Montgomery County, state and federal officials and the 187th Fighter Wing to secure Dannelly Field as one of two Guard/Reserve bed-down locations for the F-35. This included providing access to additional land for a new entrance to the 187th Fighter Squadron headquarters as well as purchasing additional acreage to extend a secondary runway to accommodate the F-35 or other aircraft required to enhance the readiness and mission capabilities of the 187th Fighter Wing well into the future. These efforts paid off, and in December 2017 it was announced that Montgomery's 187th Fighter Wing was selected to receive the new F-35 Lightning II jet — the newest, technologically advanced fighter in the nation's military arsenal — to replace their retiring aircraft.

The 187th was one of five Air National Guard sites in the U.S. considered for the Air Force's F-35 Joint Strike Fighter mission. The project will include $3 billion in investment and the addition of 1,000 jobs in the coming years, a significant economic win for the River Region and for all of Alabama.

Knight-Fleming said acquiring the F-35 at Dannelly Field will not only bring tremendous economic opportunities for Montgomery and central Alabama, it also demonstrates the continued commitment to the military and will perpetuate the legacy of Wright Field, the Tuskegee Airmen and the 187th Fighter Wing. "The 187th is important as a legacy unit of the famed Tuskegee Airmen – the Red Tail fighters – who defied stereotypes and overcame racism as the first African-American fighter pilots fighting in World War II," Knight Fleming said.

Besides the military partnership, Montgomery Regional Airport (Dannelly Field) is perfectly positioned for continued growth, both aeronautical and non-aeronautical. Montgomery is centrally located between other aeronautical developments such as Boeing to the north and Airbus to the south, and the land surrounding the airport is generally comprised of flat acreage that is development-ready. With more than 2,000 acres of land at its disposal, Montgomery Regional Airport can readily identify property for cargo, storage and other aviation-related operations. It also has sufficient land to develop non-aeronautical industries and diversify the airport's revenue stream.

"Montgomery Regional Airport is not encumbered by natural or man-made barriers that would normally hinder an airport's expansion and economic growth. Our land, location and proximity to major interstates and waterways make us an ideal candidate for economic development," Knight-Fleming said.

Photo courtesy of Montgomery Chamber of Commerce

Photo by Robert Fouts

Fly MGM

The Montgomery Regional Airport is one of six commercial airports that serve Alabama and generate nearly $4 billion in output. It is also the fundamental force that drives our area's growth and is Montgomery's connection to the world, according to Tammy Knight-Fleming, Chair of the Montgomery Airport Authority. "The Airport enables people and products to efficiently move between states, regions and nations around the world, which in turn encourages economic growth on a global scale. The Hyundai manufacturing facility located a few miles south of the airport, for example, and the nearly 100 automotive suppliers in central Alabama that support that facility are located here in no small measure because of the accessibility of convenient, affordable air service in Montgomery. Our airport also helps sustain and encourage the economic growth necessary for job creation. The high-paying jobs that airports attract require a well-educated workforce, an efficient ground and rail transportation system, affordable housing and high-speed access to the internet highway, which in turn raises the standard of living for everyone in the area," she said. And our airport keeps getting better, with constantly upgraded services and amenities. Knight-Fleming believes a place like Montgomery deserves a great airport and the opportunities and benefits it brings. "Montgomery is such a great place to live, with a deeply rooted sense of community. I see its families and businesses proud of recent growth and progress and encouraged about what's still to come. That's why our airport is important. As Montgomery's tech economy continues to evolve and expand, it will enhance upon the city's historical and cultural significance, creating opportunity and inspiring a new generation of entrepreneurs, businesses and citizens to call Montgomery home. And the Montgomery Regional Airport will be here to serve them," she said.

- **Tammy Knight-Fleming,
Chair of the Montgomery Airport Authority**

Trains have rumbled through the River Region for almost two centuries, moving goods and people all over and connecting the area to the rest of the country. An example of railway prominence still stands in Montgomery's Union Station and Trainshed, a former train station built in 1898 by the Louisville and Nashville Railroad. Rail service is still an important transportation system for the region's manufacturers today.

Photos courtesy of the Montgomery CVB / Carter Photography & Design, LLC

MONTGOMERY WATER WORKS & SANITARY SEWER BOARD

Investing in Our Community Infrastructure

After nearly 50 years at the corner of Coosa Street and Madison Avenue, Montgomery Water Works has a new home within Interstate Park off Perry Hill Road. The move took place in the spring of 2018, and now the 80,000-square-foot, four-story building is headquarters for nearly 300 employees.

"As all the growth downtown began to occur, it was exciting to see," said Buddy Morgan, who has served as General Manager of Montgomery Water Works since 1989. However, the increased pressure on downtown parking affected customer access, and the relocation made sense from a customer service standpoint. It also made sense financially. The existing property was sold for hotel and restaurant development, and the profit from the sale enabled the board to purchase and renovate the expansive space off Perry Hill Road.

The new location is also more central for a citywide customer base. Along with customer service representatives for in-person account management, the building offers four kiosks – two inside and two outside – for customers to pay their bills. Additionally, Water Works redid its website a few years back and now offers many online account features, including bill payment and stop/start service links. Plumbers and contractors can also apply online for construction permits. Montgomery Water Works is a quasi-municipality set up by an act of the state legislature. The City of Montgomery nominates and elects the nine-member board. However, Water Works is not a City department or agency, though the entities work well together. For example, customers will recognize that the services of the City's Sanitation Department are included on the bill they receive, yet that department is a separate entity. "It's for convenience. We bill the garbage on our water bill because we have a connection to every house," Morgan said.

When the utility was first established in 1949, it was located inside City Hall. The board purchased the historic 1850-built Murphy House in 1969 and moved in the next year. Water Works soon expanded to include an adjacent warehouse built in the early 1900s. But the time for change had come again. "These buildings were not conducive to what we were

> "We've been recognized across this nation for some of the things we've done. For us, it's just the best way to do it."
>
> - Buddy Morgan, General Manager of Montgomery Water Works

trying to do," Morgan said. Now with customer service, information technology, permitting and other management functions under one roof, the water-quality testing laboratory currently outside the city will also eventually move here.

In addition, the relocation made room for continued downtown redevelopment. "It's going to enhance what's going on there," Morgan added.

As it serves customers, Water Works looks long-term. "We have a 50-year long-range plan that we update every five years," Morgan said. The utility also takes a bottom-up approach to planning by involving every discipline in the discussions. "All those folks have a place at the table. The engineers are great, but these folks know what will work. We want their input."

Unlike other utilities, Water Works does not report to shareholders or a rate-setting agency. "We set our own rates," Morgan said. "Our rates are among the ten percent lowest in the nation right now." He also added that Water Works is one of the top ten in the nation in terms of financial solvency. Yet all its resources goes back into the system that serves customers. "We're spending about $35 million a year to rehab or replace sewer lines," Morgan said.

"We have $3 billion worth of major infrastructure in the ground. All of our funding goes straight back into the ground. We put all of our money back into rehabbing the system, not into someone's pocket."

Maintaining the system is also a part of maintaining quality. Montgomery Water Works releases an annual consumer confidence report on water quality, and works hard to test and maintain quality. "We pull 80 water samples a day, seven days a week to make sure we're in compliance," Morgan said.

Water Works also works with industries whose processes negatively impact waste water. "They have to pretreat it before it gets to us. Otherwise, we clean it and penalize them," Morgan said. "We put them on a pretreatment contract to make sure we're not subsidizing an industry on the backs of rate payers. Most of our industries have done a great job."

Reducing grease clogs in the sewer lines is also an important initiative to maintain the infrastructure. For example, fast food restaurants have grease traps that have to be pumped periodically. "We stay on top of them to maintain grease traps," Morgan said. Water Works also offers a grease recycling program for homeowners.

"We have run this like a business," Morgan said. "We have tried to treat our customers with the most respect we possibly can. We've been recognized across this nation for some of the things we've done. For us, it's just the best way to do it."

The Airforce Information Technology and Cyberpower conference hosted in Montgomery brings together Air Force IT experts, prominent IT academics and America's best cyber security. The three-day conference revolves around the ways we can better defend America from cyber-attacks, advanced persistent threats and proactively lead in this in this increasingly digital world.

Photos courtesy of Montgomery Chamber of Commerce / Carter Photography & Design, LLC

ALABAMA POWER COMPANY

More than 100 years ago, William Patrick Lay, a Gadsden steamboat captain, envisioned a better Alabama, and the path to that vision was found in Alabama's rivers and shoals. On Dec. 4, 1906, Lay founded Alabama Power Company and began plans to build a dam on the Coosa River between Chilton and Coosa counties.

From left: William Patrick Lay, James Mitchell and Thomas Martin.

Like many innovators, Lay's idea wasn't without obstacles. He found that investment capital in the state and interest by investors on Wall Street were hard to come by. In 1911, James Mitchell, a Massachusetts engineer, visited a proposed dam site on the Tallapoosa River. He reached out to Thomas Martin, a Montgomery attorney familiar with the state's dam laws. Mitchell had connections with a London investment company that had allowed him the resources to purchase several companies formed to build dams but was short on the capital to complete the projects. One of these companies was Alabama Power Company. On May 1, 1912, Lay transferred ownership of the company to Mitchell and associates. "I now commit to you the good name and destiny of Alabama Power Company. May it be developed for the service of Alabama," Lay said.

Today, Alabama Power serves more than 1.4 million homes across the state and 194,000 customers in the Southern Division. More than a century has passed since the company's inception, but its mission remains the same—to make Alabama better.

"A commitment to elevating our state has guided Alabama Power for more than 110 years, and remains strong today," said Chairman, President and CEO Mark Crosswhite. "Providing reliable electricity, partnering to drive economic development and being active members of the communities we serve are the foundations of our business."

The Alabama Power Foundation supports a wide spectrum of nonprofit organizations throughout the state, and Alabama Power employees and retirees volunteer their time and resources to support communities through the Alabama Power Service Organization and the Energizers retiree service organization. In the River Region, these organizations served more than 2,000 hours in the community in 2016.

In today's world of rapidly changing technology, the spirit of innovation that Lay brought to the early days of Alabama Power continues to shine brightly. The company is focused on developing innovative products and services that help customers use energy more easily and efficiently.

Leslie Sanders, Southern Division vice-president, said the company is committed to partnering with the River Region to advance the community and its residents.

"Alabama Power is proud to partner with communities throughout the River Region. We work every day to deliver reliable, affordable and safe electricity," Sanders said. "More broadly, our company continually invests in our communities, whether through economic and job creation efforts or education and health initiatives. Alabama Power has embraced this mission for more than 100 years and will continue to look for ways to meet the challenges and opportunities afforded in the future."

Working to build a better Alabama is the heart of our mission, and we are honored to partner with our communities and citizens as we all work to elevate Alabama.

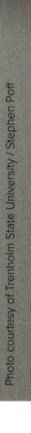

The TechMGM Vision

The City of Montgomery's Cyber Coordinator Carl Barranco has been on the forefront of the IT industry in the River Region for the last 15 years, leading the development of Warren Averett's IT company when he worked there. He's now spreading the message of technology's importance to the city's future and helping merge the work of the public and private sectors to keep recent progress going. "We have to move in this direction as the role of technology grows in all of our lives," he said. "With partnerships and relationships between the military, our academic institutions and the city, county and state governments, Montgomery has all the pieces necessary to make the city's and Chamber's TechMGM vision a reality."

- Carl Barranco,
the City of Montgomery's
Cyber Coordinator

WARREN AVERETT TECHNOLOGY GROUP

Technology Solutions to Help You Thrive

Though keeping up with escalating information technology demands is a challenge for today's businesses, Warren Averett Technology Group eases the burden. The Firm helps clients maximize the use of technology to drive growth, streamline costs and improve performance. Their team of professionals does so through a broad range of solutions, including security services, proven business and accounting software applications, risk and compliance solutions, system infrastructure support, cloud solutions, and outsourced IT services.

Warren Averett Technology Group, an affiliate company of Warren Averett, LLC, is headquartered in Montgomery, Alabama, and provides cutting-edge technology services. The Firm, which was ranked in the Top 130 Managed Service Providers in the world by MSPmentor 501, provides solutions to a wide array of industries, including legal, health care, government contracting, manufacturing and insurance, just to name a few. Their team members have extensive experience, not only through education and certifications, but also in specific industries so they are able to step into a client's shoes and understand their needs seamlessly. Some of the team's specialized certifications include:

- Certified Information Technology Professionals (CITP)
- Certified Information Security Managers (CISM)
- Certified Ethical Hackers (CEH)
- Microsoft Certified Information Technology Professionals (MCITP)
- Certified Information System Security Professionals (CISSP)
- Project Manager Professionals (PMP)
- Microsoft Certified Product Specialists (MCPS)
- Microsoft Certified Network Product Specialists (MCNPS)
- Microsoft Certified System Administrators (MCSA)
- Microsoft Certified Solutions Experts (MCSE)
- Microsoft Certified Technology Specialists (MCTS)
- Microsoft Certified Business Management Solutions Specialists (MBSS)
- Cisco Certified Entry Level Network Techs (CCENT)
- Microsoft Dynamics and Sage 100
- Network+, Security+ and A+

Whether a company is interested in minimizing risks and increasing security measures, or trying to streamline technology processes to maximize efficiency, Warren Averett Technology Group creates an individualized plan to meet their needs. Industry-certified consultants analyze a client's unique needs as the starting point for the design of a powerful, productive IT strategy. Focused on strengthening IT capabilities and boosting business results, they deliver the tools needed to protect data as well as maximize network performance and efficiency. In addition, software consultants with expertise across a variety of industries install and support proven solutions to streamline business functions, such as HR, payroll and enterprise resource planning. With cyber crime on the rise over the last few years, one of the focuses of Warren Averett Technology Group has been cyber security. From risk assessments and remediation to cloud-based back-up solutions and hosting, their goal is to help businesses prevent and prepare for possible attacks.

Warren Averett Technology Group is committed to providing the highest level of service in order to ensure a trusted partnership for years to come. Services are offered in the following areas:

- Business Software Evaluation, Implementation and Consultation
- Software Integration
- Cloud Hosting
- Cloud-Based Backup and Storage
- Disaster Recovery & Continuity Planning
- Remote Desktop Services (RDS)
- Risk Assessments
- Vulnerability Scans
- Penetration Tests
- Risk Remediation
- Compliance Consulting for PCI, HIPAA, FAR and DFARS
- Managed Service Provider (MSP) Solutions
- Network Engineering and Management

> "The River Region has something even more important, the feeling of family that surrounds all of us."
> - Quincy Minor

Focus on Tech

"The River Region's tech sector was traditionally defined by the public-sector market, but over the past 10 years, we have seen an additional focus on the commercial markets. We have the most technically advanced automobile manufacturing facility in the United States at Hyundai Motor Manufacturing Alabama. That and health care have provided an additional focus in the River Region requiring new and different capabilities, and this has led to a broad breadth of technology solutions provided by local companies. These local companies are providing some of the most technically advanced solutions in the industry, resulting in higher revenues and payroll. The RSA Data Center and the Montgomery internet exchange have also provided significant progress for the area. These assets have increased competition and allowed companies to keep their data local. With the increased competition comes increased service offerings, allowing our region to consider Smart City and Smart Base initiatives, which allow for better traffic flow on our roadways, better safety and security with lighting improvements and surveillance, better consumer services, plus many more benefits. I see a future of continued growth and prosperity in every industry here. But beyond all of the amazing strides made in the tech sector and in other industries, the River Region has something even more important, the feeling of family that surrounds all of us. That's something that does not exist in many other communities."

- Quincy Minor, President, Information Transport Solutions

Photo by Robert Fouts

INFORMATION TRANSPORT SOLUTIONS

Customer Service Is Our Passion; Technology with Integrity Is Our Mission

Information Transport Solutions was founded in 1993 by Tomi Selby. The company's mission was to provide information technology services to small companies who could not afford to hire a full-time IT team. ITS took root when the company landed a cabling contract with Montgomery County Public School System.

ITS has grown into an INC. 5000 corporation with nearly 100 team members today. From its three offices in Wetumpka, Montgomery and Mobile, ITS provides managed fiber and broadband Internet, network solutions, low voltage cabling services, network management, data center design, and virtualization services.

A reflection of its founder's passion for education, ITS first made its mark servicing K-12 Alabama schools. However, as the company grew, so did the industries it serves. Today, ITS is proud to work with universities, health care systems, financial institutions, manufacturing corporations, and mid-to-large size businesses, in addition to K-12 systems, across the Southeast.

ITS' team of highly-trained and certified professionals has more than 200 years of combined experience. ITS partners with some of the most influential tech companies in the world, including: Cisco Systems, Microsoft, Apple, VMWare, NetApp, Adtran, SMART Technologies and many more.

Montgomery's close proximity to some of the biggest metropolitan areas in the Southeast, combined with the convergence of two major interstates to connect them, makes the city a prime location with the transportation necessary for distribution and the access needed to support continued economic development. Photo by Lee Drumheller

BACHELER TECHNOLOGIES

"We have all the tools, resources and knowledge to do a great job, and we are looking for long-term relationships."

— Craig Bacheler, founder and owner of Bacheler Technologies

"We take care of networks and IT needs, but we also take care of our clients. Customer satisfaction is our primary goal," said Craig Bacheler, founder and owner of Bacheler Technologies. "We want our clients to become raving fans and not just be satisfied, but elated by the service we provide." Bacheler knows that despite the new opportunities and challenges that advances in technology provide businesses, understanding and protecting the interests of clients will always be his number one responsibility.

It's why he founded his company in 2008 to give the River Region a more personalized approach to IT services and consulting. "I was in advanced electronics in the Navy, and then I worked for other companies that do what we do," he said. "I felt like Montgomery and the tri-county area needed an IT company that looked out for the client, so I created one." He realized local business owners didn't just need someone to keep their networks running, they needed someone dedicated to helping them achieve their business goals. "That's the mission of Bacheler Technologies: to support the mission of every client," he said. "We learn our clients' businesses so we can match their processes with the appropriate solutions."

The company's employees, along with Craig, all work diligently to meet the IT needs of area businesses with strategic IT consulting, network management, system management, threat management, backup strategies and network budgeting. Everything the company does is state of the art thanks to partnerships with industry giants like Dell, Microsoft, Ingram Micro, CDW and Cisco. Plus, each client is supported by not just one technician, but the company's entire team who manages and maintains clients' networks to minimize downtime and maximize results. "We are dedicated to a high level of customer service, which means each client is supported with preventive maintenance, dependable backups, powerful virus protection and software updates, as well as a number of monthly and quarterly reviews to ensure the most efficient and effective network possible," Craig said.

Bacheler Technologies doesn't just provide services; it provides peace of mind. "We take ownership of managing and monitoring our client's IT so they can focus on their business," Craig said. "We help our clients leverage technology to help their businesses reach their full potential." The company's client list includes a wide array of industries and business sizes in Montgomery, the River Region and all over the Southeast. No matter what comes next, Bacheler Technologies will be ready. Its team of certified technicians and engineers routinely undergo continuing education to stay on the leading edge.

In the end, service is what sets Bacheler Technologies apart from the crowd and contributes to its success, growth and high client retention rate. "We view our clients as partners," Craig said. "We have all the tools, resources and knowledge to do a great job, and we are looking for long-term relationships."

Made in the River Region
Manufacturing, Creatives, Makers & Entrepreneurs

To most, manufacturing means factory floors with hundreds of workers putting together a product, assembly-line style. That's accurate, but the word really encompasses so much more, including this traditional image as well as the skilled artisan creating a one-of-a-kind object with their hands, and everything in between. Montgomery and the River Region are home to manufacturing and making at every level; the area has always been full of folks who dream things and then create or construct them, giving us a wide range of products we can designate: "Made in the River Region."

From an artistic textile seamstress who repurposes old materials into beautiful new items to a family-owned business that's been making sweet amber syrup for more than a century and a massive company using state-of-the-art robotic technology to build automobiles shipped across the globe, an array of products and goods of all shapes, sizes and purposes is fashioned and formed right here.

But there's something else being made in abundance in our area, something intangible but oh-so important: an entrepreneurial spirit and an enthusiasm for innovation that's generating even more progress. This emphasis on ingenuity is drawing a new creative class that's taking advantage of proven wisdom while blazing a new trail, both shaping and harnessing the vision of the next generation.

All combined, our artists, entrepreneurs and both new and established manufacturing companies are integral to the River Region's continued growth and success.

SABEL STEEL SERVICE, INC.

"There aren't many businesses that are run by the fifth generation. They don't usually make it that far," said Keith Sabel, who took over his family business in 1990. Eventually, Sabel Steel Service will extend that record yet again. "My son Sean is here training for the sixth generation," he added.

Founded in 1856, Sabel Steel Service is one of the longest-operating businesses in the country. The company was initially formed in Louisville, Kentucky, by Marx Sabel.

"We don't know why he came south or why he stopped in Montgomery," Sabel said, referring to his great-great-grandfather. Regardless, the founder brought his business to Alabama sometime before the Civil War broke out. "They sold leather goods to anybody who would buy them." The company bought and sold furs, including beaver and fox, as well as cow hides.

After the Civil War, however, the economy in this area took a hard hit. "There was no money," Sabel said. "How do you trade your product if you don't have money to buy it? They decided to accept scrap iron." Since farmers had tools laying around, the company offered to buy their farm implements. This transition marked the first of many transitions Sabel Steel Service would make over various economic cycles, wartime interruptions, and changing consumer needs in order to assure its survival. Since that transition Sabel Steel has recycled millions of tons of scrap metal in its 160 year history.

As the 20th century arrived, the company had a hiccup in its original business model. "Leather goods went out of style when the automobile came around," Sabel said. "Buggy whips were hard to sell." But the company stayed in the cowhide business untill the 1970s, when changes in the meat distribution industry led to a reassessment. "We closed the hide business because it wasn't viable," Sabel said. "We were able to pivot from that in time."

The company endured the Great Depression perhaps, as Sabel suggests, out of ignorance. "What keeps a business in business is either being really, really smart or too stupid to know," Sabel said. In hindsight, a smarter business decision might have been to go out of business when the country faced the dire economic conditions of the 1930s. Yet they rebounded again.

"Over the years, my family fortunately has been able to adapt to conditions presented by business decisions, war, political changes, economic conditions," Sabel said.

During World War II Sabel's father and uncle served in the military, as their uncle took the reins of the company. When the war was over they realized it was going to be tough to support three families out of the scrap business. That's when Sabel's father, Jim, and his uncle Mark suggested another pivot. "They decided we needed to sell

Band saw lines in Montgomery.

Left: Overview of Sabel Steel's headquarters in Montgomery.
Bottom: Sean and Keith Sabel.

steel," Sabel said. However, demand was high and supply was down after the war and Sabel says it was difficult to get into the business. But the company persisted and bought the first loads of steel from U.S. Steel in Fairfield, Alabama, in 1952. "About 10 years later, my dad thought we ought to be in the rebar fabrication business," Sabel said. "He ran that until he retired."

Today, Sabel Steel Service continues to thrive as a diversified steel company with six steel service centers, two scrap yards, a rebar fabrication division and a wholesale center. Sabel's full-service scrap division operates from two locations in the central Alabama region — Sabel Steel Service headquartered on North Court Street in Montgomery and as Montgomery Iron & Metal Company (MIMCO) on Day Street in Montgomery.

The Fabrication & Engineering Division is a full-service concrete-reinforcing steel detailer and fabricator on North Court Street. Whether one ton or 10,000 tons, every order received by Sabel Steel receives the attention to detail that the customer needs, and the company maintains strict accordance with the Concrete Reinforcing Steel Manual of Standard Practice as prepared by the Concrete Reinforcing Steel Institute (CRSI).

The company also operates a wholesale center on North Court Street. Sabel Wholesale Center is a full-service wholesale operation specializing in plumbing, industrial and marine supplies, specialty and general use hardware, chains, cables, and pipes. Established in 1956, at the 100-year-mark for the company, Sabel Wholesale Center was the first company in the Central Alabama region to introduce and stock PVC pipe.

Sabel Steel Service also operates five additional service centers in Mobile, Dothan and Woodstock, Alabama, as well as in Newnan, Georgia, and Baton Rouge, Louisiana.

The company's customers come in all sizes. "We rely on individuals, really big companies, and everything in between to maintain our business," Sabel said. And the company has many long-time employees to help it get the job done. According to Sabel, the secret to the company's longevity is, "paying attention to the markets, taking care of your customers, and taking care of your employees."

Photo courtesy of HMMA

Photo by Brooke Glassford / Colorbox

The Alabama Industrial Development Training agency (AIDT) is ensuring manufacturers in the River Region and the entire state have the workforce they need to get business done. Its primary purpose is to recruit and train a skilled workforce to attract new industries to the state and to expand existing industries. It helps close the skills gaps that too often keep people needing jobs and job openings from matching. Through multiple programs at various centers and with on-the-job training, AIDT provides a wide range of highly customizable offerings, all at no cost to employers and the trainees.

Photo by Brooke Glassford / Colorbox

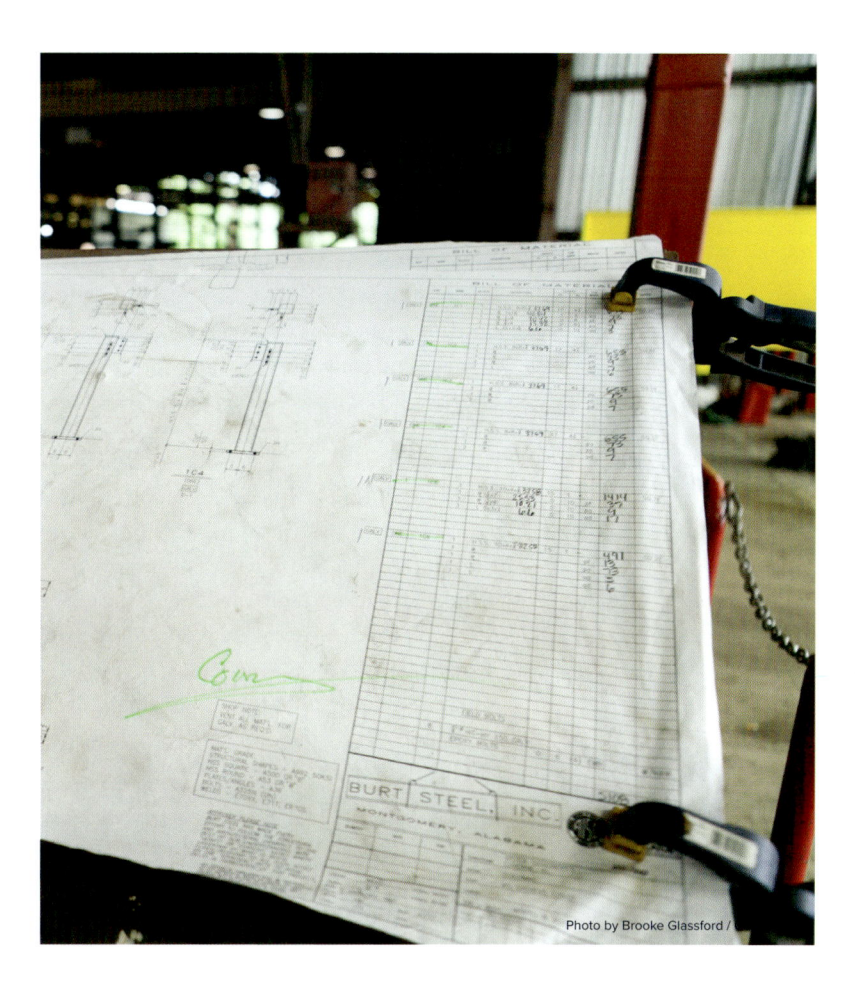

Photo by Brooke Glassford / Colorbox

Photo by Brooke Glassford / Colorbox

NEPTUNE TECHNOLOGY GROUP

Impacting the World of Water from Alabama's River Region

Innovations that continue to make a difference

Each day across North America, thousands of water utilities are helping their customers measure, manage and conserve the water they use. Those efforts are made possible by hundreds of people in Tallassee, Alabama, at Neptune Technology Group.

Now celebrating 125 years in the water industry—and the last 45 at its headquarters in Tallassee—Neptune is a leading provider of smart water utility systems and software, including automatic meter reading (AMR) and advanced metering infrastructure (AMI) technology, managed services, and water meters. Neptune's systems collect data from more than 30 million utility meters per month.

Neptune's Headquarters, Technology & Innovation Centers in Tallassee

Neptune's impact is felt far beyond the River Region, both in the everyday lives of water consumers as well as on the water industry as a whole. Many of Neptune's employees have dedicated decades to providing the highest-quality metering products and systems. That commitment comes with a need to continually build on the company's achievements.

From Neptune's lead free, bronze-body water meters to advanced radio frequency technologies to industry-leading software solutions, nearly all of its products and systems are made in America at the company's headquarters, technology and innovation centers in Tallassee. Research and development as well as manufacturing (including Neptune's own on-site foundry) are all in one location, ensuring control over all processes with absolute commitment to quality. As Neptune adds new software applications, smart metering components and technologies to its AMR/AMI system offerings, these innovations work seamlessly with existing products in which utility customers have already invested. This backward compatibility builds trust, because utilities know they can count on Neptune to support their needs in the years to come.

In addition, Neptune makes the path forward—what it calls migration—as simple as possible for utility customers, while allowing them to choose when and how to adopt new technology. Its innovative systems and software enable utilities to change between meter reading methods any time they need. They can use a handheld data collector, a car-mounted data collector that saves the meter reader time while increasing safety and productivity, or meter-reading data collected hourly from smart AMI network data collectors transmitting directly to the utility office. The best part is that utilities can implement new technology at their own pace, depending on what they need at the moment and the resources they have on hand.

The perfect place to grow an impact

In the past few decades, Neptune has proven it's much more than a meter manufacturer. As a technology company, it innovates so that utility customers can connect and leverage all their various resources—human, financial, technological and environmental—to best meet their individual needs.

The saying "grow where you're planted" certainly applies to Neptune and the River Region. Since relocating to Central Alabama in 1972, it has done exactly that. And continued to grow, both in terms of personnel and capabilities. While Neptune has offices in the Unites States, Mexico and Canada, its Tallassee headquarters houses nearly 500 of the company's total 700 employees.

To provide cutting-edge solutions, Neptune continually invests in people and facilities. The company averages more than 20 hours of training per employee per year, and invests in excess of $5 million annually in new equipment and upgrades. In April 2010, Neptune completed and opened a new 19,000-square-foot Innovation Center.

Neptune works equally hard to establish a safe, productive, and supportive work environment for all its employees. Just as the River Region has provided the company with opportunities to grow, Neptune is committed to returning the favor, providing ways for area residents to challenge themselves, grow their skills, and build rewarding careers. The company promotes a shared sense of pride and a feeling of "family" among those who've joined its ranks over the years.

Neptune bases its success on more than the bottom line. After it received the 2011 River Region Ethics in Business and Public Service Award, company leadership reflected the importance of giving back to the community.

A company doesn't simply reach an installed base of more than 30 million water meters, 18 million AMR/AMI radio transmitters, and a loyal customer base of 3,000 utilities overnight. It takes years of innovation. Of service. Of experience and commitment to being trusted as their most valued partner. That difference is made every day through teamwork, by people driven by excellence toward a common goal. Neptune is proud of its employees, and proud to be a part of Central Alabama's River Region.

Clockwise from above: AMI Network Collector for Smart Meter Data Collection; Wireless Technology Design and Testing; Our 19,000-square-foot "Kullmann Innovation Center."

NEPTUNE
TECHNOLOGY GROUP

The creative department of Stamp Idea Group housed in the historic Confederate Post Office building located at 111 Washington Avenue in downtown Montgomery.

Photo courtesy of STAMP

The River Region is blessed with a vibrant group of productive creatives, from artists, craftspeople and designers to writers, photographers and more.

Photos courtesy of Southern Makers

1957

2017

BURT STEEL, INC.
Erecting Steel Structures Across the Southeast

Albert Burt was a teenager in the early 1900s when his father, a blacksmith in Montgomery, passed away. To help support his family, the young man found a job at a local boiler works, and remained there for 40 years. The family tradition of metal works continued as he rose to become general manager of the plant. His son William Raymond Burt became the foreman. After he completed military service during World War II, he and his father, Albert, decided to pool their experience and expertise and start their own business.

In 1945, father and son opened Burt Boiler Works in downtown Montgomery. Originally, the company repaired boilers for sawmills, laundries and schools in the area. But the scope of their work shifted when they began to bid on structural steel jobs for construction projects, and they quickly outgrew their company name.

Today, the third and fourth generations of the family business lead a team that works with general contractors to build structural steel frameworks for building projects all over the Southeast, with a specialty in shopping centers. The projects are accomplished through two companies – Burt Steel, Inc. and B&S Erection, Inc. – and are headed by William Raymond's sons, Raymond "Bo" Burt, who serves as president, and Hampton G. "Sonny" Burt as senior vice president. The fourth generation is represented by Jeremy Burt, Bo's son, as the project manager, and Lee Burt, Sonny's son, as production manager.

A staff of 45 people fabricate and erect the structural steel framework for shopping centers, offices, schools, medical facilities and other large buildings. Burt Steel, Inc. is the steel fabrication side. In the last 10 years it has added more than $2 million worth of equipment and building expansions. Last year it added the Python X Beamline, an innovative computerized, robotic plasma cutting system that has revolutionized structural steel fabrication. "All of the fabrication is done from our modern 80,000 square foot fabrication shop located on North Decatur Street," Lee Burt says. After it's fabricated, it is loaded onto Burt Steel trucks and sent to its jobsites. Once the steel is on the jobsite, B&S Erection, Inc. sends its crews to erect the steel structures. Burt Steel, Inc. and B&S Erection, Inc. are two separate companies that work together as one.

Right: Burt Steel, Inc. received an award at The 27th Annual Business In The Arts Awards at the Renaissance Montgomery Hotel & Spa at the Convention Center in 2013. The award reads, "In great appreciation to Burt Steel, Inc. for creating the 1903 Wright Flyer sculpture proudly displayed at Wright Brothers Park. Montgomery, Alabama."

In Burt Steel's early years, the company helped build many of the area's landmark sites, including the east side of Cramton Bowl, Paterson Field, Normandale Shopping Center, East Brook Shopping Center, Cloverland Shopping Center, Forest Hills Shopping Center and the Montgomery Fair store.

More recently, Burt Steel, Inc. has built structural steel frameworks for a lot of familiar retail names, such as Target, Best Buy, Kroger, Whole Foods, Winn Dixie and Publix. In addition, the company has recently begun building Dialysis Clinics throughout the Southeast.

"One of our favorite projects has nothing to do with structural steel buildings," says Mr. Burt. In 2013 the City of Montgomery began developing The Wright Brothers Park, in downtown Montgomery. It was to honor the aviation pioneers, Orville and Wilbur Wright, and their decision in picking Montgomery, Alabama as the location for the first ever civilian flight school, which later became Maxwell Air Force Base, the home of the U. S. Air War College. The City of Montgomery wanted an airplane to go in its park, and Burt Steel, Inc. wanted to build it. Burt Steel and its employees wanted the opportunity to show their talent and ability to build something special, a piece of art and a piece of history to pass down to their children and grandchildren and future generations. Most everything they build gets covered up by brick, sheetrock, and ceiling panels but this 25 foot by 40 foot replica would proudly be displayed soaring over the riverbank for all to see. At nighttime it shines brightly, commemorating this special time in Montgomery's history.

Burt Steel, Inc. and its employees were extremely proud of their accomplishment and were so pleased to donate this project to the city for all to enjoy.

Burt Steel typically works with around 15 to 20 general contractors, and its clients keep coming back for future projects. "It's because of our service and experience," Jeremy Burt says. "The market we're in is very fast-paced and we meet their scheduled delivery dates, and that's why they keep coming back. We deliver a quality product on time."

The company has many long-term employees who've been on board for 30 or 35 years. While it's been a family business from the beginning for the Burts, it has also been a family business for others as well. "Several generations of families have worked together here," Sonny Burt said. "We are grateful to be in Montgomery and thankful for our dedicated employees. We celebrate our past, while we look forward to many years serving our community," says Bo Burt.

Providing grants, resources and advocacy and forming all-important connections, the Alabama Launchpad is fostering increased entrepreneurship in the River Region, helping companies start, stay and grow here.

Photo courtesy of Montgomery Chamber of Commerce / Carter Photography & Design, LLC

Photo courtesy of Alabama Launchpad

291

REGITAR U.S.A.

For Dr. Yu-Tueng (Y.T.) Tsai, the work he does at his automotive electronics company Regitar U.S.A. is a family affair. His wife, two sons, three sisters, three brothers, as well as other family members all work together. And while much of his extended family stays busy at Regitar's outpost in Taiwan, their North American headquarters is in Montgomery. It's where Y.T. and his wife Dr. Chau L. Tsai started it all in 1987, a decision driven in part by the hospitality they found here.

Born in Taiwan, Drs. Y.T. and Chau Tsai came to the capital city to teach at Auburn University at Montgomery (AUM) in 1985. "We didn't think we'd stay here long, but we were welcomed by so many friendly people," Y.T. said. Montgomery quickly felt like home and a few years later, the Tsais got the entrepreneurial bug. "In addition to teaching, we wanted to start a business," Y.T. said, "but since we didn't know anything about running a business in the United States, we started a warehousing and distribution center for goods from overseas, mostly from Taiwan."

First, they imported shoes and power tools. Next, they began importing and selling auto parts. Today, the company is focused exclusively on car components, specifically high-tech parts, and has a solid global reputation as a sales and distribution center for quality electronic components.

"Anything electronic under the hood is our 'bread and butter,' such as parts for the ignition system, modules and coils, various sensors, voltage regulators, and even safety systems like backup cameras, Tire Pressure Monitoring Systems (TPMS) and more," said Gary Tsai, Y.T.'s son who oversees Regitar's operations.

Orders for almost 5,000 products used in domestic and imported cars produced in Regitar's Asian manufacturing centers come to Montgomery and are processed, packed and shipped from its 53,000-square-foot warehouse, which will expand to 100,000 square feet by June 2018. The company is also doing some light assembly and has grown from doing $250,000 of business in its first year to hitting that figure daily in 2017.

Regitar serves customers in North, Central and South America, as well as the Caribbean. Gary likes to point out that when Regitar began, it was the first Asian automotive company in Alabama. It's a point of pride for Y.T. and his sons, including Henry, who works for the company as the Director of Global Sourcing and Procurement. "We raised our boys here, and they had so many opportunities that came from the size of this town and from the inclusive attitude in this town," Y.T. said. His company felt welcomed too. "We got so much support from the city and Mayor and the Chamber of Commerce when we started," he said. "The resources from the Chamber especially proved invaluable. That meant a lot, and we're still getting that support today, so we want to support this community and give back. That's why we stayed here."

Today, Regitar provides jobs for 40 people in Montgomery, as well as many more in California, United Kingdom, Brazil, China and Taiwan. And as much as Montgomery means to the Tsais, the ties of family mean even more, something Gary believes benefits the company and its customers. "It's part of our success, the fact that we are a family business," he said. "It provides a level of comfort and trust because we share the same vision and have common ideas on how to grow the company and move it forward." Henry echoed his brother's sentiments by saying, "Being a family business gives us stability. That inspires confidence in our customers."

Another key component of Regitar's success is its product line and assembly. "We offer unique products known for quality, and we keep putting out new products," Gary said. "We are continually doing research and development and always innovating." Price matters too, but they know stellar service counts even more. "We're competitive in our pricing, but we've never tried to be the least expensive in the industry. We strive to be the best in terms of quality and service. That's what our customers want," Gary said.

Regitar also emphasizes repeat business over the one-time sale, which is made possible by its family-focused culture and customer-first philosophy. "It helps us remain flexible, and that means we can provide great service while building long-term relationships with our customers," Gary said. Those relationships keep paying off for both parties. "Most of our customers we have had from the beginning," Y.T. said. "And we rarely lose customers."

While Regitar is thriving and enjoying its success, Y.T. plans to keep the company on the cutting edge of the changing automotive and transportation industry. "Down the road, we'll be moving into electric cars, as we see sensors, one of our biggest product lines, as the key components of electric cars," he said. "We're already manufacturing parts for electronic buses in Taiwan."

Currently, some of Regitar's products are rebranded before hitting the retail market. Going forward, the company is working to increase its name recognition. "One of our major goals is to be more of a name brand in the market," Gary said. "We've been behind the scenes, but we are ready to be brand-forward." Regitar's Montgomery headquarters could also see some additional manufacturing onsite. "We recently celebrated 30 years, and we're already thinking about the next 30 years, about our future," Y.T. said. "Montgomery keeps moving in the right direction, and it is home. It will remain a part of our future."

regitar.com

Automobile Manufacturing

While River Region companies make more than cars, Hyundai Motor Manufacturing Alabama is still a heavy hitter. Its role in the region's economy is huge, representing a $2.4 billion impact in Montgomery County and a $4.8 billion overall economic impact in the state annually. As of 2014, HMMA employed 3,732 people, and the company's Tier 1 and 2 suppliers collectively employ 8,900 in Alabama. Other automakers and their suppliers have followed HMMA to the area. In 2016, Montgomery was selected as the location of the first North American facility for Gerhardi Kuntstoftechnik. The German automotive supplier is investing $37.9 million and employing more than 200. Montgomery is home to four of the Top 10 global automotive suppliers – Denso, Mobis, Faurecia and Lear.

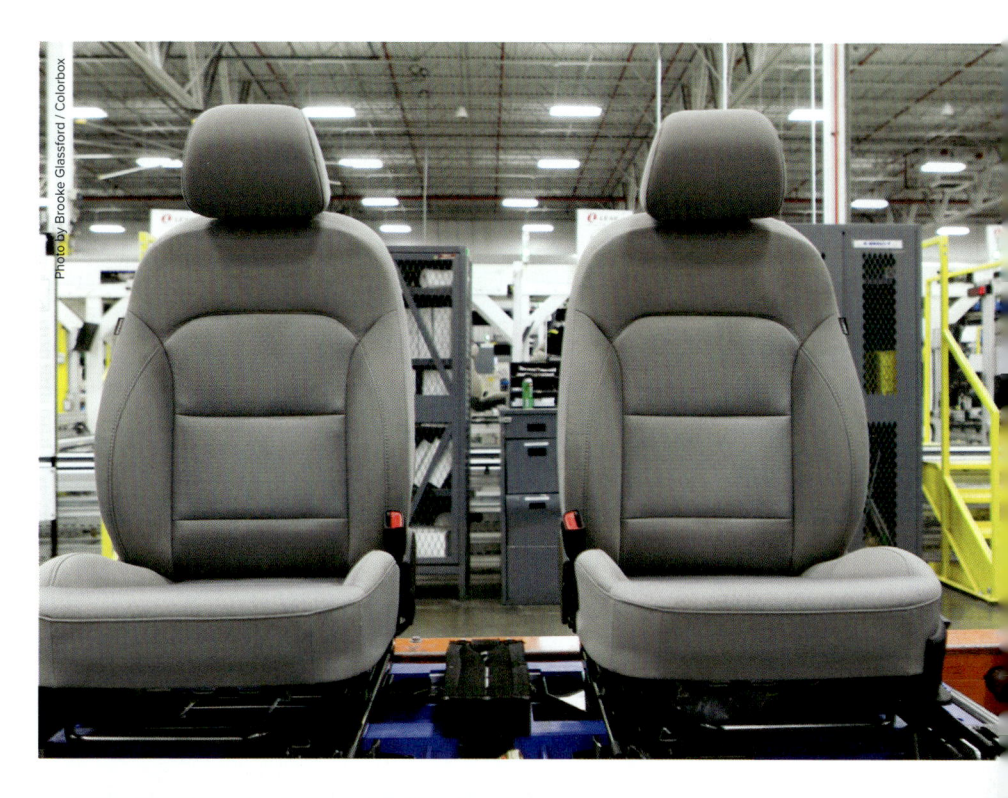

"Hyundai Motor Manufacturing Alabama brought a lot of jobs to the area. It gave a lot of people a means and a chance to take care of their families. It provides good benefits and opportunities to its thousands of team members. It is also a company that embraces diversity. I love my co-workers and management team. I enjoy the positive atmosphere and togetherness. And while my job is challenging, it keeps my mind sharp. I always try to find ways to make my work better."

- Hyundai Motor Manufacturing Alabama Team Member Kerra Taylor, a sander in the paint shop

ALABAMA MACHINERY & SUPPLY COMPANY

Serving Customers for More than 100 Years

> "We're an excellent, honest company that believes in serving our customers."

Founded in 1902, Alabama Machinery & Supply Company is one of the state's oldest businesses. This longevity, said company president C.M. "Mike" Reinehr, "demonstrates we're an excellent, honest company that believes in serving our customers."

His family took ownership of the business in 1966 when his father, F.G. "Mickey" Reinehr, purchased the company. It had been established by brothers Arthur and William K. Pelzer at the turn of the 20th Century in response to the state's growing industrial, lumber and mechanized farming business.

"When my father bought this business, we were still receiving merchandise in railroad cars. You would purchase your inventory in annual amounts," Reinehr said. Purchase orders were submitted by mail, rush orders were placed by phone, and products were (and still are) delivered by common carrier. Though much about commerce has changed over the last 100-plus years, in many cases, Alabama Machinery & Supply sticks to the traditional way of doing things. "It hasn't changed how we do business with our customers," Reinehr said. "We're still out in the customer's plant talking with the customer about their needs every day."

While their service to customers is still in person and personal, how they work with suppliers to get the products their customers need is one aspect of their service that has changed. "Through the use of modern technology our inventory is maybe 10 percent of what it was 50 years ago, and our range of products is much broader," Reinehr said. "Our mission has always been customer service. Now we have additional tools to service our customers."

This customized approach provides insight that can be quickly translated into action. "Product knowledge is more important than inventory," Reinehr said. "Customers may or may not know what they need. We know what they need. We also know where we can source it." Alabama Machinery & Supply's strongest sales tool is indeed its seasoned and knowledgeable staff. Many have been with the company 20 to 30 years or longer. With this combined experience, Reinehr said, "We have a lot of product knowledge."

Alabama Machinery & Supply sells manufacturing, repair and operating supplies to a customer base made up primarily of manufacturing companies and large general contractors. Products include personal safety gear, work boots, hand tools, power tools and other recurring supplies. The company has been in its current location since the mid-1990s, when they purchased and moved into the former Brewbaker Buick dealership building on Bibb Street in downtown Montgomery.

VT MILTOPE

"Reliable in the Extreme!" is how VT Miltope has built an enduring reputation with its customers. Their ruggedized laptops, tablets, wireless access points and peripherals are purpose-built to be genuinely tough – not merely commercial or industrial-grade products resold with a metal wrapper.

Miltope Corporation was founded in 1975 to develop ultra-rugged hard drives, printers and other peripherals for military use. While forty years of innovation has led Miltope from tape drives and dot matrix printers to laptops and wireless access points, an underlying dedication to product quality and customer support has been key to the company's continued success. This success led to its acquisition by Vision Technologies Systems, Inc. in 2003 and a change in name to VT Miltope.

Customers know they aren't buying just a product, they are buying a relationship built on dedication to the customer. Today, Miltope's products are being used around the world and are in the hands of many of the country's Warfighters, and can be found crisscrossing the globe onboard the fleets of leading airlines. VT Miltope has an unparalleled dedication to supporting its products and customers where they are, whatever environment they are in.

The company's history with Alabama goes back to the early 1980s, when Miltope opened a 65,000-square-foot manufacturing facility in Troy, Alabama to expand its manufacturing capabilities. In 1994, the company relocated its headquarters from New York to Montgomery; where it has resided ever since.

Today the company provides some of the world's most rugged laptops, tablets and wireless access devices that exist for both military and commercial applications. The facility located in the Montgomery city limits provides the company with the ability to accommodate all phases of product life cycle, from concept to design all the way to full-rate production. The company's ability to adapt to the ever-changing needs of its customers means that even though its products may change, its dedication and support to its customers never will.

While VT Miltope is part of a large global company, the Alabama operations are able to provide customers with the individual support and care that has made it known for its reliability.

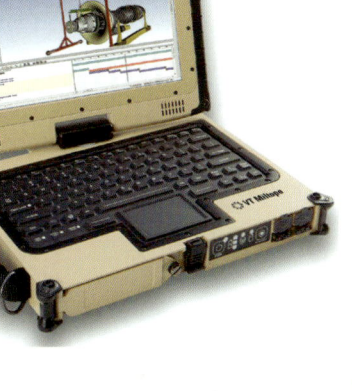

Different by Design

"I am honestly first, and at heart, a missionary and then a designer by default. I'm so incredibly blessed that God has allowed me to create beauty with my hands. Some of the women we help have experienced such rejection and abuse and believe there's no way beauty can come from all they've experienced. What they don't see, but I, and all of us at Re-Invention do, is that these situations and experiences have added such richness and texture to their lives, and it's truly humbling to see how their pain and hurt can be turned into something beautiful that impacts everyone around them. So, they inspire me personally and inspire my work. And it is why we say every piece is a declaration exclaiming that the pieces and parts of our lives come together to create something beautiful, and nothing is ever wasted. I'm also inspired by Montgomery. The old firehouse where I live and run my business is located in the 5 Points neighborhood, right smack in the middle of Montgomery's history at the end of the Selma to Montgomery Trail. Not a day goes by that I don't stand in awe of what happened right where I wake up and create. While we still have a long way to go, I believe this is a pivotal time here. There is a new generation rising who is making real efforts to reconcile the tensions birthed from our city's history. It's exciting and a privilege to be living here right now, and I have a front-row seat for what I believe is a 'for such a time as this' moment."

-Kellie Guthrie, owner/founder/designer at Re-Invention, a Montgomery-based social business that re-purposes leftover and vintage materials to make new items like pillows and bags and hires local women in need and teaches them basic job skills as well as textile-specific skills.

299

FASTENING SOLUTIONS, INC.

Smart. Effective. Solutions.

"We provide more than nails and staples. We provide 61 years of industry knowledge, the best products and the best customer service and support." - Will Rue

Fastening Solutions, Inc. (FSI) was co-founded in 1956 by Bill Rue Sr., and today is led by his grandsons, Will Rue and Les Rue Jr., who are first cousins and represent the third generation of a family business known for offering a wide array of products as well as a deep knowledge of how their customers use these products.

Headquartered in Montgomery with 85,000 square feet of warehouse space on Selma Highway, the company has an additional 18 sales and service centers in 10 other states, including six distribution warehouses in each of the regions served.

The company is best known for selling collated fasteners, such as nails and staples, and the tools that drive them. FSI also services the tools in any of their 19 locations. Primary customer groups include industrial customers, dealers and large contractors.

For the industrial sector, customers are drawn from industries that include those specializing in furniture, cabinetry and millwork, fence panels, window manufacturing, pallet/crate assembly and repair, in-plant manufactured housing, lumber processing, truss/component manufacturers, and boat/RV manufacturers. The FSI team evaluates each customer's unique fastening and strapping needs and recommends the products that best meet individual requirements.

For lumberyards and hardware dealers, FSI is able to recommend the best mix of fastening products from a variety of well-known national brands, including FSI's own EZ Fit brand of fasteners, compressors and accessories.

The company's continued success can be traced to two key strengths – outstanding employees and solid, dependable vendors. "The experience of our associates, combined with their commitment to customer satisfaction, is one of FSI's keys to success," said Les Rue. "Additionally, our vendors provide us with a definite advantage." He added that FSI puts a high priority on vendor selection, working with those who deliver long-term quality products and who are responsive to FSI's – and their customers' – requests.

In 2010, FSI added a division that services and sells equipment for packaging products for palletizing. This addition enabled the company to leverage its existing service personnel while also expanding its offerings to customers. Packaging products include strapping/banding, stretch film and edge protection, as well as the highly specialized tools and equipment used by industrial customers.

Since 1956, having earned the reputation of being the best in the industry, the FSI team has become an integral part of its customers' success stories by offering a range of quality products and demonstrating a unique understanding of how customers can use them. "We provide more than nails and staples," Will Rue said. "We provide 62 years of industry knowledge, the best products and the best customer service and support."

Above: "Our Strength Comes From Within"
Pictured left: Larry Hutchinson, Dennis Morgan, O'Neal Davis and Lewis Alexander in 1980.

PRODUCTION AUTOMATION, INC.

Production Automation Inc. (PAI) was formed as a partnership between O'Neal Davis and Dennis Morgan in 1978 as D.M. & Associates. Engineer Lawrence "Larry" Hutchinson joined the group in 1980 and it became D.M.H. Company. In April 1981, the group incorporated in Montgomery, Alabama as Production Automation Inc., a manufacturer of high speed/low speed palletizers, depalletizers and automated material-handling equipment that provides automatic means for stacking cases of goods or products onto a pallet. Since its inception, the company has proudly maintained the same location at 2075 Exchange Street, Montgomery, Alabama 36116.

The high value, strong work ethic and commitment to excellence by the original three principles are still evident in every aspect of PAI. O'Neal Davis and Larry Hutchinson are now deceased, but the ideals forged with Dennis Morgan remain in effect. Today, Dennis Morgan and the Davis Family Trust are active in daily operations. Terry Davis, son of O'Neal Davis, serves as the CEO with various Davis family members serving as department heads.

PAI has one of the fastest, most energy efficient, high level palletizers available on the market today. Its first palletizer was sold to Southeast Canners, a Pepsi-Cola franchise in Columbus, Georgia. Its first depalletizer was sold to Buffalo Rock, a Pepsi-Cola franchise in Birmingham, Alabama. Throughout its history, the company has shown a strong presence in the state of Alabama as well as states across the nation, including Hawaii. PAI is well-respected in the automated material-handling industry with national and international recognition in Canada, South America, Mexico, British West Indies, Puerto Rico and Taiwan.

Any commodity seen in a grocery or big box store is a potential or existing customer. PAI, with its long established innovative design, enjoys a high-profile client base in water bottling companies, pet food companies, wineries/breweries, food/beverage companies, with familiar names such as:

- Coca-Cola
- Pepsi-Cola
- 7UP
- Dr. Pepper
- Shasta Beverages
- Labatt Breweries
- E&J Gallo Winery
- Yuengling Brewery
- Tito's Vodka
- Gatorade
- Campbell Soups
- Quaker Oats Company
- Heinz
- Delmonte

PAI is a leader in the palletizer industry with a product that signifies the nation's best in quality of engineering, manufacturing, installation and customer service. PAI has approximately 60 employees, 50 percent have more than 20 years with the company. There is opportunity for employment with training in a variety of positions on many different levels in a safe, healthy, positive work environment. PAI believes in giving back to its community by participation and contribution to various charities. It is also known as an animal friendly business. Employee and customer pets are always welcome.

"Innovation." "Dedication." "Discipline." "Teamwork." These words by the three original partners describe the motivation behind the high standards that resonate within the walls of PAI, reflective of 40 plus years of success. "You are only as good as the people you have around you...the people you surround yourself with." CEO Terry Davis, the Davis Family Trust, Dennis Morgan and dedicated employees continue the tradition.

Since 1947, the Montgomery Curb Market has been drawing locals and visitors alike to enjoy purchasing fresh flowers, produce and specialty foods made and grown right here in the River Region.

Photo by Michelle Consuegra Lambert

Prevail Union Montgomery was rated the Best Coffee in the State of Alabama by *Food and Wine* Magazine in 2018 and is one of the first new shops opened in the newly renovated Kress building.

LEAR CORPORATION

It is truly a rare occasion when you can find a product on the shelves today that was first made by a company a century ago. Maintaining a quality product and successful business for 100 years is exactly what Lear Corporation, founded in 1917, has accomplished in the automotive seating industry.

Lear's success is not only based on superior quality products but a customer-focus mindset that encompasses operational excellence. Lear was the first North American seat manufacturer to introduce "Just-In-Time" manufacturing for improved efficiency, a streamlined supply chain and customer value-added service.

Lear Montgomery opened in 2005 to service an important partner, Hyundai, and since that time has been building seats for their Sonata, Elantra, and Santa Fe vehicles that are assembled at Hyundai Motor Manufacturing of Alabama. Lear Montgomery is one of nearly 260 Lear facilities located in 38 countries that employ more than 160,000 people around the world.

As the most vertically integrated seating manufacturer in the world and the largest provider of premium automotive leather, Lear is the world leader in providing luxury and performance seating. Lear's E-Systems business segment also provides seat components as well as its ConnexUs™ suite of connectivity products, including cybersecurity and more for the automotive future.

Lear serves every major automaker in the world and its local teams work every day to help realize its customers' goals for consumers everywhere. Lear Montgomery takes great pride in helping Hyundai work toward its future success and in the past contributed to such accolades as the Elantra winning a North American Car of the Year title and "Highest ranked in compact car segment for initial quality" according to J.D. Power and Associates in 2014.

Lear's Core Values include Integrity, Diversity and Community Service, and Lear Montgomery's three-shift operation provides opportunities for 400 team members, with 90 percent living in the River Region.

With so many employees from the area, Lear has a strong sense of local pride and is proud to be an active participant in community events and charities such as the River Region United Way, Habitat for Humanity, Prattville YMCA and the Montgomery Easter Seals, to name just a few. A creative and fun "Red Nose Day" at the plant saw the team raise approximately $3,000 that went to purchase and install playground equipment for local Head Start efforts.

CAPITOL CONTAINER, INC.

Corrugated Packaging Delivered with Personalized Service

From its location in Gunter Industrial Park, Capitol Container, Inc. designs and manufactures corrugated containers for customers across the Southeast. "Our customers manufacture a product that needs to be boxed. We make the boxes they need," said Bill Kennedy, who founded the company in 1992. Kennedy had worked as a plant manager in the packaging industry when a series of mergers led him to establish his own company – one that was independent, customer-service focused and responsive to industry trends. "We make a quality product, provide the best customer service and our customers' satisfaction is our top priority," Kennedy said.

In recent years, the trend has moved toward just-in-time and point-of-use delivery. As corrugated sheets are transformed into boxes of almost any type, shape and size imaginable, the company's team delivers them to customers at the time and the location they are required.

"In the old days, manufacturers would place an order and get them in a week's time. Now they want them within an hour," said Robby Brantley, the company's vice president. "We bring it to you within the hour of when you need it and where you are going to use it on your floor." In the case of one of their customers, Brantley added, "We keep employees at their location, and we push what they need to that part of the plant."

As son to owner Susan Kennedy, Brantley has seen first-hand how the company has evolved in its customer-centric services. "We're also a third-party logistics company," he said. "We are a fulfillment center for our existing customers with out-of-town suppliers." This service fits the just-in-time delivery model in that Capitol Container warehouses supplies so that customers don't have to add them to their inventory until needed.

Capitol Container's original building is 130,000 square feet and is where boxes are designed and manufactured. The company operates a jumbo press that is one of only two in the Southeast. A few years back, the company bought a neighboring building and expanded it to a 60,000-square-foot warehouse for shipping and receiving. "We handle all of our own delivery," Brantley said.

In addition to their customer-service focus, Capitol Container stands out for its engineering expertise as well. Boxes are custom designed for customers, with particular attention given to weight in order to aid customers in holding the line on shipping costs. Capitol Container also designs and manufactures corrugated store displays.

BEERS & ASSOCIATES
Telling Stories That Celebrate Communities

Anyone who knows Ron Beers knows he loves a good story. In 1981, Beers' passion for stories became his profession when he went to work for a publishing company that published history books on cities and states throughout the country. In 1989, Beers went out on his own. Over the next 30 years, he founded and built two successful publishing companies pouring his experience and heart into over 160 titles on more than 120 different communities throughout the United States and Canada. When he started Beers and Associates in 2005, he decided to keep things manageable enough so he could do what he really loves to do: listen to stories about the birth of a city and stories about the start of a business.

"People love to tell stories, and we have the privilege of publishing them," says Beers. "Through our books, we tell their stories to people across the street and around the world."

Beers and an experienced team of writers, editors, photographers, designers and associates, publish two types of books: community history books and contemporary image books. These beautiful, oversized, hardcover volumes are sponsored by the local chamber of commerce or historical society in return for a royalty on the sale of corporate profile space to local business owners. Over his career, Beers' books have returned more than $3 million in royalties to their sponsors.

"In years prior, the cost of producing a coffee-table book like this came right out of the sponsor's budget. We take the financial burden off the sponsor and actually creates a significant stream of non-dues income," Beers says. The dollars generated from profile sales underwrite the cost of producing the book. "It's a 'win-win' for both the sponsor and the participating businesses."

Participating businesses get to see their story published in a hardcover volume right alongside the story of the city or state where their business is located without having to fund the venture themselves. "Our business model allows them to partner with other members of the business community and each pay a significantly smaller portion of the total cost," Beers says.

Additionally, everybody benefits from each other's distribution of the book. Every time the hospital in town gives a copy to the new doctor in town, the bank benefits. And when the bank gives a copy to a new customer, the realtor benefits. And when the chamber of commerce gives a copy to a company looking to relocate, and they do, the whole community benefits. Ultimately, the book becomes a local best seller and so it goes. "We love to tell stories," Beers says. "You have a story, too. Let us tell it."

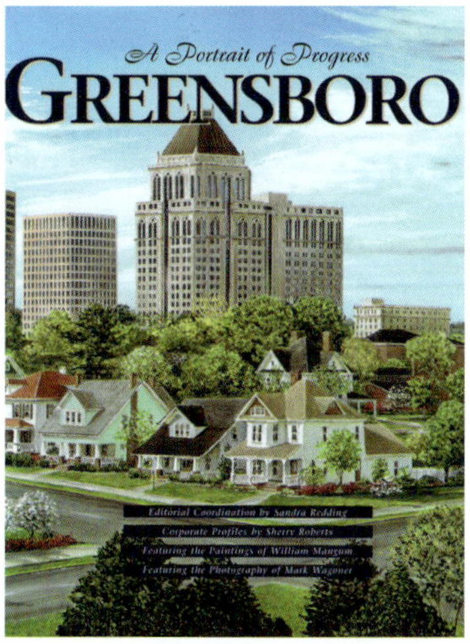
A Portrait of Progress
GREENSBORO

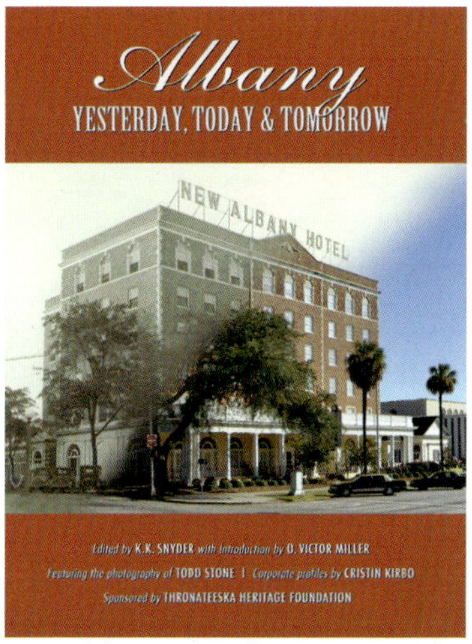
Albany
YESTERDAY, TODAY & TOMORROW
NEW ALBANY HOTEL
Edited by K.K. SNYDER with introduction by D. VICTOR MILLER
Featuring the photography of TODD STONE | Corporate profiles by CRISTIN KIRBO
Sponsored by THRONATEESKA HERITAGE FOUNDATION

BIRMINGHAM
Magic City Renaissance
by Joe O'Donnell
Corporate Profiles by Ruth Beaumont Reuse
Featuring the photographs of Don Newton, Jr.

Hampton Roads
GATEWAY TO AMERICA'S EAST COAST

Columbus
CELEBRATES THE MILLENNIUM

HEART OF AMERICA
KANSAS CITY
BY JANE MOBLEY • CORPORATE PROFILES BY SHIFRA STEIN
FEATURING THE PHOTOGRAPHY OF ROY INMAN

New Orleans
RIVER REGION RENAISSANCE

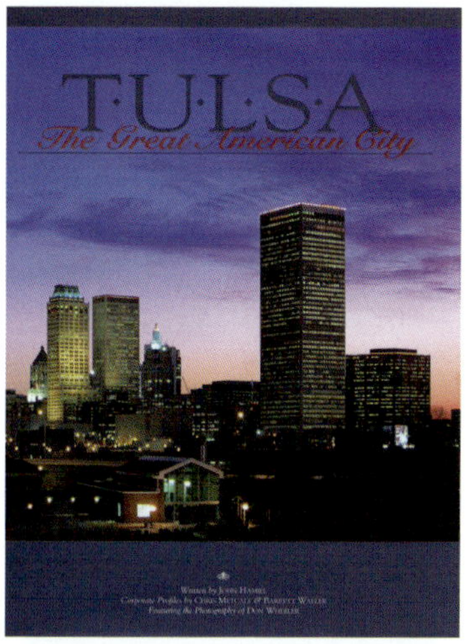
TULSA
The Great American City

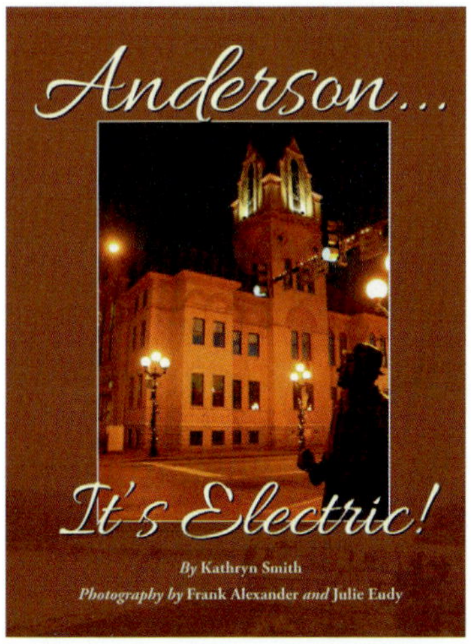
Anderson...
It's Electric!
By Kathryn Smith
Photography by Frank Alexander and Julie Eudy

Atlanta
The Making of a World Class City

Long
ISLAND
AN ENVIRONMENT FOR SUCCESS

Fort Worth
Catching the World's Attention

MOBILE BAY
Yesterday, Today & Tomorrow
MICHAEL V. R. THOMASON | CAROL ELLIS
Featuring the photography of
CATT SIRTIN
Corporate profiles by
ELISABETH A. DOLHRING
HARDY

MARY ANN NEELEY
MONTGOMERY and the RIVER REGION
yesterday, today & tomorrow
featuring the photography of Robert Fouts
Corporate profiles by Charles Barnette

The Shoals
Cities in Harmony
LAURA ANDERS LEE
Photography by
SHANNON WELLS
Corporate Profiles by
NANCY MANN JACKSON

TUSCALOOSA
Yesterday, Today & Tomorrow
By Donald and Hannah Brown
Featuring the photography of Barry Fikes,
Porfirio Solorzano and Alice Wilson

There aren't many things more Southern than a tall, icy-cold glass of sweet tea, and the Montgomery-based Alabama Sweet Tea Company, founded by Montgomery natives Wes Willis and Golson Foshee, is making some of the best. The company uses a custom blend of whole-leaf black tea to create several different versions, and none of them contain preservatives or anything artificial.

SABIC *Chemistry That Matters*

Whether it's everyday objects like refrigerator trays, food containers and storage bins, or "out of this world" objects like NASA astronaut helmets – they all have their start at SABIC.

Saudi Basic Industries Corporation established its plastics portfolio in September 2007 with the acquisition of GE Plastics. Today, SABIC has operations in more than 50 countries with a global workforce of over 35,000 talented individuals. The 6,300-acre Burkville, Alabama facility opened in 1987, and is one of the world's largest polycarbonate production facilities.

SABIC produces plastic pellets and resin for companies which then mold the plastic to make materials for everyday use, like mobile phone and computer casings and even automobile signal lighting. The Burkville facility supports the LEXAN™ Resin portfolio and ships this product both domestically and to multiple countries around the globe. Key markets include: automotive, consumer goods, construction, medical, aircraft, and business equipment. The Burkville facility employs 340 people from 13 counties in Alabama– primarily Montgomery, Autauga, Elmore, Dallas and Lowndes.

Sweet Home Alaga

"Montgomery has been a fabulous spot for Whitfield Foods. The company has been here since 1906, and is quite proud to call Montgomery home. The community, the history, the Southern charm and, most significantly, the citizens of Montgomery are all benefits to being here for the last 112 years. While there is no denying that Alabama was critically hurt with the demise of the textile industry, in the last two decades the state has rallied wonderfully with the advent of the automobile industry. This has led to better training and education for local industry, which in turn is now encouraging other industries to locate here. My favorite part of my job is our people. We take great pride in employees that have worked here for 10, 20, 40 years and more. I also love our customers. People tell us, 'I was raised on Alaga Syrup,' and that puts a smile on my face every time I hear it."

-Les Massey, President & CEO of Whitfield foods, Inc., a family owned company that produces Alaga Syrup and other products as well as serving as a contract packager for several national food and beverage companies.

WESTROCK

Integrity. Respect. Accountability. Excellence. These are the values that make WestRock a leading provider of differentiated paper and packaging solutions that answer unique local needs.

WestRock's 45,000 team members develop and deliver products with a worldwide perspective, executed with local precision, at more than 300 manufacturing facilities, design centers, labs, and sales offices around the world. One of those facilities is located in Montgomery. The 95-person team is responsible for creating and shipping corrugated boxes and sheets to other converting facilities in Alabama—an important link in the WestRock process.

WestRock is known as a partner that provides a competitive advantage, delivers consistent quality and superior service, and fuels innovation to foster real, sustainable growth. Innovation is key to WestRock's aspiration to be a premier provider of differentiated paper and packaging solutions that help customers win in the marketplace.

Photo by Brooke Glassford / Colorbox

Quality of Place
Events, Tourism, the Arts, Sports & Recreation

The Montgomery Symphony Orchestra's annual summer Pops Concert on the lawn of the Alabama Department of Archives and History downtown is a highlight of the region's cultural calendar.
Photo by Carter Photography & Design, LLC

The River Region is alive with culture, from large-scale productions and exhibits of classic works to ballet-school recitals and funky folk art. It's also an area packed with a wide array of activities and multiple entertainment offerings. But it's the friendly feel of its many close-knit communities that gives the area its warm, welcoming sense of place.

The arts are an essential component of any thriving area and are truly alive in the River Region thanks to longstanding institutions like the world-class Alabama Shakespeare Festival. This remarkable place surrounded by the serenity of Blount Cultural Park routinely stages work that rivals Broadway productions, and it packs its two state-of-the-art performance spaces with more than 120,000 theater-goers each season.

On the other end of the spectrum, Montgomery's Cloverdale Playhouse, Prattville's Way Off Broadway Theatre and Wetumpka's Depot Players put homegrown talent on the stage and in the spotlight and offer more intimate theatre experiences.

Also tucked into the grass-covered hills of Blount Cultural Park, The Montgomery Museum of Fine Arts boasts an impressive collection of American art, Old Master prints and Southern-based paintings as well as rotating exhibitions. The Montgomery Symphony fills the city with the sounds of music at several concerts every year, and The Alabama Dance Theater brings both ballets and modern choreography to area audiences. Together, these organizations provide a firm foundation of continuing creativity on which numerous other arts groups throughout the River Region across all disciplines are building.

continued on page 316

The Montgomery Museum of Fine Arts

Photo by Becca Beers

The Davis Theater for the Performing Arts
Image courtesey of Montgomery CVB

Alabama State University's Center for the Study of Civil Rights and African-American Culture showcases Montgomery's powerful role in shaping the modern Civil Rights Movement.

The River Region is blessed with several dance companies teaching and performing everything from classical ballet to jazz and more contemporary forms of the art.

THE MONTGOMERY MUSEUM OF FINE ARTS

The Montgomery Museum of Fine Arts is Alabama's oldest fine arts museum, founded in 1930. The facility in the Blount Cultural Park opened in 1989, and after two significant expansions, now encompasses more than 60,000 square feet devoted to the exhibition, care and study of art. In 2018, a three-acre sculpture garden opened on the grounds, offering new ways for visitors to experience art in a natural setting and fresh approaches to art education in its outdoor learning spaces. The galleries of the Museum are routinely filled with touring exhibitions as well as art from the Museum's own collections, which consist of American paintings, sculpture, and works on paper, with a special emphasis on the art of the southern region of the United States. The Museum also holds more than 500 etchings, engravings, and woodcuts in its Old Master Prints collection, as well as both historical and contemporary glass. Examples of traditional African art, self-taught art by regional artists, and American photography are also part of the Museum's always expanding collections.

From its earliest days, the Museum has placed a special emphasis on art education, particularly programs designed to serve school children in the River Region. Through on-site tours, outreach programs, and other learning opportunities for elementary-age children, the Museum inspires more than 10,000 students each year to embrace art and creativity in their lives. Its chief educational resource for children and families is ARTWORKS, a dynamic and immensely popular interactive learning environment that features many tactile and multi-sensory exhibits, as well as programs for computer-based exploration. In addition, the Museum annually offers diverse educational experiences in the arts for all ages and features many opportunities for lifelong learning through its gallery-based lectures, art-themed courses, and evening-schedule enrichment programs.

The Museum embraces its role as an important cultural resource for all Montgomerians and strives to create a space that is accessible and welcoming to all. Through a successful partnership of public funding by the City of Montgomery and private support solicited through the Montgomery Museum of Fine Arts Association, the Museum strives daily to meet its mission to collect, preserve, exhibit, and interpret art of the highest quality for the enrichment, enlightenment and enjoyment of

Opposite page: The MMFA is a landmark in Montgomery's Blount Cultural Park. Clockwise from top left: Students of all ages attend classes and summer workshops in the studios. Visitors enjoy a rotating selection of artwork in the galleries. Interpretive signage and audio tours engage visitors in exhibits. ARTWORKS offers hands-on, multi-sensory, and entertaining ways to engage with art.

ARTWORKS and gallery photography by Windham Graves

its public. As one of the premier visual arts institutions in the Southeast, the Museum attracts more than 140,000 local, regional, and national visitors annually.

The Museum's building and grounds also host large-scale family events celebrating the local military community, national holidays, and native peoples. The annual centerpiece celebration for families and the community is the Flimp Festival, which is held on the first weekend in May. The Museum Store features artwork created by Alabama and regional artists and craftspeople and supports their ability to earn a livelihood through their creative efforts. Café M is designed for those who love a relaxing and delicious meal in style and comfort, situated with an outstanding view of the Museum's lake and abundant waterfowl. During hours when the Museum is not open to the public, its spaces often are alive with receptions, concerts, and performances in the Wilson Auditorium.

The Montgomery Museum of Fine Arts is frequently the only major art museum many of its visitors will access, and it is proud to offer a free experience of art and learning for all citizens of the city and region. Through its strong collection, partnerships with other community organizations and institutions, outstanding education initiatives, and exhibition programs, the Museum delivers amazing, distinctive art experiences to audiences of the River Region.

Whether you're an avid athlete or simply a spectator, sporting events in Montgomery are scoring big points. The Montgomery Biscuits keep racking up wins and awards and keep filling Riverwalk Stadium with both baseball devotees and those simply in search of a nice evening outside enjoying the ballpark's fabulous food and ice-cold beer.

River Region leaders have worked hard to bring even more sporting events to the area, capitalizing on its central location, mild climate and affordability by building and renovating athletic facilities and harnessing the resources needed.

continued on page 320

Photo courtesy of Montgomery CVB

317

MONTGOMERY SYMPHONY ORCHESTRA

Performing the Great Music of the Ages for More than 40 Years

Blake Thomas was hired in July 2017 as the Montgomery Symphony Orchestra's third executive director since its founding more than 40 years ago. Yet he's been preparing for this role since childhood. "I'm part of the first generation that got exposed to orchestral music by the Symphony and got opportunities through the Symphony," Thomas said. A native of Montgomery, Thomas enrolled in the city's magnet schools, and several of his strings teachers – starting as early as kindergarten – played with the Symphony. Eventually, the late Helen Steineker, who began serving as MSO manager in 1986, took notice of the young musician and encouraged his continued involvement.

At age 12, Thomas became involved with the MSO's StringFellows Summer Music Seminar, which is a seven-day residential music camp for students of violin, viola, cello and bass. "It provides young musicians with the opportunity to have an introduction to intensive orchestral studies," he said. Around that age, he also began playing double bass with the Montgomery Youth Orchestra, which is also under the MSO auspices. He began playing double bass with the Symphony at age 14.

The programs that Thomas was able to participate in – along with many other educational and performance programs that enrich the community – were hardly on the radar when the Symphony first came into being in 1976.

"It began with a group of musicians who wanted to find locations to play orchestral music," Thomas said. "They didn't have an outlet for playing orchestral music, so this was a way for everybody to come together to rehearse and perform."

Wind, brass and percussion players were organized by John Dressler, music director at First United Methodist Church, and their first performances were to accompany the church's choirs. The MSO rehearsed at the church and, as it grew, began to offer concerts in the community. "It was a small chamber ensemble orchestra when it first started," Thomas said.

Maestro Dressler guided the young orchestra until retiring from the podium in 1979, even as the structure continued to grow. A Board of Directors was formed in 1980 and incorporated in 1981, and the Montgomery Symphony League was formed a year later. "They were all

"I am part of the first generation that was exposed to orchestral music by the Symphony and provided opportunities through the Symphony."

- Blake Thomas, Montgomery Symphony Orchestra Eexecutive Director

volunteer – volunteer management and volunteer conductor – at that time," Thomas said. "They played just about anywhere they could find."

Following a year-long search for a new Music Director and Conductor, Thomas Hinds stepped onto the MSO's podium at the beginning of the 1983-1984 season, where he remains today. His debut as Music Conductor coincided with the MSO's debut on the Davis Theatre stage.

In the late 1980s the organization turned its combined efforts toward nurturing the artistic development of the Orchestra. The Fellowship Program brought a world-class violinist into the MSO's midst to help lead and inspire the strings. Since that time, the MSO has welcomed more than 30 fellows from such countries as Russia, Germany, Bulgaria and Czechoslovakia, as well as from California, Kentucky and Tennessee in the U.S.

A focus on music education inspired the development of several programs in the 1990s. For example, the Montgomery Symphony Radio Show first aired in 1992 and continues today, providing a weekly opportunity to educate listeners on all aspects of music. Two other programs, the Trawick Players and the StringFellows Summer Music Seminar were initiated to provide musical learning opportunities for elementary and junior high students. Each year, approximately 70 young musicians from public and private schools throughout central Alabama participate in the Montgomery Youth Orchestra. In addition, the Montgomery Music Project provides educational opportunities for students from 3 to 13 years old.

The MSO's annual Subscription Concert series includes performances that feature an artist-in-residence (one of the fellows), a classical concert, a guest artist, and the winner of the Blount-Slawson Competition, which is a concerto competition for pre-college instrumentalists.

The Symphony also performs three pops concerts each year – a holiday concert at the Davis Theatre, a Memorial Day concert at the Alabama Department of Archives and History, and a Broadway Under the Stars concert at the Alabama Shakespeare Festival. In addition, the Symphony performs annual Children's Concerts for public and private school students in the River Region.

"Ours is a unique organization," Thomas said. "We are a non-profit community orchestra." People from all types of professions, such as dentists, lawyers, tellers, government and teachers, come together to play. "They all have the common theme of passion for orchestral music, and they come together for that."

Through the years, hundreds of musicians have devoted nearly a half million volunteer hours to rehearse and perform the great music of the ages. Many musicians have pledged their Monday nights to the MSO for 30 years or more, including several charter members. The maturity they bring to the Orchestra's performances undergirds its artistic success. In appreciation, they have been supported by the time, energy and resources of an entire community and sustained by the enthusiastic applause of a grateful audience.

Each fall, the Alabama National Fair brings massive crowds to Montgomery from the surrounding River Region and beyond. They come to fill their senses with the sights, sounds, smells and tastes of the fairgrounds — fried foods, spun sugar, farm animals and thrilling rides all lit by the glow of neon shining brightly from the midway. The annual Southeastern Livestock Exposition Rodeo also draws folks in droves with its blast of buckin' broncos, cowboy clowns and intense barrel racing and bull riding competitions.

Other events put residents right in the middle of the activity. The Dragon Boat Race draws hundreds to the Riverfront to have fun and do good, either as part of one of the teams doing battle with paddles on the Alabama River or by simply watching the action and cheering, all to raise money for a local non-profit.

The popularity of each spring's Taco Libre event, a food fest focused on south-of-the-border fare, is proof that the area's culinary scene is cooking. Residents have more ways than ever to satisfy their appetites thanks to the continued success of time-honored eating establishments like the century-old Chris' Hot Dogs (still owned and operated by its founding family) as well as the rise of new chef-driven restaurants with a focus on farm-to-fork dishes and innovative takes on regional favorites.

Add the area's easy access to nearby getaways like sparkling lakes, sugar-sand beaches and major metropolises, and it's simple to see why quality of life is one of the River Region's most valuable and appealing assets.

Montgomery's annual Dragon Boat Festival features fierce competition and serious fun each summer on the Riverfront with eating, drinking, rowing and racing, all to raise money for local charities.
Photo courtesy of Montgomery CVB / Carter Photography & Design, LLC

Lightning Line MGM, a group that works to create experiences to bring the community together, hosts two tasty eating events each year, the MGM Burger Bash and Taco Libre.

Innovative Events

"Lightning Line's purpose is to create experiences where our local community comes together as friends, families, neighbors, businesses organizations and non-profits to celebrate the great things our city has to offer, by having a good time and supporting a good cause. It really kicked off when Adam and I were on a trip to Nashville and saw some cool events that were going on there. We both wished Montgomery had similar things to keep people in town and bring in visitors. We decided to create some, starting with the first Burger Bash competition, and got Steven Lambert of Cotton & Pine on board. That's how Lightning Line was born. Next, we held the first Taco Libre event. Both food fests were successful and both have grown, and we've got more plans for the future. But it's not just us. I think the creative and entrepreneurial environment here is growing too. You can feel it. People are staying here or moving here and wanting to make Montgomery a better place. I can't wait to watch it keep growing and to continue to help build a city that people want to be a part of."

- Avery Ainsworth, owner of Fleet Feet Sports Montgomery and co-founder of Lightning Line with Adam Warnke and Steven Lambert

Photo courtesy of Montgomery CVB

Photo by Sam Moody

Photos by Robert Fouts

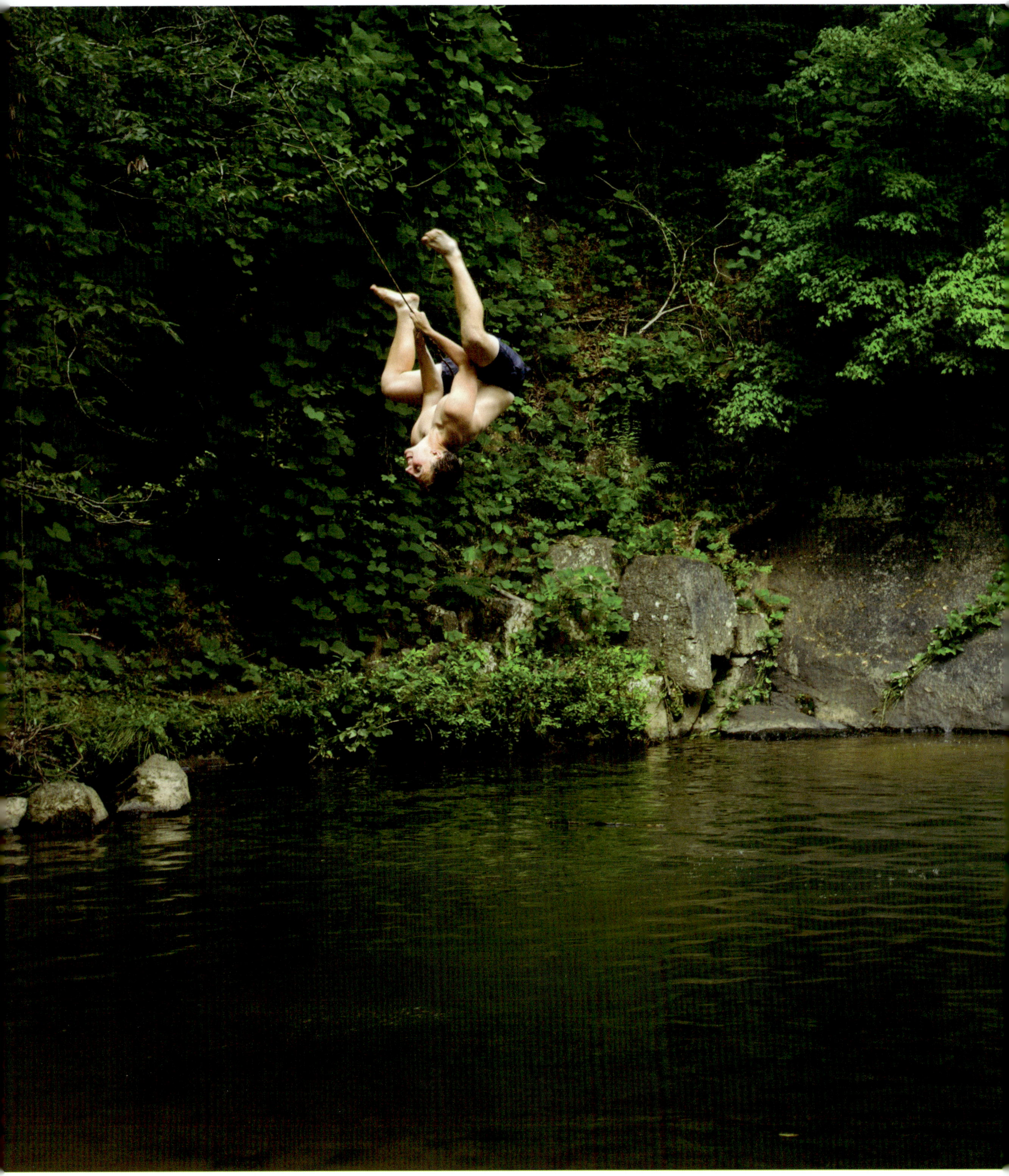

MONTGOMERY ZOO & MANN WILDLIFE MUSEUM

For decades, thousands of residents and visitors to Montgomery have taken a walk on the wild side, spending an hour or an entire day exploring natural, barrier-free habitats filled with 500 amazing animals at The Montgomery Zoo. They come to get an up-close-and-personal look at a wide array of creatures, species they might spot in their own backyards and exotic animals hailing from the most far-flung locations around the globe and ranging in size from the tiny squirrel monkey to a 6,000-pound African elephant.

These more intimate encounters have made the Zoo one of the area's most popular and important attractions, as Marcia Woodard, Zoo Director, explained. "The Montgomery Zoo is a valuable resource to the City of Montgomery and the River Region since it appeals to people of all age groups and all walks of life," she said. "We are able to bring people as close as possible to viewing animals in a natural environment."

These environments are divided into distinct continental realms, representing five diverse geographical areas: Africa, Asia, North America, South America and Australia.

It's different from the way many zoos are organized and speaks to the broader purpose of the Zoo, one that extends beyond entertainment to provide in-depth education through on-site signage, creative bulletin boards and events. "We are as much about education as anything and see it as important that we teach our visitors about the animals in our collection," Woodard said. "Communicating information about the region the animals come from, the food the animals eat and if the animal is endangered or threatened is key to help our Zoo visitors understand the importance of taking steps for conservation efforts." The Zoo makes it part of its mission to encourage its visitors to make a difference by actively conserving water, electricity and recycling when possible. "Collectively these actions help to save animal habitats globally," Woodard said.

The Zoo recognizes that the best way to get someone interested in protecting animals by preserving habitat is to catch them early. "We strongly believe that young kids who care about animals and the planet we share with them will continue to care about the way they affect the well-being of animals," Woodard said. And the best way to capture a child's interest is to engage their imagination. Interactive activities during the Zoo's Animal Enrichment Days and the Earth Day Safari plus hands-on activities offered through education programs are designed to forge connections and impress upon people of all ages their place in the world relative to animals and how we impact them by impacting the environment.

This approach has been a foundational element of the Zoo since it moved to its current site in 1972, relocating from its original location in Oak Park, where it first opened as a small children's zoo in the 1920s. It has grown from a 6-acre complex to a 42-acre, modern zoological facility that draws just shy of 300,000 visitors each year. And today these visitors have the opportunity for even richer, one-on-one experiences with additions like the Giraffe Encounter, which allows hand-feeding of the Zoo's geometrically embellished gentle giants; Parakeet Cove, where cheerily chirping brightly colored birds land on shoulders, heads and hands to peck at seed-covered sticks; and the newest Zoo attraction, Stingray Bay, where Zoo guests are encouraged to stroke stingrays and other aquatic creatures as they swim in a shallow pool. "When you have this interaction with an animal, you identify with them more and want to do the things that can benefit their survival. Plus, it's just such an awesome experience," Woodard said.

The Zoo's commitment to conservation continues behind the scenes as well and reaches outside the River Region. It is a member of the Species Survival Plan (SSP), which allows it to help keep the populations of threatened and endangered species healthy by participating in the SSP breeding network with other zoos. "Many people are surprised to learn that we trade animals with other zoological facilities," Woodard said. "Many species have a coordinator assigned to them that makes recommendations for breeding based upon the animal's genetic make-up."

Promoting conservation is key, but pure fun is still a major part of the equation on any visit to the Zoo, thanks to diversions like pedal boats, a train that traverses the property and the Skylift, which affords a birds-eye view of several large animal exhibits. "Where else can you soar over lions and cheetahs?" Woodard said. And the Mann Wildlife Learning Museum, which joined the Zoo in 2004 and lets visitors touch the fur and feel the hides of the animals in its large collection of North American species, adds another level of discovery.

There are so many ways to enjoy the Zoo, and being able to "do it your way" is part of the appeal. "You can go just to the Zoo, to just the Museum or both, and with all the rides and encounters, there are so many options," Woodard said. "The Montgomery Zoo is really one great big outdoor classroom where we are creating a true adventure for our visitors."

Fireworks light up the night sky over the capital city.

The Alabama Shakespeare Festival is the official state theatre and produces some of The Bard's most famous works as well as contemporary musicals and favorite children's plays each season.
Photo courtesy of Montgomery CVB / Stephen Poff

Taking Center Stage

Rodney Clark has been acting at The Alabama Shakespeare Festival for 22 years, inhabiting countless characters while performing in 100 plays and engaging audiences of all ages. He counts himself fortunate to grace the stage at ASF. "ASF is renowned throughout the theatre world as one of the best regional theatres in the country and is certainly one of the most beautiful and functional facilities," he said. "It produces more shows than any other theatre in Alabama, employs more actors and artisans, and draws audiences from all over the United States and many other countries."

He thinks by being in Montgomery, ASF is exactly where it ought to be. "The River Region and Montgomery are a vibrant area. I don't believe Birmingham could support this theatre the way Montgomery has and does," he said. "There is a love of arts and a community feeling in Montgomery that I'm not sure exists in any other part of the state."

His wife and fellow ASF actress Greta Lambert agreed. "There is an active unified effort to make our region a diverse cultural center, welcome to everyone in our community. The number of arts organizations is growing, giving us more theatre, more dance, more music, more crafts, painting, sculpting and design. The talent in our area is tremendous and growing," she said. She also praised the large group of folks who work together at ASF to make each season's productions happen. "Our people are what make ASF a wonderful place to work. There are so many dedicated, talented artisans who work in our shops and costume, set, sound, lighting and props departments."

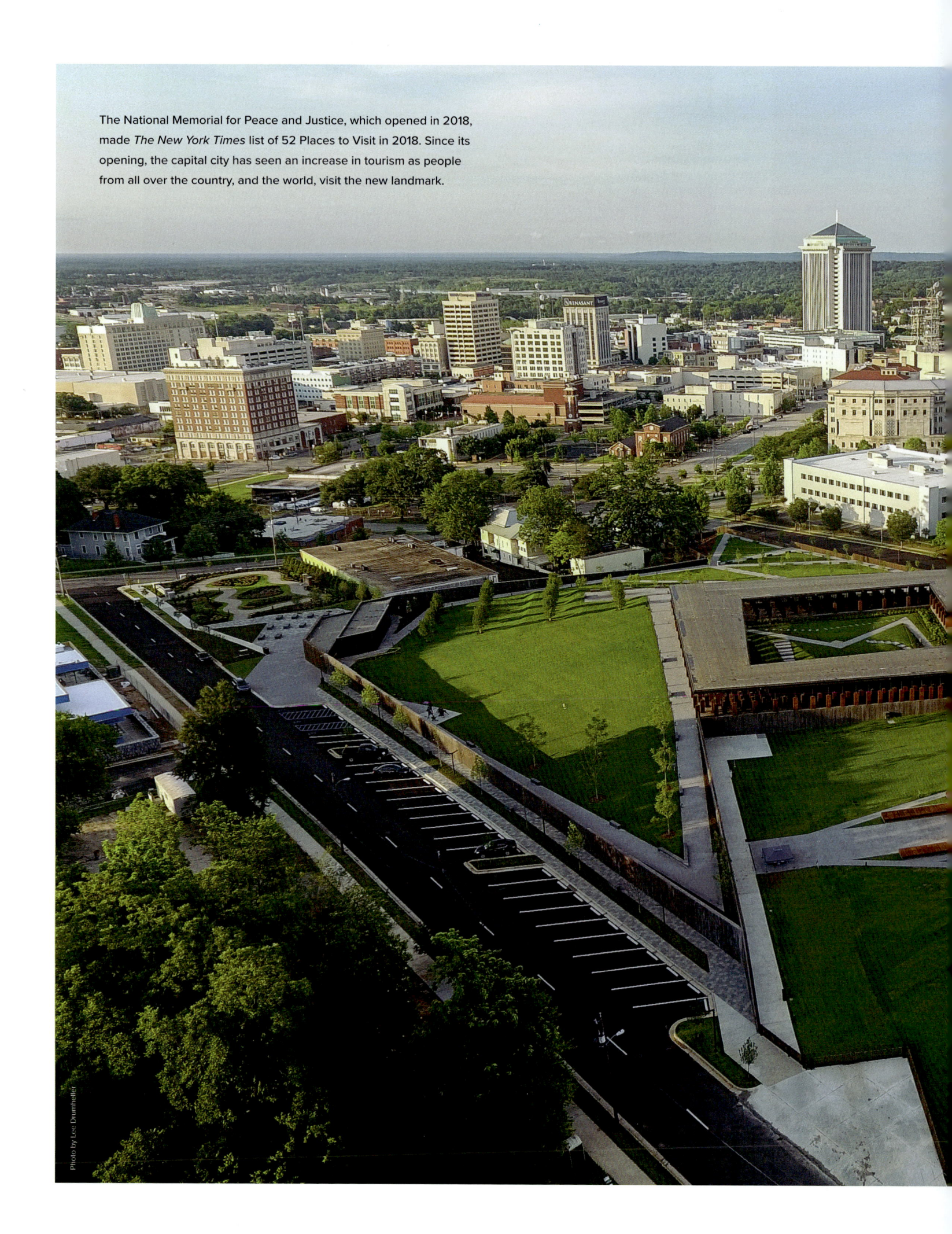

The National Memorial for Peace and Justice, which opened in 2018, made *The New York Times* list of 52 Places to Visit in 2018. Since its opening, the capital city has seen an increase in tourism as people from all over the country, and the world, visit the new landmark.

Photo courtesy of F. Scott Fitzgerald Museum / Thomas Lucas

Photos courtesy of Montgomery CVB / Carter Photography & Design, LLC

329

Downtown Montgomery is packed with things to see and do. Explore Civil War history at The First White House of the Confederacy. Find almost everything there is to know about the Yellowhammer state at the Museum of Alabama. Learn about the deep roots of civil rights struggles at the Rosa Parks Museum, the Dexter Avenue King Memorial Baptist Church and the compelling Maya Lin Civil Rights Memorial. Or get to know a country music legend a little better at the Hank Williams Museum.

Photo courtesy of Montgomery CVB

...UNTIL JUSTICE ROLLS DOWN LIKE WATERS
AND RIGHTEOUSNESS LIKE A MIGHTY STREAM

MARTIN LUTHER KING JR

As the birthplace of the Civil Rights Movement, the capital city is home to some of the best and worst moments and memories of that struggle, and with The Equal Justice Initiative's Legacy Museum & National Memorial for Peace and Justice, Montgomery is making a dramatic statement, shining a powerful bright light on racially based injustices and oppression that have happened here, across the South and the world.

Photo by Eric Salas

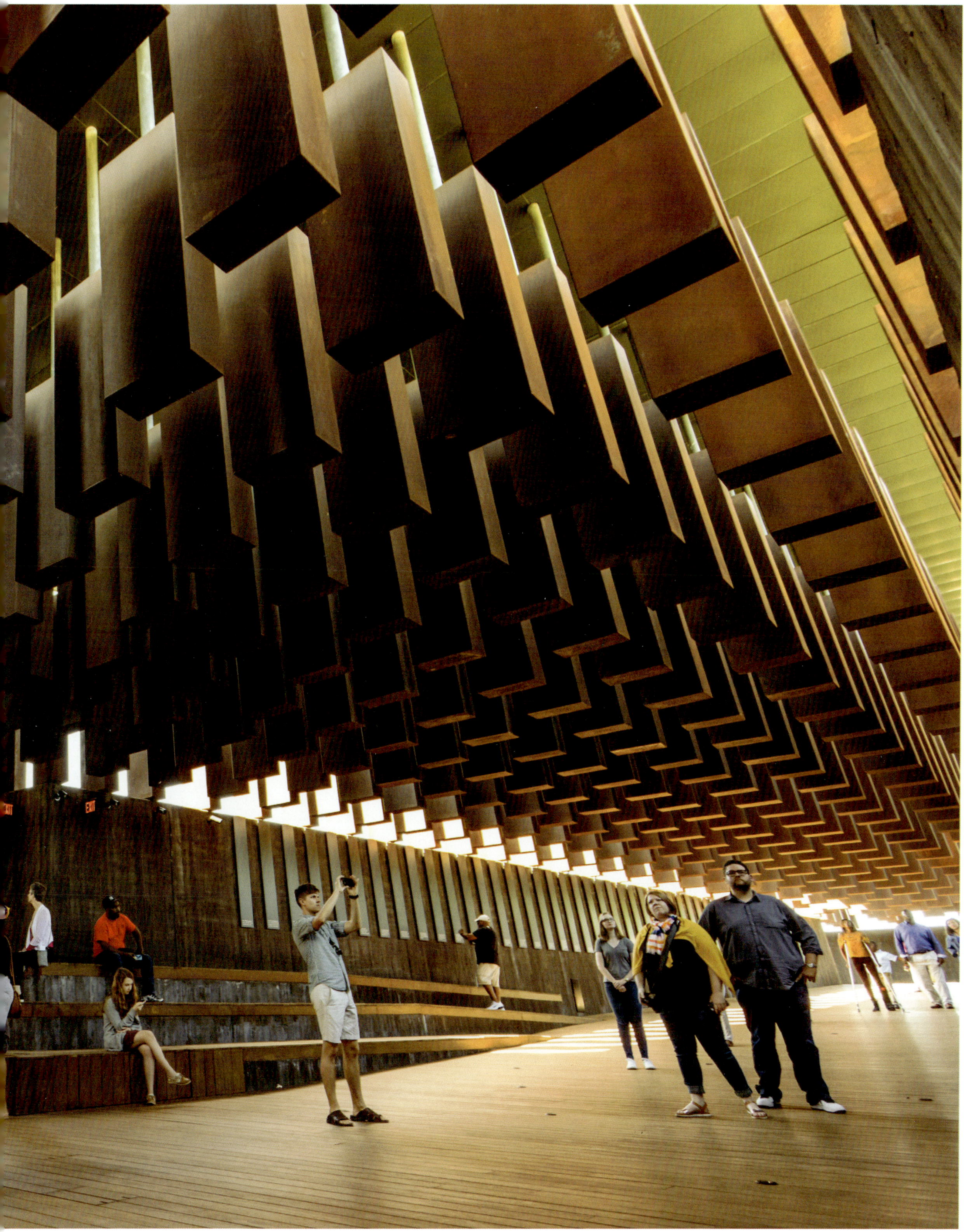

The world-class courses at Capitol Hill in Prattville are often considered the "crown jewel" of the highly praised Robert Trent Jones Golf Trail. The rolling fairways and verdant greens of all three courses (The Judge, The Legislator and The Senator) consistently garner impressive rankings from national media, including Golf Magazine, and continue to attract countless golfers, everyone from casual duffers to the pros.

Photo by Robert Fouts

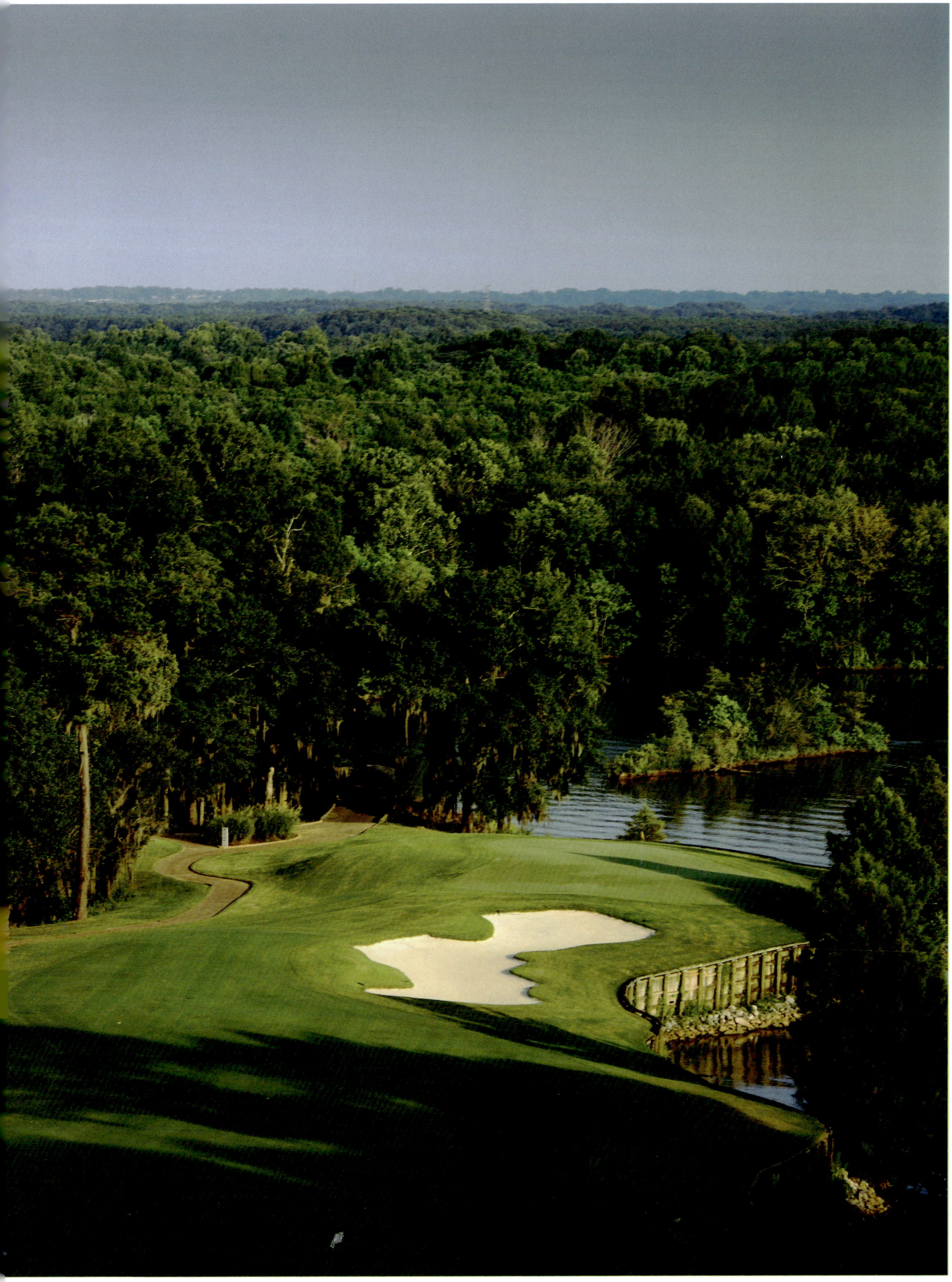

The River Region has outdoor events and activities galore. Hunting and fishing opportunities are abundant, and the Annual Southeastern Livestock Exposition Rodeo brings some of the country's best cowboys and cowgirls to show off their roping and riding skills.

Hunter Chambliss, an avid sportsman. Photo courtesy of the Chambliss family.

Jasmine Hill Gardens in Wetumpka welcomes guests to wander through acres of beautiful blooms dotted with statuary representing mythical Greek heroes and gods.

Photo courtesy of the Montgomery CVB / Carter Photography & Design, LLC

KOUNTRY AIR RV PARK

The story of Kountry Air RV Park, located in Prattville, actually began thousands of miles away in the high desert of northern Nevada. On a snowy day in 2011, Don and Gigi Deselms left life out west and headed to Alabama. The result of their "amazing leap of faith" was a brand new adventure for them. Owning and operating an RV park was full of unknowns and Gigi had never even been to Alabama before. But their risk proved successful. For the past six years, the Deselms have used their love for the outdoors to create a unique place for travelers to relax close to nature and experience southern hospitality.

Gigi says that revitalizing the place that is now Kountry Air is a blood, sweat and tears story of hard work to renew the beautiful piece of property they call their "little piece of heaven." Kountry Air has become a premiere family-oriented RV park with first-class amenities and beautiful surroundings that attracts guests from all walks of life.

The Deselms' mutual love for gardening, bird watching and cooking are on full display at Kountry Air. Guests enjoy beautiful landscapes maintained by the couple, and Don's specialty: Hungarian stew.

The same faith that led the Deselms to open Kountry Air is the same faith that keeps the park running today. "We continue to run on faith every day," says Gigi. "We are blessed by our family, friends and guests that have crossed our path."

The tranquil Bamboo Forest in Prattville. Photo by Sam Moody

The fictional town of Spectre, a location for the filming of several scenes in the movie "Big Fish," is a fun spot to explore on Jackson Lake Island in Millbrook. Photo by Barry Chrtizerberg

WINGATE BY WYNDHAM

Montgomery brings you its best when staying at Wingate By Wyndham. Its 82 guest rooms, conference room, banquet space and amenities—complimentary hot breakfast, free high speed internet, outdoor pool, business and fitness center—provide the perfect getaway for you. Other tremendous room features, which guests love, include tempur-pedic mattresses and Wolfgang Puck Coffee as well as a serene view of the hotel's private lake from the guestrooms. Furthermore, the hotel places you nearby the famous Alabama Shakespeare Festival, Montgomery Museum of Fine Arts, and Downtown Montgomery.

"At Wingate By Wyndham Montgomery, our staff treat every guest as their own family members," says the General Manager Anna Yu. Visitors range from family members coming for reunions to military or government workers, and those on business trips. Travelers all around the world take advantage of the Wyndham Reward Program that could get you a free night simply for staying at any Wyndham properties. The Wingate By Wyndham will make its guests feel welcomed and have an impeccable experience here in Montgomery.

The River Region's warm hospitality is always on display at area hotels, like the Renaissance Montgomery Hotel & Spa. The WindCreek Casino and Hotel in Wetumpka, operated by the Poarch Band of Creek Indians, has plenty of gaming good times.

Serving as the center for entertainment in downtown, the Montgomery Performing Arts Center is a state-of-the-art facility large enough for first run Broadway shows, yet intimate enough with 1,800 seats to view a wide variety of concerts, opera, comedy, dance and children's shows.

Photo courtesy of Montgomery CVB

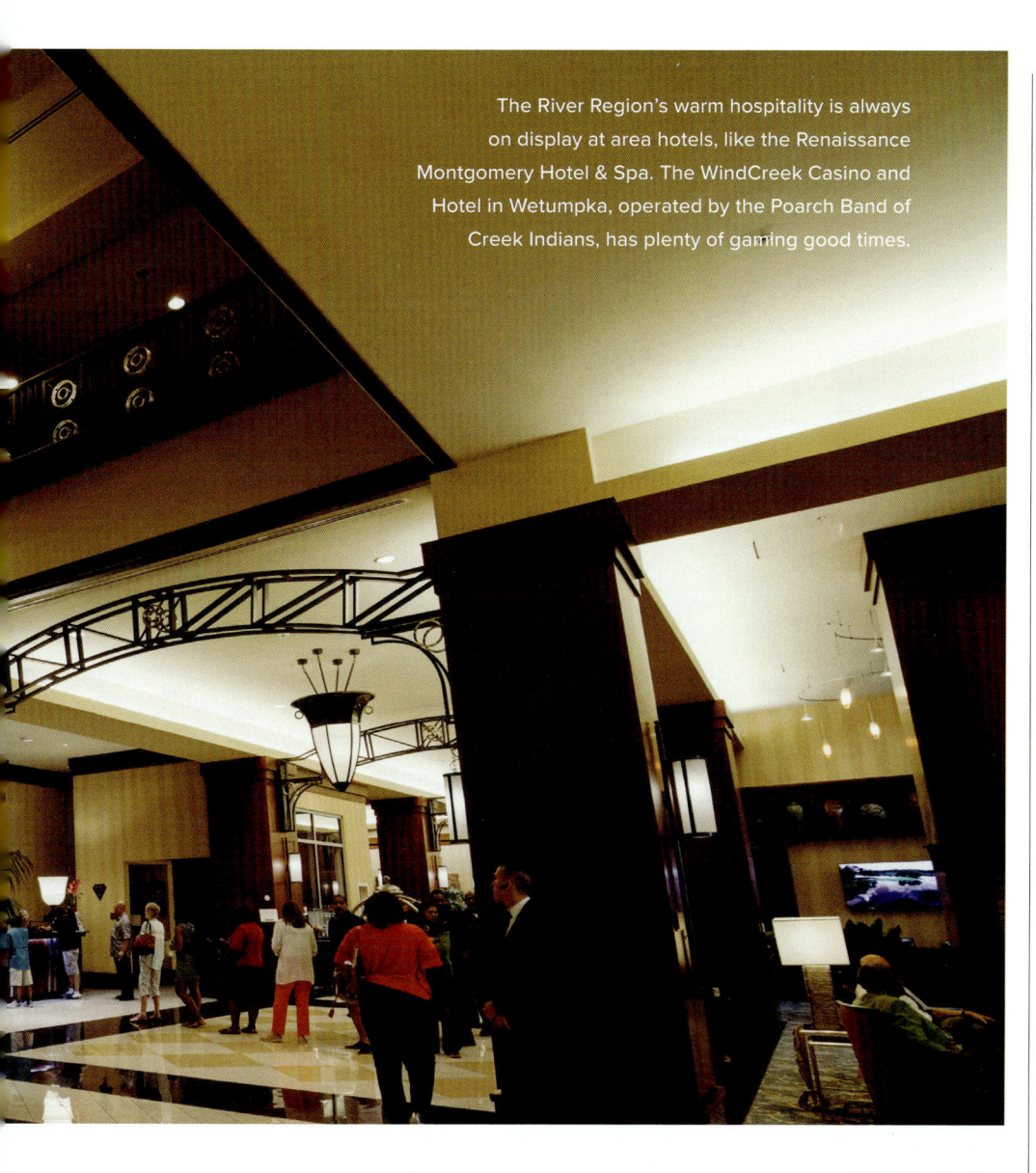

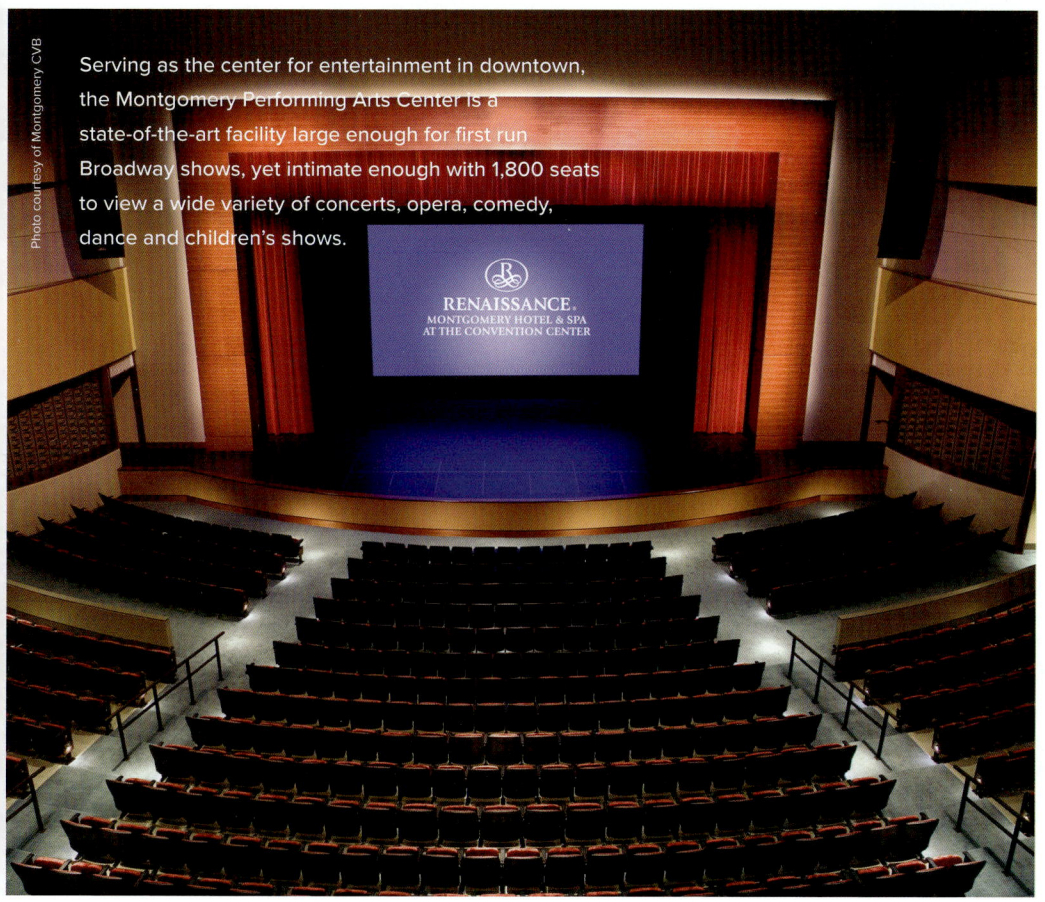

THE KELLY FITZPATRICK MEMORIAL GALLERY

The Kelly Fitzpatrick Memorial Gallery was born in 2011 to honor Wetumpka native and favorite son, John Kelly Fitzpatrick, and to foster the development and recognition of a vibrant visual arts community in Elmore County. "The Kelly" is an all volunteer organization, housed in beautiful exhibit space provided by The City of Wetumpka.

Formed as a hybrid between a museum and a gallery, The Kelly is building several permanent collections, including one that features the work of the gallery's namesake. Each year brings a series of stellar exhibitions featuring the work of artists living and dead from throughout Alabama and the southeast.

The Kelly has a strong educational component, including a monthly lunch-and-learn series called "Tuesdays With Kelly." The gallery has given the community a new meeting place, convivial social gatherings, free and open to the public, and enhanced cultural opportunities for citizens and visitors. The Kelly Fitzpatrick Memorial Gallery is proud to add new depth and texture to the Elmore County Arts community and to enhance quality of life for residents, newcomers and people looking for a vibrant, forward-looking place to call home.

Corporate Sponsor Index

Adams Family Enterprises, LLC
10 East Jefferson Street
Montgomery, AL 36104
(334) 301-0597
pp. 60-61

AIDT
1 Technology Court
Montgomery, AL 36116
(334) 242-4158
aidt.edu
pp. 96-97

Alabama Christian Academy
4700 Wares Ferry Road
Montgomery, AL 36109
(334) 277-1985
alabamachristian.org
pg. 111

**Alabama Machinery
& Supply Company**
323 Bibb Street
Montgomery, AL 36101
(334) 269-4351
ams-co.com
pg. 296

Alabama Power Company
200 Dexter Avenue
Montgomery, AL 36104
(800) 613-9333
alabamapower.com
pg. 271

ALFA
2108 E. South Boulavard
Montgomery, AL 36116
(334) 288-0375
alfainsurance.com
pp. 188-189

Amridge University
1200 Taylor Road
Montgomery, AL 36117
(334) 387-3877
amridgeuniversity.edu
pg. 104

Answered Prayer Home Care Services
4101-C Wall Street
Montgomery, AL 35106
(334) 356-3911
answeredprayercare.com
pg. 131

Aronov Realty Management
3500 Eastern Boulevard
Montgomery, AL 36116
(334) 277-2700
aronov.com
pp. 158-159

Auburn University at Montgomery
7440 East Drive
Montgomery, AL 36117
334-244-3000
aum.edu
pp. 80-81

Bacheler Technologies
7005 Brockport Court
Montgomery, AL 36116
(334) 669-4530
bachelertechnologies.com
pg. 277

Baptist Health
301 Brown Springs Road
Montgomery, AL 36124
(334) 273-4389
baptistfirst.org
pp. 114-117

Beers & Associates
113 Washington Avenue
Montgomery, AL 36104
334-396-2896
beersandassociates.net
pg. 306-307

**Borden Morris Garner
Consulting Engineers**
903 South Perry Street
Montgomery, AL 36104
(334) 269-0329
bmg-eng.com
pg. 231

Brown Studio Architecture
401 Madison Avenue
Montgomery, AL 36104
(334) 834-8340
brownstudio.com
pg. 204

Burt Steel, Inc.
920 N. Decatur Street
Montgomery, AL 36104
(334) 265-9268
burtsteel.com
pp. 288-289

Capital City Gastroenterology
4126 Carmichael Court
Montgomery, AL 36106
(334) 495-2600
ccgastro.net
pg. 127

Capitol Container, Inc.
2555 Container Drive
Montgomery, AL 36109
(334) 277-5644
capitol-container.com
pg. 305

Cedric Bradford
420 South Lawrence Street
Montgomery, AL 36104
(334) 262-5100
statefarm.com
pg. 220

Central Alabama Community College
1675 Cherokee Road
Alexander City, AL 35010
(256) 234-6346
cacc.edu
pp. 92-93

Chip Nix, Attorney at Law
7505 Halcyon Point Drive
Montgomery, AL 36117
(334) 279-7770
nixattorney.com
pg. 241

DAVMOOR
8650 Minnie Brown Road
Montgomery, AL 36117
(334) 244-5044
davmoor.com
pg. 208

Edwards Plumbing and Heating
1540 Jean Street
Montgomery, AL 36107
(334) 834-6120
edwardsplumbing.com
pp. 196-197

eSolution Architects
3325 Kessinger Drive
Montgomery, AL 36116
(334) 532-3663
e-sainc.com
pg. 217

Fastening Solutions, Inc.
3075 Selma Highway
Montgomery, AL 36108
(334) 284-8300
fsiusa.com
pg. 300

Faulkner University
5345 Atlanta Highway
Montgomery, AL 36109
(334) 386-7140
faulkner.edu
pg. 101

Frazer United Methodist Church
6000 Atlanta Highway
Montgomery, AL 36116
(334) 272-8622
frazer.church
pg. 169

Garner Electric
2701 Main Street
Millbrook, AL 36054
(334) 285-0101
garnerelectricinc.com
pg. 228

Goodwyn, Mills and Cawood
Lakeview Center
2660 East Chase Lane #200
Montgomery, AL 36117
(334) 271-3200
gmcnetwork.com
pg. 209

Holt Street Memorial Baptist Church
1870 S Court Street
Montgomery, AL 36104
(334) 263-0522
holtstreetmemorialbaptistchurch.net
pg. 43

Information Transport Solutions
335 Jeanette Barrett Industrial Boulevard
Wetumpka, AL 36092
(334) 567-1993
its-networks.com
pg. 275

Jackson Hospital
1725 Pine Street
Montgomery, AL 36106
(334) 293-8000
jackson.org
pg. 121

Jackson Thornton
200 Commerce Street
Montgomery, AL 36106
(334) 834-7660
jacksonthornton.com
pg. 225

Jenkins Tire & Automotive
38 E Jefferson Street
Montgomery, AL 36104
(334) 262-1996
jenkinstireandauto.com
pg. 235

JMR+H Architecture, P.C.
445 Dexter Avenue, Suite 505
Montgomery, AL 36104
(334) 420-5672
jmrha.com
pp. 180-181

The Joe Hubbard Law Firm
325 N. Hull Street
Montgomery, AL 36104
(334) 312-2697
joehubbardlaw.com
pg. 247

Jones Drugs – Fairview Avenue
59 W Fairview Avenue
Montgomery, AL 36105
(334) 676-2900
jonesdrugs.com
pg. 130

Joy to Life Foundation
2350 Fairlane Drive
Montgomery, AL 36116
(334) 284-5433
joytolifefoundation.org
pp. 136-138

The Kelly Fitzpatrick Memorial Gallery
408 S. Main Street
Wetumpka, AL 36092
(334) 567-5147
thekelly.org
pg. 341

Kountry Air RV Park
2133 U.S. Highway 82 W.
Prattville, AL 36067
(334) 365-6861
kountryairrv.com
pg. 338

Larry E. Speaks & Associates, Inc.
535 Herron Street
Montgomery, AL 36104
(334) 262-1091
lespeaks.net
pg. 212

Lear Corporation
200 Folmar Parkway
Montgomery, AL 36105
(334) 286-4504
lear.com
pg. 304

The Lilly Baptist Church
820 Hill Street
Montgomery, AL 36108
(334) 269-2592
p. 162

McPhillips Shinbaum, LLP
516 South Perry Street
Montgomery, AL 36104
(334) 262-1911
mcphillipsshinbaum.com
pg. 243

Merrill Lynch
4001 Carmichael Road
Montgomery, AL 36106
(334) 409-5800
ml.com
pg. 224

The Montgomery Academy
3240 Vaughn Road
Montgomery, AL 36106
(334) 272-8210
montgomeryacademy.org
pg. 105

The Montgomery Area Chamber of Commerce
41 Commerce Street
Montgomery, AL 36104
(334) 834-5200
montgomerychamber.com
pp. 176-177

Montgomery Catholic Preparatory School
5350 Vaughan Road
Montgomery, AL 36116
(334) 272-7220
montgomerycatholic.org
pg. 108

The Montgomery Museum of Fine Arts
1 Museum Drive
Montgomery, AL 36117
(334) 240-4333
mmfa.org
pp. 314-315

Montgomery Regional Airport
4445 Selma Highway
Montgomery, AL 36108
(334) 281-5040
flymgm.com
pp. 264-265

The Montgomery Symphony Orchestra
507 Columbus Street
Montgomery, AL 36104
(334) 240-4004
montgomerysymphony.org
pp. 318-319

Corporate Sponsor Index

**Montgomery Water Works
& Sanitary Sewer Board**
2000 Interstate Park Drive
Montgomery, AL 36109
(334) 206-1600
mwwssb.com
pp. 268-269

**Montgomery Zoo
& Mann Wildlife Museum**
2301 Coliseum Parkway
Montgomery, AL 36110
(334) 625-4959
montgomeryzoo.com
pp. 324-325

Neptune Technology Group
1600 AL-229
Tallassee, AL 36078
(334) 283-6555
neptunetg.com
pp. 284-285

Prattville Area Chamber of Commerce
131 N Court Street
Prattville, AL 36067
(334) 365-7392
prattvillechamber.com
pg. 201

Prattville Christian Academy
322 Old Farm Lane N.
Prattville, AL 36066
(334) 285-0077
prattvillechristianacademy.org
pg. 110

Prattville YMCA
600 East Main Street
Prattville, AL 36067
(334) 365-8852
prattvilleymca.org
pg. 145

Production Automation, Inc.
2075 Exchange Street
Montgomery, AL 36116
(334) 281-4970
palletizers.com
pg. 301

Publications Press, Inc.
884 Lagoon Commercial Boulevard
Montgomery, AL 36117
(334) 244-0436
publicationspress.com
pp. 192 - 193

Ralph Smith Motors
427 Jefferson Street
Montgomery, AL 36104
(334) 263-1347
ralphsmithmotors.com
pg. 233

Renal Associates of Montgomery, P.C.
4760 Woodmere Boulevard
Montgomery, AL 36106
(334) 288-0814
renalmgmal.com
pg. 124

Realty Connection
2066 Fairview Avenue
Prattville, AL 36066
(334) 491-0049
realtyconnection.biz
pg. 163

Regitar U.S.A.
2575 Container Drive
Montgomery, AL 36109
(334) 244-1885
regitar.com
pp. 292-293

Riverfront Facilities
200 Coosa Street
Montgomery, AL 36104
(334) 241-2100
funinmontgomery.com
pg. 65

River Region Dermatology and Laser
2060 Berryhill Road
Montgomery, AL 36117
(334) 676-3366
rrdermatologylaser.com
pg. 125

River Region United Way
3121 Zelda Court
Montgomery, AL 36106
(334) 264-7318
riverregionunitedway.org
pg. 146

Robinson and Associates Architecture, Inc.
906 S Perry Street
Montgomery, AL 36104
(334) 269-5590
robinsonandassociatesarchitecture.com
pg. 221

Ross-Clayton Funeral Home, Inc.
1412 Adams Avenue
Montgomery, AL 36102
(334) 262-3889
rossclaytonfh.com
pg. 232

Sabel Steel Service, Inc.
749 N Court Street
Montgomery, AL 36104
(334) 265-6771
sabelsteel.com
pp. 280-281

SABIC
1 Plastics Avenue
Burkville, AL 36752
(855) 201-9620
sabic.com
pg. 308

Saint James School
6010 Vaughn Road
Montgomery, AL 36116
(334) 277-8033
stjweb.org
pg. 100

ServisFirst Bank Montgomery
One Commerce Street
Suite 100
Montgomery, Alabama 36104
(334) 223-5800
servisfirstbank.com
pp. 184-185

Stanley Steemer
850 Plantation Way
Montgomery, Alabama 361117
(334) 277-0002
stanleysteemer.com
pg. 230

The Town of Pike Road
9575 Vaughn Road
Pike Road, AL 36064
(334) 272-9883
pikeroad.us
pp. 152-155

Trenholm State Community College
1225 Air Base Boulevard
Montgomery, AL 36108
(334) 420-4200
trenholmstate.edu
pp. 84-85

Trinity School
1700 E Trinity Boulevard
Montgomery, AL 36106
(334) 213-2100
trinitywildcats.com
pg. 109

Troy University
231 Montgomery Street
Montgomery, AL 36104
(334) 241-9500
troy.edu/montgomery
pp. 88-89

United Heating and Air
3045 Mobile Highway
Montgomery, AL 36108
(334) 262-0247
unitedheating.net
pg. 229

VT Miltope
3800 Richardson Road
Hope Hull, AL 36043
(334) 284-8665
mymiltope.com
pg. 297

**Warren Averett CPAs and Advisors
/ Warren Averett Technology Group**
3815 Interstate Court
Suite C
Montgomery, AL 36109
(334) 386-4800
warrenaverett.com
pg. 205, pg. 273

Wealth Management Partners, LLC
575 S Lawrence Street
Montgomery, AL 36104
(334) 230-9676
wmpcpa.com
pg. 213

Corporate Profile Credits

**Wesley Gardens
Retirement Community**
1555 Taylor Road
Montgomery, AL 36117
(334) 272-7917
methodisthomes.org
pg. 129

WestRock
111 Folmar Parkway
Montgomery, AL 36105
(334) 281-4600
westrock.com
pg. 309

Wetumpka Area Chamber of Commerce
116 E Bridge Street
Wetumpka, AL 36092
(334) 567-4811
wetumpkachamber.com
pg. 203

Wingate by Wyndham
2060 Eastern Boulevard
Montgomery, AL 36117
(334) 245-4684
wyndhamhotels.com
pg. 340

**Woolard Brothers
Commercial Contracting, Inc.**
531 Oliver Road
Montgomery, AL 36117
(334) 277-3770
woolardbrothers.com
pg. 216

The following profiles were written by Minnie Lamberth:

Adams Family Enterprises
AIDT
Alabama Machinery & Supply Company
Amridge University
Auburn University at Montgomery
Baptist Health
Borden Morris Garner Consulting Engineers
Burt Steel, Inc.
Capital City Gastroenterology
Capitol Container, Inc.
Cedric Bradford
Chip Nix, Attorney at Law
Edwards Plumbing and Heating
eSolution Architects
Fastening Solutions, Inc.
Garner Electric
Holt Street Memorial Baptist Church
Jackson Hospital
Jackson Thornton
JMR+H Architecture, P.C.
Larry E. Speaks & Associates, Inc.
McPhillips Shinbaum, LLP
The Montgomery Academy
The Montgomery Symphony Orchestra
Montgomery Water Works and Sanitary Sewer Board
Prattville YMCA
Realty Connection
Renal Associates of Montgomery, P.C.
Riverfront Facilities
Robinson and Associates Architecture, Inc.
Sabel Steel Service, Inc.
Trinity School
United Heating and Air
Warren Averett CPAs and Advisors
Warren Averett Technology Group
Wealth Management Partners, LLC
Wesley Gardens Retirement Community
Woolard Brothers Commercial Contracting, Inc.

The following profiles were written by Jennifer Kornegay:

ALFA
Bacheler Technologies
Goodwyn, Mills and Cawood
Joy to Life Foundation
Merrill Lynch
Montgomery Zoo & Mann Wildlife Museum
Publications Press, Inc.
Regitar U.S.A.
ServisFirst Bank Montgomery
The Town of Pike Road

The following profiles were written by Rachel Fisher:

Answered Prayer Home Care Services
Central Alabama Community College
Jenkins Tire & Automotive
Joe Hubbard Law Firm
Jones Drugs
The Kelly Fitzpatrick Memorial Gallery
Kountry Air RV Park
The Lilly Baptist Church
Ralph Smith Motors
Ross-Clayton Funeral Home, Inc.
SABIC
Stanely Steemer
WestRock
Wingate by Wyndham

The following profiles were submitted by the company or organization:

Alabama Christian Academy
Alabama Power Company
Aronov Realty Management
Brown Studio Architecture
Central Alabama Community College
DAVMOOR
Faulkner University
Frazer United Methodist Church
Information Transport Solutions
Lear Corporation
The Montgomery Area Chamber of Commerce
Montgomery Catholic Preparatory School
The Montgomery Museum of Fine Arts
Montgomery Regional Airport
Neptune Technology Group
Prattville Area Chamber of Commerce
Prattville Christian Academy
Production Automation, Inc.
River Region Dermatology and Laser
River Region United Way
Saint James School
Trenholm State Community College
Troy University
Wetumpka Area Chamber of Commerce

Photo by Becca Beers

Contributing Photographers

BECCA BEERS is a local photographer who loves to capture images of places and people. An avid traveler and Montgomery dweller, she is always aiming to bring more life to a place through her lens. You can find her work at becbeephoto.com.

BRYAN CARTER Bryan Carter is a photographer and graphic designer living in Montgomery, Alabama. He currently runs a small photography and design business, where he works with clients such as Montgomery Area Chamber of Commerce Convention & Visitor Bureau, Alabama Department of Archives and History, *Montgomery Visitor Guide*, The River Region United Way, Saint James School, The YMCA, Auburn University Montgomery, Volunteers of America, *Know the Community, Alabama Living, Montgomery Business Journal*, Wells Fargo & Co., Partners Realty, The Shoppes at EastChase and many more. You can find his work at carterphotodesign.com.

ELMORE DEMOTT Passionate about getting people to connect with nature, Elmore DeMott is a photographer with award winning work in private and corporate art collections, galleries, and museums. Flowers and mighty pine forests — her signature subjects — are featured in publications, presentations, and arts collaborations, and her Camera Journey in pursuit of images that offer a unique perspective takes Elmore throughout her home state of Alabama and beyond. Her photography and books can be found at elmoredemott.com.

LEE DRUMHELLER Lee Drumheller is a local aerial photographer who enjoys aviation and owning his own business. He knows there's no better way to capture the sights and sounds of the city than in the air. Always excited to share his experiences, Lee also loves sharing his passion for aviation with others.

ROBERT FOUTS is a commercial photographer working out of Montgomery and serving the Southeast. His work has appeared in many books and publications over the years. He holds a Master's and a Craftsman's degree from the Professional Photographers of America and has received over 150 awards from print competitions, including several Best of Shows and seven Kodak Gallery Awards. His clients include architects, advertising agencies, industry, hospitals, artists and museums. You can find his work at photofouts.com.

BROOKE GLASSFORD is a professional photographer based out of Montgomery, Alabama. Brooke received a public relations degree from Auburn University in 2010, and she began her photography career in 2011 as the photographer for Colorbox, a division of Kim Box Photography. Brooke's photography focus is weddings, but she has been proud to document for the River Region book as she was born and raised in Montgomery. Brooke's work can be found at colorboxphotographers.com.

JONATHON KOHN is an Alabama based photographer. He employs a photojournalistic approach with minimal direction to his commissioned work, in that it remains both honest and impartial, in order to extract the most factual record of a given moment in time. Jonathon's work can be found at jonathonkohn.com.

MICHELLE CONSUEGRA LAMBERT Michelle Consuegra grew up in the South and calls Montgomery, Alabama home. She became a firm believer in the work of validating a human soul within their experience, as she worked alongside various relief organizations overseas and within the states. As an invested listener and observer she aims to honor the dignity of a life within its ever unfolding narrative. Her work is inspired by the ways people connect in an environment and bring value to one another through relationship. You can find her at michelleconsuegra.com.

AUBRIE MOATES Aubrie Moates, a Florida-native and now happy Alabamian, has a passion for birth photography that comes first-hand as a mama to two growing boys. Knowing the images of mama's happy tears and her baby's first breath will become more precious and more priceless each year, she captures birth not as a single moment, but as a story made up of extraordinary emotions. Find her work at hellobabyphoto.com.

ERIC SALAS served as an active-duty Air Force instructor at Maxwell-Gunter Air Force base until 2018 when he moved to the west coast. In January of 2017, Eric launched his photography business, ESVINGETTES, and decided to follow his love for photography full time. His images of the River Region are captured using his unique point of view. You can find him at esvingettes.com.

THE MONTGOMERY CVB – The Montgomery Convention and Visitors Bureau provided a gallery of images to help showcase Montgomery and the River Region. When noted, we provided the names of the photographers. Included in this volume are images provided by the CVB by Carter Photography & Design, LLC.

@EXPLOREMGM, an Instagram account, helped us locate photographers whose images we were able to use in the book such as Sam Moody and Madeline Burkhardt.

CONTRIBUTION OF ADDITIONAL IMAGES provided by Benjamin Bevilacqua, Barry Chritzerburgh, Nancy Fields, Josh Moates, Grace O'Connor, Scooter Painter, Stephen Poff, Erika Tracy and Josh Whitman.
Page 16 and 67: Photo by JNix courtesy of Shutterstock
Page 53: Photo by JNix courtesy of Shutterstock
Page 211: Photo by Syda Productions courtesy of Shutterstock
Page 25: Photo by McCallk69 courtesy of Shutterstock

This volume is dedicated to the loving memory of
Hunter Alan Chambliss
June 17th, 1993 - February 4th, 2018

Hunter was loved more than words can express by his family and countless friends. A great athlete, outdoorsman, and the kind of kid every man would want for a son - a hard worker, and a "yes, sir", "no, sir" kind of guy. His life was defined by his exuberant love for his family and the outdoors. Hunter loved life and shared it fully with those around him. He was especially passionate about his extended family and felt closest to God in a tree stand. He never met a stranger and his fun-loving personality made everyone laugh and feel at ease - no one ever stood alone in a crowded room if Hunter was in it. In his 24 years, Hunter got more out of life than most of us do in a much longer lifetime.

A native of Montgomery, Hunter was a lifetime member of Frazer United Methodist Church and attended Trinity Presbyterian School from kindergarten until he graduated in 2012. He excelled in football and led the Trinity baseball team to a state championship as a team captain. Hunter continued his education at Auburn University where he was a member of Kappa Alpha Fraternity and received a degree from the McWhorter School of Building Science earning his bachelors degree in Building Construction.

Upon graduation from Auburn University in May of 2017, Hunter began work with Brasfield & Gorrie Construction Company, leading a project expanding Centennial Hospital in Nashville, Tennessee. Brasfield & Gorrie, along with their partners, established a room in the hospital, in memory of Hunter, dedicated to the use for families of stillborn babies.

Hunter has been recognized by having a Team Room on the main floor of the new Brown-Kopel Engineering Student Achievement Center at Auburn University named the "Hunter Alan Chambliss Team Room" in his honor. It will remain named this for the lifetime of the facility.

The "Hunter Alan Chambliss Memorial Endowed Scholarship" in the McWhorter School of Building Science at Auburn University has been established by family and friends. This scholarship will allow Hunter's work ethic and determination to live on through future men and women.

The first annual Hunter Alan Chambliss Turkey Rodeo, benefitting the Auburn University scholarship established in his name, was held in April of 2018, thus celebrating one of his most-loved outdoor activities.

The Capital City Optimist Club sponsors the Alabama High School Athletic Association's All Star Baseball Game each year. Hunter was recognized in 2018 when the club dedicated the game in memory of Hunter.

Numerous gifts have been received in his name at Valiant Cross Academy to further the education of young men in Montgomery, Alabama.

Hunter was a great son, loving brother, and a reliable, loyal friend. Hunter made an impact on many during his short life and his legacy continues to influence lives each and every day.